31 December 2016
For Chris & Nick,
Wishing you
love for life!
Jan

HOW *Two* LOVE

Making your relationship work and last

Jan Resnick PhD

AMYGDALA
PUBLISHING

Amygdala Publishing
PO Box 6135
Swanbourne
Western Australia 6010
info@amygdalapublishing.com
amygdalapublishing.com

© Jan Resnick 2016 all rights reserved

This work is copyright. Except under the conditions described in the *Copyright Act 1968* of Australia and subsequent amendments, no part of this publication may be reproduced, stored in a retrieval system, or transmitted in any form or by any means, electronic, mechanical, photocopying, recording or otherwise, without the written permission of the copyright owner, Jan Resnick.

Editors: Afra Wilder, Con Coroneos, Joanna Moore and Liz Sheean
Cover image: *Heavenly Kiss*, a sculpture by Ayad Alqaragholli, with permission
Cover photograph: Christian West, copyright 2011, with permission
Cover design: Kiryl Lysenka – gnibel.com
Typesetter: Andy McDermott, Liz Sheean, Gwynneth Cavilla – gdesign.com.au
Indexer: Jenny Browne – webindexing.com.au

National Library of Australia Cataloguing-in-Publication entry
Creator: Resnick, Jan, author.
Title: *How Two Love: making your relationship work and last* / Jan Resnick, PhD.
ISBN: 9781925254013 (paperback)
Notes: Includes index.
Subjects: Love. Interpersonal relations. Interpersonal relations--Psychological aspects. Couples--Psychology. Emotions.
Dewey Number: 158.24

The recommended reference for this publication is:
Resnick, Jan 2016, *How Two Love*, Amygdala Publishing, Perth.

Questions regarding the use of this material should be directed to the publisher above.

Disclaimer: The material contained herein should not be taken as advice of a specific nature pertaining to your relationship. The ideas are of a general nature and may be applied as you see fit. Neither the author nor publisher accept any responsibility for consequences arising from the use of this material. We recommend you seek professional advice for personal issues pertaining to love and couple relationships.

Cover image acknowledgment: I am grateful to Christian West for the use of his photograph of Ayad Alqaragholli's beautiful sculpture *Heavenly Kiss* (alqaragholli.com). Ayad has exhibited his work widely in the Perth area, most notably at the annual *Sculptures by the Sea* events, and internationally. This immensely talented artist captures a unique combination of qualities – how love can make our spirits soar but is built on a precarious foundation (represented by chairs piled on top of each other). The openness of the figures' hands suggests an offering of ourselves to each other, ultimately the most personal offering. That is the intention of this book – to show how two love.

*For Cath
who brought magic
to a love I never knew was possible
and for
Sean, Mischa, Lauren, Reece, Josh and Gabriel*

Meaningful Living Series
by Jan Resnick

visit meaningful.life

Including upcoming working titles

How Two Love
Making your relationship work and last

50 Ways to Lose Your Lover
... or nearly

How Meaning Happens
The origins of creativity

The Psychosomatic Metaphor
The psychology of health and illness

The Psychology of Money
Symbol of transformation

Empathic Parenting
Raising emotionally healthy children without going mad

The Power of Dreams
Adventures in discovery, meaning and emergence

Contents

Acknowledgments.................................i
Preface..iii
Introduction: The Making of Love................v

1. **Attracting Love**..............................1
   Neediness
   Emotional self-sufficiency
   Vulnerability
   Connectedness

2. **Relating**...................................17
   Perception
   Trust
   The dance of love
   The place of romance

3. **Is This the One?**...........................41
   How do you know?
   Being objective, subjectively
   The in-love feeling
   Crazy love

4. **Love and Desire**............................61
   Love as esteem
   Know thy partner
   Desire: an introduction
   The dialectic of desire
   The matrix of desire

5. **Making Love and Making Sex**.................77
   Understanding the difference
   The function of sexual activity
   Suggesting sex
   Emotional safety
   Passion
   Vanilla sex and unconventional sexual practices

6. **Co-sexuality** 103
   What is co-sexuality?
   Foreplay and before-play
   Being a good lover
   Communicating sexual needs and preferences
   Sex as a barometer

7. **The Lifespan of Love** 125
   Addressing issues
   Mutual responsibility
   Acceptance, and its limits – parts 1 and 2
   Forbearance, tolerance and forgiveness

8. **Partnership Unity** 153
   Trust and trustworthiness – revisited
   The rules of engagement
   The contract

9. **The Ecology of Successful Relationships** 167
   Emotionally honest communication
   Reciprocal attunement
   Empathic negotiation – parts 1 and 2
   Affective compromise

10. **The Best Relationship You Can Have** 205
    For better, for worse
    Each other's best interest
    The power of love and the love of power – parts 1, 2 and 3
    Realizing the dream

11. **Couples Therapy** 237
    An independent perspective
    The therapy process
    My approach
    Healing and repair

12. **Ever After** 267
    The lessons of love
    Living lovingly

End Note 277
About the Author 279
Index 281

"That simple light may arise out of complicated darkness"
— **Bread and Puppet Theater**

Acknowledgments

Family, friends, colleagues and professionals provided much help and they are briefly, though no less gratefully, acknowledged here.

My friend Afra Wilder provided constant enthusiasm and editorial attention that has made for a better book. Con Coroneos helped me find my voice and mentored my transition from therapist to writer. He contributed to the development and more articulate expression of the ideas. My dear friend Sally Richardson drew upon her background in theatre and literature, combined with her understanding of love relationships, and encouraged me to complete this project. Ross Bolleter, a poet, writer, musician extraordinaire, Zen Roshi and much valued friend, influenced numerous drafts. As professional editor, Joanna Moore provided careful line-editing, offered reactions, and suggested alternative constructions to the entire manuscript that have improved the book immensely. Mal Mckimmie revealed much I had been blind to, resulting in a more coherent and better written text. My friend and colleague, Marie-Laure Bromley-Davenport, a London-based Lacanian psychoanalyst, gave many valuable insights. Tony Africano, friend and colleague, drew from his own clinical experience to provide pertinent perspectives on the issues faced by couples. Sue Lutton provided encouragement and support. Dick Marek, senior editor with an extensive career in publishing, read the manuscript and made useful comments. My six children all read and contributed to the manuscript. I appreciated their comments, especially those from Sean, Mischa, Josh and Lauren. Lauren deserves recognition for her ingenuity in realizing the title *How Two Love*. Peter Hoffman, Mia Lalanne, Jim Goodbourn, Sue Volzke, Felice Watt, Annette Mackereth, Ros White and Dave Shutler made helpful comments. Liz Sheean has edited and published my writing for the past 20 years. She contributed both editorial and typesetting suggestions, and deserves special mention for her influence upon my formation as a writer.

Last, and certainly not least, my wife Cath read every draft and participated in countless discussions with me. The book is not about our relationship, but our relationship has been the wellspring from which some of the content has been drawn. I am grateful to Cath for her determination for this book to be seen through to production, for her seminal contributions to the text, her constant enthusiasm and, most of all, for her unwavering love. Cath taught me what 100 per cent means.

Preface

We are conceived as the product of two people. In the womb, we are tied to the placenta by the umbilical cord. After birth, babies bond with their primary carer and a loving dyad seems to work best to promote healthy early development. Perhaps it is not surprising that adults often seek a partner with whom to couple and share their life.

Polyamory refers to loving more than one person at the same time. It sounds attractive but culturally, most people are orientated toward exclusive coupling. Perhaps this is a logical extension of our earliest origins. I find polyamory attractive philosophically, but in practice it is often accompanied by intense pain, jealousy, complicated messy boundaries and ambiguities around the meaning of love. Without prejudice toward multiple partners in love, sex and intimacy generally, this book examines how couples can make their love work and their relationships last.

This is a guide for getting into a 'good' relationship or improving an existing one. The motivation to write *How Two Love* arises from this thought: there are very few adequate teachers, sets of instructions or roadmaps for how to be a couple and make a love relationship work well over the long term.

Most relationships are far from ideal; typically, they are a 'work in progress'. There is certainly no pretense that mine have been perfect. I've learned many lessons and many more still need to be learned. What I *have* learned is that there is much that can be done that I wish I had known earlier. Now I have put that in writing.

Decades of psychotherapy practice have provided a rich source of real life examples employed liberally throughout this book. Some are composites that bring themes together. To protect privacy and ensure anonymity the stories are de-identified, names are pseudonyms and some personal details changed.

Unless otherwise specified, 'love relationships' refer to heterosexual, homosexual, and bisexual equally. Though gender equality is desirable, our culture is still far from achieving it. Some of my case examples reflect this.

The grammatically incorrect use of the pronouns 'they' and 'them' when referring to the singular are used deliberately to avoid privileging the pronoun 'him' or 'her' when it could be either. The terms 'client' and 'patient' are used interchangeably.

Take your time with this. Give it thought. Feel your way.

For it to be all it can be, love deserves to be given time.

Jan Resnick
Perth, Australia
March 20th 2016

INTRODUCTION
The Making of Love

> *"For one human being to love another;*
> *that is perhaps the most difficult of all our tasks,*
> *the ultimate, the last test and proof,*
> *the work for which all other work is but preparation."*
> **— Rainer Maria Rilke**

Amy arrived for her first consultation looking a little lost. She was of average height and weight. I wondered why she wore so much make-up.

Her first words were: *I'm just lonely and I want someone to talk to.*

What would you like to talk about? I replied, knowing that the word 'just' usually means 'not just'.

Amy told me that since her ex-husband left their marriage she had been out with others, but never felt satisfied. She had friends but it was difficult to speak of certain subjects.

She hesitated, I held the space. *I suppose I am looking for love,* Amy finally added.

Amy had someone interested in her named Walter. She said they had been friends for a while and went out together occasionally. Now, he wanted to have sex with her but she wasn't interested.

Why not?

Amy explained that Walter didn't turn her on. He was overweight and while that wasn't a total obstacle, she felt he didn't look after himself. She also said that he took her for granted, didn't pay enough attention to her, didn't phone her after she'd been away and then expected them to be lovers anyway.

I can easily understand that, I said. *I don't see any reason why you should feel that you have to have sex with him if you don't want to.*

Amy responded: *Well, at 82 years old I don't feel I have many choices ...*

I was so struck by how these same issues could apply to a 16 year old, a 45 year old or an 82 year old – looking for love, struggling with choices, wondering whether to have sex or not. And so, after many formal and informal discussions about how to be a couple, I set out to write what would be most helpful.

Love is at once one of the best and most dangerous experiences. When lovers live together as a couple and as partners, home can be a refuge; the site of intimacy or it can be the site of war. I have seen people die because love has gone wrong. And more murders are committed in the bedroom than any other room of the house.

Love broken, betrayed, destroyed, or simply lost can rock us to our core. It fragments and disintegrates us in ways that can make the experience of serious illness seem mild by comparison.

> *Love is a matter of life and death.*
> *And life is a matter of love and death.*

Prevention is better than cure. Understanding is required to pre-empt problems and to rectify those that haven't been avoided. The primary message of this book revolves around what to do – how two love – to sustain the emotional health of your relationship, minimize damage and heal love's inevitable wounds. To do this, it is essential to understand the difference between living as an individual and living as a couple.

Love relationships often struggle when we fail to make the transition from operating as an individual to being together with another, as a couple, even as there is overlap between these roles. And, if children appear on the scene and we need to function as a family, further transition is required.

These transitions have to be 'made', involve a 'doing', and don't just happen because you find yourself in a relationship. Often, they don't happen at all. A lasting love relationship depends upon each person balancing their needs and identity as an individual with those of being partners in coupledom. This balance will vary in different relationships.

○○○

I came to better understand this distinction through my own relationship. My wife Cath and I had a fight. We never fight. But one Saturday night we did.

It was the end of an enjoyable day and evening out together. We'd had a walk on the beach, then later been out to dinner and the theater with friends. Arriving home, without a word to Cath, I put a recording of the last part of my team's final football match of the season on the television. Cath *hates* the football. She let me have it, claiming I ruined the end of a good day by inconsiderately turning on the 'footy', which she definitely did not want to listen to.

She was right of course, but at the time I didn't see it that way. I couldn't believe the fuss for what turned out to be about 30 minutes of screentime. I was angry and my anger lingered into the next morning.

Cath is a generous person; on waking she said sorry for sounding off at me and gave me a hug. Though I was quite ready to go another round or two (I still believed I was right), she gave me an opportunity to let it go, and I took it. I decided it was better to move on.

On reflection, I had been acting as an individual and not as a partner in a couple. This theme – the tension between these two positions that we occupy simultaneously – needs negotiation and thoughtfulness way beyond my actions.

If you continue to act solely as an individual, then the fallout can be full of hurt, anger and resentment. And resentments, if left unresolved, grow and become corrosive.

I know Cath well enough to know that she would hate my flicking on the football, especially without discussion. I ignored that and did what I wanted anyway. Maybe my aggressive disregard of her was born out of a feeling that I had given a lot in the day and was entitled to something in the evening, the right to do what I wanted. *But it doesn't work like that.*

(And, my team lost! Again.)

I admonished myself: you are full of earnest declarations of love, romantic gestures, sexual intimacy, and convincing expressions of commitment such as *I want to grow old with you* but at the same time *do not expect me to press pause on sport!* Initially, it was more important for me to be right than to be close to Cath. The compelling belief that my actions were justified, and her reactions out of order, informed my position and attachment to the fight.

> *When 'being right' positions you against your partner, it becomes 'being wrong' in your relationship.*

Being right, and being invested in being right, becomes competitive. It can turn a couple's relationship into a power struggle, a contest of wills. Competition for dominance pits you, as two individuals, against each other which is destructive, not loving. Ultimately, if your relationship becomes structured in this way, it can be the deciding factor in love dying an early and sometimes agonizing death. If this occurs, you will surely feel that you haven't fulfilled love's potential.

○○○

You may fall in love – or into something that you call 'love' – with someone you hardly know. Sometimes, after decades of living together, you may still know little of what your partner really thinks or feels. Each of you might reveal to your therapist, in confidence, what dwells in the most private regions of your minds, but you will not reveal the same to your own partner. How bizarre!

Is this not a charade? As you say: *good night darling, I love you*, are you, at the same time, protecting your partner from the truth of who you are and how you really feel? Pretense is not love.

You may fear that you won't be loved if you reveal your honest thoughts and feelings. But what does being loved mean if you are not allowing yourself to be seen? What does relationship mean if you only partially know each other?

> *Prepare to be visible and vulnerable in order to love and be loved.*

To develop and achieve a true sense of knowing, let go of who you would like your love partner to be, who they could be if only they fulfilled their potential, in favor of accepting your partner as they are. Letting go of the ideal and not holding out for it is expressed in the traditional marital vow: 'for better, for worse'.

Whenever you get together with another, it is always a 'package deal'. You get together with their past, with their assets and liabilities, their children, their parents, their traumas, their debts, their scars, their medical history and so on. Such past occurrences often define us in the present. You get together with the 'emotional baggage' that each person carries into the next relationship, even if sometimes we like to imagine we have left it all behind. As a therapist, I've often heard from clients *I've already dealt with that issue* and I believe that. But it doesn't mean that it's gone completely.

Letting go of your portfolio of agendas of what you want from your partner, of how they should be, or how they should look, what you want them to do for you, even how they act, may feel challenging. But by doing so space opens up for truly knowing and accepting one another.

'Knowing' involves shared experience and a paring away of:
- the transferences of the past
- the projections of parts of ourselves onto our loved ones in the present
- the illusions we harbor for the future.

This enables us to reach toward acceptance.

Acceptance, however, is not absolute. Or should you put up with anything?

ooo

Culturally, there is a pervasive idea that love should be unconditional. Let's think this through.

The feeling of love is not the same as a relationship. Have you ever heard the following statement? – *I will always love you but can no longer stay with you.*

> *Love is not unconditional, nor should it be.*

When 'love' refers to the committed relationship, do you really believe that you stay with your partner no matter what? Forever?

Or are you only in it for the good times? This is a hard call. How much of 'for worse', 'for poorer', and 'in sickness' are you prepared to put up with? Consider the following:

- Your partner becomes permanently disabled the week after your wedding.
- Your partner turns out to be infertile when your life dream is to have your own children.
- Your spouse goes to jail for a long time.
- Your partner has changed into a radically different person from the one with whom you fell in love.
- Your partner falls into a protracted mental illness.
- Your partner acts in a way that is malicious, corrupt, destructive, greedy, violent, perverse, or just plain weird.
- Your spouse loses all you own, radically changing your way of living.
- Your partner fails to live up to their vows – should you?

Promises to our partners may take the form of marital vows or de facto agreements, and these promises are based on explicit understandings or implicit assumptions. Explicit or not, lovers are often shocked to the core when these promises are broken. However, there are many contingencies and conditions that challenge these promises. Whatever the nature of your couple agreement, there are conditions to be met, and if not, there probably should be. The following chapters spell out how I see these conditions.

Love relationships, and the conditions that make them work, require work. The making of love isn't all hard work but accepting that this is a part of it and worth the effort, can make all the difference. The 19th century Bohemian-Austrian poet Rilke says: *it is the work for which all other work is but preparation.*

When things go flat or lifeless, when sex dries up, when bad feelings or arguments take center stage, what then? Turning the situation around requires an attitude of openness and honesty and a willingness to address what's wrong, and to do so in the spirit of a committed loyalty to the union of partnership.

How Two Love shows you how to do just that – what you need to know, how to renovate a relationship, how to restore and renew the energy between you, how to enliven your sexual connection, and how to *enloven* the bond of faith, trust and commitment.

ooo

There are as many forms of love as there are people to experience them. Love is ineffable; it resists definition, analysis and explanation. There is always more to it. Love is exquisitely personal, particular, and distinguished by its immediate and historical context. This means that the love that two people experience is not identical with any other love, ever. I am mindful of this when generalizing about love.

Your story of love is yours. Staring dreamily into each other's eyes may be a part of it, but love takes place in and through the practicalities of living. For love to be a dream come true, leave your work at the office, come home to one another, switch off the TV (even the football!) and switch on to each other, especially if the love you are living now feels wanting.

Love is the most important subject of our lives; it can make the difference between whether life feels worth living or not. Love is one of the most powerful motivational drivers. Love is life-giving in all of its diverse shapes and forms. It brings eros to ordinary living.

Our way of life is meaningless without love. What are we here for? To accumulate a portfolio of assets? What's the point of acquisitiveness without someone to share it with?

The expression *love is a matter of life and death* captures the urgency of our task to transform feelings of love into relationships that work and last. Then, the love that unfolds is a magical experience that fulfills its potential. Love gives meaning to wealth and gives value to what we mean to each other.

To have love, you must *be* love. When it comes to relationships, *being* love refers to how you act, both toward your partner and when on your own. The being of love is not a static or passive state, rather it needs to be ec-static, electric, eclectic and eccentric.

Love needs daily renewal much as the body needs daily replenishment. The fundamentals of physical health include eating well, drinking water, breathing clean air, exercising, maintaining good hygiene and getting restful sleep. How do you look after your relationship to support its health and longevity? And how does your partner? What do you do together to make love work and last?

It takes two.

CHAPTER 1

Attracting Love

> *"And in the end, the love you take is equal to the love you make."*
> — **Paul McCartney**

How can you attract love? Even though love needs to be made – that is, requires action – try as you might you *cannot* make someone love you. Love must not be forced. It may be the case that no matter what you do, your beloved may never love you in return, or never love you as you would like.

Attraction is a mysterious subject. How is it that you can walk into a room of a dozen strangers and be attracted to a particular one? What is it about this one and not the others? Why does one stand out and affect you, sometimes powerfully before you have even spoken? Sometimes, you don't discover the answers until you have become involved and grown to know each other well. Sometimes you don't find out the answers at all.

Whether it is up to God, fate or destiny, the stars or the magic of interpersonal chemistry, there are factors over which you can have some influence when it comes to attracting love.

Neediness

We all have emotional needs, but if your need to be loved is extreme then few people will want to requite your love in order to be a solution to your problem. You become a deficit seeking a supplement; this is not love. It is attempting to fill a void. You are trying to compensate for a felt-lack in yourself. This is an individual issue that exsists independently of the relationship.

> *Excessive emotional need turns love off.*

If a person is drawn by your need, a limited dynamic is established, a one-way street. *You have this need; I meet it, or try to; that is mainly what we do.*

> Josephine needed constant reassurance. She needed her partner to convince her that he loved her (he did), that she was beautiful (she was), that he would never leave her (he had no wish to), that he preferred her to every other woman in the world (well, he was with her and no one else), that he felt passionate desire for her (he did, but it was wearing thin because of her neediness), and that he wanted to spend all his time with her (he probably would have but he needed a break from her constant demands for reassurance).

Josephine could resolve this dilemma by realizing that her neediness originates prior to, and outside of, her relationship, and that therefore it is unlikely that her partner could reassure her enough. She could work at containing these feelings, understanding their origins, and not imposing them in a destructive fashion. Otherwise, she might drive her partner away and lose him (thus *re-creating* the conditions underlying her need for constant reassurance) and create what she most wants to avoid.

Josephine is an example of someone with excessive emotional need. Oppositely: if you don't need *anything* there is nothing that another person has to offer you. Where is the love in that? It is a question of balance.

Emotional self-sufficiency

Generally, we become more attractive when we are able to be by ourselves, live by ourselves (without a partner – I don't mean that we have to live alone), function by ourselves, and still feel reasonably well. Being emotionally self-sufficient does not mean that you are absolutely complete in yourself, that you don't need a love relationship or that you are better off without a partner. It means that you can look after yourself, emotionally and practically, and therefore you have a choice. Consider the following questions:

- Are you okay on your own?
- Are you comfortable living alone?
- Do you mind spending the evening alone?
- What about the whole day alone or a number of days?
- Would you choose to go to the movies or dinner by yourself?
- If you go to a party alone, does that feel okay?
- Does going to a social or family gathering on your own bother you?

The answers to questions such as these will indicate whether you are emotionally self-sufficient, or the degree to which you are not.

If the idea of being on your own is too disagreeable, you may feel an internal pressure to stay in a relationship that doesn't make you happy, or to enter into a relationship despite knowing it is unsuitable. There is a risk you will put up with what you shouldn't, or hold back expressing your grievances, because you need the relationship. Eventually, you break up because the relationship wasn't satisfactory, or you are rejected and so have no choice. Then you start all over again.

It is better to work at developing emotional self-sufficiency than to pursue a relationship that is unduly compromising, dysfunctional or stifling. If you are successful in getting yourself 'together' – in feeling you are enough on your own – it will be more fulfilling when you get together with someone else.

From a more self-sufficient position, you can freely exercise your choices in your own best interest.

How do you develop emotional self-sufficiency? The guiding principle is to acknowledge and address what is unresolved, hurting, or deficient developmentally. In this way you can work through core issues that keep recurring in your life. You may have a series of relationships and notice that the same or similar problems and conflicts arise, even though your partners are quite different. You are the common denominator – what is it within you that is contributing to the origination and perpetuation of these patterns?

In psychotherapy we speak of 'the unconscious'. When experience is determined unconsciously, such patterns can continue – within a relationship or from one relationship to the next – until we realize *this must have something to do with me!* Once we realize *this*, and also how blind we have been to our part in the pattern, the world takes on a dramatically different complexion.

The antecedents of these patterns are found in significant childhood experiences, early relationship dynamics and attachment styles. When we connect the past with the present we can understand and then address what is unresolved. In this way we can end the cycle of repetitions.

> *Becoming aware of destructive patterns and dismantling them leads to emotional health.*

Working toward emotional health involves a willingness to suffer an uncomfortable feeling and to allow it, to stay with it. I call this *dwelling in the discomfort zone*. It is the opposite of remaining in our comfort zone. The discomfort zone is a challenge and a trial. The point is not that it is a virtue to suffer, but that there can be value in tolerating feelings that cause discomfort, and holding them, rather than trying to avoid them.

Joan couldn't bear the feeling of hunger. It made her anxious, and that made her eat. She would often eat more than she needed and also the wrong type of food. Then she would feel guilty. Then she would feel panicked about being overweight (even though she wasn't). Then she felt depressed.

When we worked on Joan's relation to hunger, it became clear that her mother became anxious when, as a child, Joan didn't want to eat or refused to finish her meal. Joan's mother, probably attempting to soothe her own anxiety, put a great deal of pressure on her daughter to eat and to finish everything. As a result, Joan had a very low tolerance for hunger or even the possibility of hunger. Often she ate *before* she felt hungry, in anticipation of feeling it.

The more Joan grew to be able to tolerate hunger and stay with it, regardless of her discomfort, the more she was able to make healthier choices. She began to feel in control of food rather than feel controlled by it. Joan found that once she could master the feeling of hunger, it became less threatening and less agitating, and she could cope with it for longer periods of time. She also realized that her anxiety over hunger began with her mother; that she had taken on her mother's anxiety and had taken it into herself.[1]

This pattern around food is both incredibly common and notoriously difficult to help. Its relevance to love relationships lies in analogy — when it comes to love, there are many different types of hunger.

When feelings of separateness and aloneness threaten, allow the feelings to arise, stay with them, tolerate them, and watch where your mind goes as a result. While doing so, consider:
- Do the feelings worry you?
- Do they make you feel paranoid?
- Or sad?

---

1. This can be taken too far in the case of anorexia nervosa, in which hunger is often allowed and endured for extreme lengths of time. This is unhealthy and dangerous and not what is being espoused here.

- Do you become self-conscious, self-critical, or self-deprecating?
- Are you bothered about what others might think of you?
- Do you imagine how you are judged?

Feelings may be uncomfortable but will not be harmful. If you can hold them without being unduly afraid of them, usually they diminish in intensity. Take your own judgements out of it; they do not serve you well. Work at being better company for yourself. The more you realize that you are fine on your own when you are fine with your own mind, the easier it becomes. Being on your own can become a pleasure.

○○○

When two people who have reasonable levels of emotional self-sufficiency fall in love, that love brings something additional – something special – to each person. Love is then not merely a way out of an unhappy place that each person occupies separately. Love becomes communion.[2] It is a shared experience between two (reasonably) whole people. If this is what you want then this is also what you have to be able to bring to the table.

The joining of two souls is radically different to filling a hole, meeting a need, or resolving a past trauma. In those cases, love is required to be more than what it is of itself, and when others sense this, their attraction wanes and their interest diminishes. They tend to take flight.

It is not that you are ever completely free of your past and can move on to the next relationship entirely unencumbered. But when you are dominated by what remains unresolved, it detracts from what is unfolding in the present.

Vulnerability

Vulnerability is the necessary condition through which love becomes possible. Am I right to make this statement so boldly

---

[2]. I'm using this term in a secular sense, no religious sense is intended or implied.

and unequivocally? Many people seeking love do everything possible *not* to be vulnerable.

> *Vulnerability is the ground of love.*

Vulnerability is not the same as need. To be vulnerable is to have something at stake, something to lose. You are affected by the other person, you care, you can be hurt. It probably means that you *will* be hurt, for we are most hurt by those that matter to us most.

> When Leroy was five years old, his baby sister was born. Until then, he had enjoyed a loving relationship with his mother and father. But when the new baby came, his mother became devoted to her, and Leroy began to behave badly. He resented the loss of his mother's attention and before long they did not get along well.
>
> Leroy's mother had expected him to understand that a new baby required a lot of care and attention and that there were times when Leroy had to occupy himself. She became critical of him and frequently let him know that she was not pleased with him.
>
> When Leroy grew up, he got together with Nancy. They enjoyed a loving relationship for five years. Just after the five-year mark passed, Nancy noticed that Leroy, strangely, had become rather critical of her. Sometimes he could be quite vocal about it and other times he kept it to himself, but she could feel it. She felt attacked by the way he raised small things such as her forgetting to put things away, and the amount of toilet paper she used. There was an underlying hostility in him toward her and, as a consequence, she became somewhat guarded toward him, and distant.

Leroy's mother died when he was 15 years old. He told me that for those 10 years from five to 15 he felt his mother had wanted him to be someone else, at least more grown-up than he could be. There had been a decade of conflict in his childhood home that grew worse and worse.

I pointed out that the change in his attitude toward Nancy after being together for five years seemed to replicate the change he felt from his mother toward him at five years old. With this in mind, he made a deliberate effort to dismantle his critical attitude toward his partner.

Shortly after, when Nancy and Leroy went away for a weekend, Leroy felt unhappy about Nancy's guardedness toward him and felt that her sexual interest had waned. He noticed that she had become withdrawn and the feeling between them had cooled. He realized that he could blame Nancy for this in a critical way, or he could recognize that it was a reflection and a consequence of his hostility toward her. He remembered that once, in therapy, I had said: *Don't blame the mirror for its reflection. It's easy to fault your partner for what you have made them feel.*

They talked about it. He opened up and apologized for having been so critical. He felt bad about attacking Nancy and he regretted the way it had detracted from the loving and sexually intimate relationship they had enjoyed. There were tears; Leroy cried when he registered that his change of attitude toward her had caused her to become guarded toward him.

The moment that Leroy became vulnerable to her, Nancy felt her guardedness go. She hadn't wanted to feel guarded, she just did, and she couldn't let it go. She didn't decide to let it go in that moment. It evaporated in response to his vulnerability. At the same time, the feeling of love and also sexual desire for Leroy, which she had missed, started flooding back.

Nancy was struck by the way her guardedness had taken over her body. She told Leroy that her body had shut down in relation to him. Her libido had diminished and her sexuality was dulled or even anaesthetized: she didn't feel as intensely during sex as she had before. She had become unresponsive – *numbed down*, she called it. Leroy's vulnerability prompted her sexual desire to return and her body became enlivened and responsive again.

This is an example of *co-sexuality*, a term discussed in greater depth in Chapter 6. Co-sexuality is the unique form of sexuality particular to a couple in a love relationship. Here, Nancy's experience of their co-sexuality moved from vital and alive to numb and compromised and back again. Nancy's own description was illuminating: *When he became vulnerable I came together within myself, I felt sexual again and attraction for him was there again, I felt enlivened and full of love; I hadn't felt that for a while. It was as if I had to connect with myself first in order to connect with him but I couldn't until he became more vulnerable and less aggressive.*

Notice how co-sexuality pivots around vulnerability.

This example also shows how vulnerability is the ground of love. When he was critical and aggressive or cold she became guarded, not surprisingly. It appeared that the problem was hers, but it did not reside solely in her. It was not a product of some individual psychopathology such as 'low libido'. Her guardedness was a direct reaction to his change of attitude. It was *relational*. She *felt* disconnected from her body, specifically her sexuality. When Leroy took ownership of his aggression and its affect upon her, they could return to a more open, connected position. Love's injury was recognized and felt. He acknowledged hurting her; he cried. His vulnerability affected a reintegration in her and also between them so they could re-connect. Their love became renewed and sexualized, charged with attraction, desire and power. The eros in their relationship was restored.

Though the physical aspect was terribly important here, it was not *just* physical. We love through our bodies, but our bodies are not separate physical objects that can be removed from who we are, from our selves.

> *Love is best expressed through the body, for our bodies are inseparable from our selves.*

When is the right time to express vulnerability?

What if, in the middle of a party or social gathering, you want to say to your partner: *When that good-looking bloke chatted you up and engaged you in an animated exchange, you seemed quite receptive to it. It made me feel terribly anxious and uncomfortable.* Is this the right time? Probably not.

Perhaps you return home a bit drunk, and decide it's best to raise the issue the next day when you're sober. In the morning, you've slept off the alcohol, and think you'd like to have a happy, uncomplicated Sunday, and don't want to risk spoiling it by bringing up the fraught issue.

It is easy for the moment to slip away. Soon it feels too late: we've moved on and bringing it up seems out of place or out of time. But somehow, sometime, this feeling of vulnerability needs to be expressed, or your partner may never realize that you are affected. Sometimes you need to manage and contain your vulnerability and sometimes you need to bring it right into the center of the relationship.

Sometimes, if your partner is not doing anything that is wrong or disrespectful, you have to take responsibility for your discomfort. Not doing so can unreasonably limit their freedom. If you restrict your partner's interaction with the outside world in this way, you will create a need to pull away from you and perhaps break away from the relationship.

In another usage, vulnerability can equate to care. In the example above, the woman might say: *Oh, I'm glad you said how you felt. He is handsome and a real charmer but I am not interested. He is just like that with everyone.* She might go on to say to a friend that she is pleased to have made her partner a little jealous because it shows he cares. Sometimes, it can be disappointing if your partner is so cool, so invulnerable as to be utterly unaffected by such encounters. You might wonder: *how far do I need to go before my partner becomes bothered?*

Vulnerability is compatible with healthy inter-dependency and emotional self-sufficiency. You can be affected without being destroyed. You can suffer an uncomfortable feeling without having to pay back, act-out or otherwise punish your partner. Vulnerability in good measure is when you can give expression to your vulnerability without breakdown or drama. Needs and emotional self-sufficiency are in balance.

Connectedness

Connectedness refers to your accessibility at a personal level. How open or ready are you to make contact? Are you present? Are you emotionally available? Are you involved in a full sense? Or are you disconnected?

> Katy had difficulties attracting someone to love her. Yet, she was noticeably attractive, fit and slim, with long hair and an appealing look. She was bisexual, and she just wanted to be loved by someone. When she first arrived for therapy, my initial reaction was: how can such an attractive young woman have difficulty finding a lover? But as therapy unfolded, I began to discover the answer.
>
> Katy was often 'spaced-out' in the consulting situation. I would sit and wonder: where are you? It felt like she wasn't really here, in the room with me. She often seemed 'off with the fairies'. There was a sense of disconnection.

> Sometimes we would begin a conversation, she would tell me something that had happened to her or that she was interested in, and then it would fizzle out. She wasn't able to stay engaged with me, or even with her own subject in the conversation. It was as if she lost interest, got distracted, or became lost in her inner world.
>
> I might ask her: *Where did you go just now? We were speaking in an animated way and then suddenly you seemed to lose the thread. What happened?* Katy would look at me with a puzzled expression, suggesting that she didn't really know what I was talking about. Then she would shrug and say: *I don't know.*

This is an example of disconnectedness. It wasn't Katy's fault. She wasn't doing it on purpose and she didn't want to be doing it. She could see that this would make it difficult for someone to forge the kind of connection with her that would enable her to reach her goal – to be loved. Perhaps this is also an example of someone blind to her own blindness. Katy didn't know she was disconnecting. She was cut off from her own cut-off. When she overcame this, she began a process of recognizing what she had been doing unconsciously. She began to notice when it happened. She began to bridge the gaps and bring herself back to the present.[3]

ooo

Happy unawareness can also be a problem.

> Mal was a friendly and naïve sort of character. When he and his partner went out for lunch, a bubbly, young waitperson raced over to their table, chatting with enthusiasm: *Hi Mal! How are you going today?*
>
> He replied: *Really well, Charlene, all the better for seeing you.* When his partner asked: *How do you know her?* he

---

[3]. Therapists will recognize the likelihood of dissociation here and it turned out that Katy did indeed have a traumatic history. Mindfulness practices are useful here as one of the range of approaches for addressing post-traumatic consequences.

answered: *Oh, I don't really know her at all, only from coming here for lunch occasionally.*

In this exchange, that seemed rather innocent, Mal felt he had done nothing wrong. He hadn't taken Charlene out secretly. He hadn't been unfaithful. He was just being friendly. However, he didn't realize that he was creating mistrust that was causing his partner to feel distant from him.

There is no moral question regarding Mal's conduct. It is more a question of who his partner is, how she feels, and her particular sensitivities. Another partner might think nothing of this friendly encounter with a waitperson. While there is nothing wrong with being friendly, there was a particular quality of intimacy in his way of being friendly that gave his partner cause for suspicion. It raised a question. It made her feel unsafe and insecure in the relationship. A 'disconnect' was created between them. His partner felt too vulnerable, exposed and a little anxious. Mal didn't mean to generate anxiety or mistrust. In fact, it was the last thing he wanted because then he would suffer the consequences of her finding it difficult to be close with him.

> Mal realized finally that the most important person was the one he was in a love relationship with, and therefore that he needed to tone down the intimate quality of his other interactions. This may have been his natural way of being friendly with people he didn't know well, or care about, but inadvertently he was cooling the connectedness between himself and his partner.

ooo

George would often tell his wife about his sexual fantasies of other women whom they both knew. He claimed that she shouldn't worry about this because by telling her he felt less of a need to act on his fantasies. But hearing it made his wife feel threatened and marginalized, certainly not special.

Without intending to, George created a disconnect in their relationship that eventually reduced his wife's desire to be sexual with him. She started to wonder if he was thinking about one of his fantasy women when making love with her, and this caused her to feel more distant.

ooo

> Sarah liked to go out and get drunk with her girlfriends. They danced, fooled around, got noisy, 'untidy' and had a lot of fun.
>
> Sarah's boyfriend Sam didn't like the person Sarah became when she got drunk. He didn't go out with her because he didn't like drinking and anyway, 'it was a girl thing.'
>
> Sarah would come home at all hours, waking Sam up and often saying things that she then wouldn't remember when sober. Sometimes, she was quite hurtful – she said Sam was no fun; he was a deadbeat and all he wanted to do was sleep. He replied that yes, at 4am, all he did want to do was sleep.

Sam felt that Sarah didn't respect him. It wasn't that she was flirting with other men, or that he worried that she would be unfaithful – he said she wasn't like that. What he meant was that he worried about her in her drunken state. She didn't know what she was doing or saying and he felt disrespected because she disregarded his concern. The resulting disconnect between them threatened the future of their relationship.

Disconnection can happen at any stage, when things have hardly begun between you, or after you have been together for decades. If you want to attract love and keep it, it is important to stay connected and to notice the ways that disconnections occur, grow, and become entrenched. The longer disconnections go on, the greater the distance between you.

ooo

It is also possible that we can become too close, too connected. The idea of 'immaculate attunement' begins with the way that a truly connected and attuned mother of a newborn baby may become intensely aware of her baby's needs at every moment. Without words (which is what the word 'infant' means: *in fans*, 'without language'), mother may sense that baby is cold and needs to be wrapped up, or that baby is hungry and needs to be fed, or tired and needs to sleep. This level of attunement is appropriate and desirable for the earliest stages of child care and serves early development well.

In an adult love relationship, especially in the early stages, lovers become attuned to each other. Each, in attending to the other, becomes aware of the other's thoughts, feelings, needs and desires. This is normal, in principle. There is, however, a degree of attunement that can become too much.

> John would wait on his partner Anthony hand and foot. He loved to cook meals, give massages, iron Anthony's shirts and even straighten his tie for him as he left for work. The level of care and attention that John bestowed upon Anthony was high by any standard. For a long time, Anthony appreciated John's attitude of devotion and love.
>
> However, after a time, Anthony began to feel that John had few other interests: he felt that he was the sole focus of John's life. If Anthony was out longer than expected, John would be on the phone: *Where are you? Are you all right? Has anything happened?* Anthony began to find John's attunement oppressive and constricting.

It became clear that this 'love' was more an expression of John's compulsive need to look after someone, and Anthony started to resent it and pull away. John's efforts to be connected were so intense that they created distance. In fact, this was a recurring pattern – John had lost every former partner because of this overbearing caregiving that was more akin to that of a devoted mother to her baby. Was he trying unconsciously to repair his own experience of early mothering?

> *True empathy should also tell you when your partner needs space.*

Empathic attunement that promotes connectedness enables, perpetuates and intensifies attraction.

CHAPTER 2

Relating

*"Love is the only reality and it is not
a mere sentiment. It is the ultimate truth
that lies at the heart of creation."*
— **Rabindranath Tagore**

Perception

Say you are attracted to someone and think you'd like to 'start something'. What should you do? Begin by growing attuned to who that person is, how they feel, their desires and preferences, their moods, values and general disposition.

How do you become attuned in this way? You begin through your perception of that other person.

It is important to distinguish between perception and conception. Perception refers to the senses. Conception refers to ideas.

What do you see?

What do you hear?

These are the first questions of perception. Attuning your senses to this person is like focusing binoculars or tuning in a radio station. But if you are dazzled by her beautiful smile or the twinkle in his eye, if you are hypnotized by the curve of her breasts or his butt, if you are intoxicated by the smell of her perfume or the pheromones of his sweat – then you are at risk of shifting from perception to conception. Why? Because being dazzled, hypnotized or intoxicated often launches us on a trip – a flight of fancy – where we travel away from our perceptions or direct experience of the other person into fantasyland. The risk is that excitement shifts us away from the immediacy of our perceptions into a constructed narrative of our own making.

Conception refers to the way your *idea* of this person begins to dominate, and become static and even sedimented. Conception then takes over from your perceptions. While conceptions can change over time, there is a risk of your idea of the other person becoming fixed. Remaining in the immediacy of your perceptions enables them to be refreshed as you go. Perception allows for difference and change with the passage of time.

There is nothing wrong with taking pleasure in the sight, sound, smell, touch or even taste of another person. But if you then go off into fantasy – if you spin out into dreaming, idealizing, conceptualizing who this person is – then you have left the site of the other, and replaced the other with yourself. Your idea is substituted for your direct experiencing of this other person, the real-time person. If you take off into a flight of fancy, you have gone on a head trip rather than a journey of getting to know someone on the road to love. Exciting, yes, but: *is it real?* Who are you relating to? The other? Or your idea of the other?

You can fall in love with a person or you can fall in love with a dream of how beautiful it will be when you come together with this other person. It is easy to do, so easy. And indeed, there is something quite irresistible, quite delightful about the in-love feelings that are generated. But is this fantasy of the other really what you are in love with? Perceptions inflated by ideas risk becoming illusions.

> *Excitement born of desire risks mistaking your idea for reality.*

You can be more invested and attached to the feeling of excitement that arises from your own ideas than the direct experience of another person based upon what happens between you. In this event, you can become addicted to your own biochemistry that produces opioid-like chemicals from the pain and pleasure of your internal trips and fantastical transportations. I'm not saying: 'don't go there'; it may be a necessary part of getting to know someone. But ensure you can get past your assumptions in order to actually know them.

In order to perceive the person, as they are, you may have to ground yourself. You have to suspend your assumptions and dismantle your mental constructions as you amend your sense of the other person. How?

A sorting process is required. What is real and what is unreal? What is perception and what is conception? What have you put there, perhaps because it is your desire to be so? Ironically, you may have turned this person, the subject of your interest, into someone else in order to love them. (They may well feel this.)

Perception refers to direct, unmediated experience, a kind of *Zen* of experience. Perception comes prior to your conceptions, prejudices and your tendency to think, or explain or interpret. Allow perceiving first, and apperception later.[4] Understanding this principle enables your ongoing experience to remain fresh rather than become stale with repetition and predictability. This will help you avoid that sense that you are experiencing 'things', people, and events in much the same ways, again and again.

Perception enables a *reading* of each other. Generally, the inner life is inscribed in facial expressions, gesticulations, other physical gestures and body movements, the lines around

---

4. Apperception is a term that has various applications in psychotherapy and psychology, in education, in science and in philosophy. It refers to the way that our direct perceptions of 'reality' in the present are interpreted in conjunction with our previous experience and understandings from past perceptions. While I think a direct and unmediated perception is desirable, it is rarely this simple. In general, we are already constituted by everything that has gone before and new perceptions are, to some degree, unavoidably mediated by the influence of past experiences. But while that may sound like a contradiction to the text above, awareness of this is key in the service of the freshness of our perceptions and experience, and the ability to differentiate the ways that the present is informed by our past experiences.

the eyes, muscle movements around the mouth, the rhythm of breathing, the tensing and flexing of the limbs, posture, gait, and prosody of tone of voice. The mood expressed varies and changes like the weather of our selves. We generate an atmosphere just as we are affected by the atmospheres of others. 'All that you are' is not visible to others, but much shows if they are perceptive enough.

Even being perfectly still, quiet and contained expresses something of who you are.

In practice, you can never fully know what is going on inside another person. You know what they say and show, you know what you see and hear, you know what you feel and intuit. Perception is reading what can be read in so far as it is present to you. In order to perceive what is there, you must first suspend your conceptions and, most of all, your pre-conceptions.

Freeing yourself of prejudices and pre-conceptions enables perceiving the other as they are. A prejudice is a pre-judgement that occurs prior to perception. You may be carrying personal biases based on what you want or don't want, based on how you want this other person to be or not to be. You may be pushing your own agenda, pursuing a goal or trying to achieve a desired result. While human, notice how this narcissistic pursuit has no love in it. It's all about me, me, me – what 'I' want. *I want you to love me! I want you to want me! I want you to like me and be like me, and like me the way I like you. Give to me as I give to you and I'll be happy, if you're happy!*

While perception can only happen from and through ourselves, it still involves getting ourselves out of the way to reach toward the other person; it is a perpetual reaching for new beginnings. Starting over ensures the freshness of experience.

> *Love flourishes through perception of difference rather than an egocentric desire for sameness.*

Put reflection on hold to allow a pre-reflective space to open up so that clear perceptions can appear.[5] Then, reflections that follow perceptions may well be of value.

Seeing and hearing clearly avoids misrecognitions and cuts through misrepresentations. I can hear when you don't really mean it and you can see when I am not entirely genuine about how I feel. He can tell when she is faking it. And she can sense when he is performing.

Perception is a means of receptivity of the other person; it is your way of experiencing that other person. You are not literally taking them inside you but you are getting an impression. Ideally, such impressions are most accurate in so far as they are free from what you put there. Then, you get the *feel* of the other, a vibe or energy, some threads from the complex weave of their being that is now becoming interwoven with your own. It helps if you are clear about what threads are yours and those that belong to this other person. Knowing how you are, where you are looking from, what you bring to the fabric of your meeting with this other person helps to clarify what belongs to you and what belongs to them.

It is fair to want something. Most of us are not so enlightened that we are entirely free from desire. But be careful that your desire does not overly determine what unfolds between the two of you. Otherwise, the fabric of your meeting consists primarily of aspects of yourself, the threads of your own projected attributions and agendas.

At its worst, two people can conceive a mutual fantasy together, *une folie a deux* (a term referring to psychotic delusion) which can be compelling and intense. It can even feel fulfilling for as long as it lasts. But such conceptions tend to have a short use-by date.

Eventually, one person wakes up as if from a dream and, as the dream is shattered by the dawning realization that love was based on an imaginary reality, a depressing sense

---

5. This is a 'phenomenological attitude' for those philosophically inclined. (See the work of Maurice Merleau-Ponty. A good place to begin is the Preface to *Phenomenology of Perception*.)

of disillusionment takes over. The two of you can no longer continue as you were; such dreams often end in tears.

Is it worth hesitating before you plunge headlong (and heartlong) into the deep water?

The aim is to develop attunement grounded in the other's experience of the world, arising from your perceptions of them. Being clear about what belongs to the other person and what belongs to you facilitates perceptions that promote attunement.

Then it becomes just as important to be perceptible as it is to be perceptive so that your partner may become attuned to you. Hence, the difference of 'otherness' becomes the beginning of relating and the origin of the possibility of love. Over time and attuned experiencing, love is cultivated and grows between you as an unfolding 'thing' beyond any previously held concept. Then your relationship involves ongoing relating through perception and perceptibility, seeing and being visible in the fullest sense.

Trust

Vulnerability is the ground of love and trust is the foundation built upon it.

Trustworthiness on its own, however, is not enough. Being *seen* to be trustworthy is also critical. When you are both trustworthy and seen as such, you create a strong foundation for your relationship. Anxiety and insecurity are reduced and your partner feels they stand on solid ground with you.

> *Trust is the foundation of love relationships.*

To be transparent and accountable promotes trust. Maybe you feel you shouldn't have to demonstrate your trustworthiness explicitly. *I know I'm trustworthy. If you really knew me, you would know that my trustworthiness is unassailable. So, if you don't trust me – that is your problem. You are not able to trust.* Don't be surprised if your partner does have a problem that they cannot resolve, even if you do deserve to be trusted.

> When Henry and his partner Kathryn went to a party Henry spent a lot of time talking to Chrissy, who he hadn't seen for a long time. Kathryn felt abandoned and neglected because she didn't know many people at the party and was left on her own and feeling awkward.
>
> Kathryn also felt threatened because Chrissy looked like a supermodel, striking and glamorous, and Henry appeared rather excited by his contact with her. Henry felt completely innocent because Chrissy was his cousin. The trouble was, Kathryn didn't know that.
>
> When Kathryn expressed her grievance to Henry he first dismissed it as being silly. Then he put himself in Kathryn's position (with empathy) and realized he should explain in detail about his family tie with Chrissy, their history (they used to play together as children at family gatherings) and the reasons behind their losing contact (her family moved away) and so on.
>
> Henry's account was credible and through spelling it out in detail he enabled Kathryn to feel better, *and her trust in Henry was restored*. Kathryn's feelings of discomfort, neglect and being threatened could likely have been avoided if Henry had introduced her to Chrissy, and included her, as the exchange was unfolding.

We are called upon to trust, even though trust doesn't come with guarantees.

Perhaps everyone has limits to their trustworthiness. There is a tension between self-interest and privileging the interest of the other person. When it comes to love, perhaps trust is privileging the interest of your significant other such that they can count on you to do so. Does this have to be absolute? I would say not.

The inherent contest between loving someone and self-interest can generate an internal debate that is difficult to negotiate. Mal, who we met in Chapter 1, had to decide whether the feelings of his partner were more important than being friendly to someone he hardly knew, Charlene, the waitperson in the café.

In a different sort of example, what if there is a bowl of chips on the table and a large bloke comes home from work ravenously hungry. There are three other people there in the family, his partner and two children. He loves them all dearly *and* he is starving. Should his share be a quarter of the total number of chips or might he have a little more? Does being the biggest physically entitle him to more? How hungry are the others? How do they measure? What is fair? How do they know? What is fairness based on? Who decides? Who decides who decides? Who's counting? Who counts?

○○○

Knowing someone for who they are is as crucial for trust as it is for love. If we want the love to grow, to blossom and to be all it can be, then we need to work on our own trustworthiness while keeping an eye on that of our partner. No one likes to be a fool or be fooled.

I am not advocating that you should trust your partner with blind faith. Being naïve leaves you terribly exposed and too vulnerable. Don't set yourself up for a fall – possibly a serious emotional injury – when the truth comes out. On the other hand, if you are too circumspect, cautious or suspicious, then love is likely to wither, and eventually shrivel up. There is a balance between being overly suspicious and asleep to warning signs.

> *You can trust someone as far as you know them.*

Some people definitely deserve not to be trusted even if they appear to be trustworthy. My therapy practice has shown me that more people lead double lives than many of us suspect.

> Lachie was a successful writer. His novels were full of sex, love, romance, passion, betrayal, deceptions, lies, cheating and risky rendezvous. It all came from his overactive imagination, he told his wife. In reality, his vivid and often florid descriptions were based on his actual experiences, many of which occurred during his marriage.
>
> His wife sometimes wondered if she recognized one of the characters in his books. But she trusted him because he was as good at concealment as he was at writing.

Either relationships grow on a strong foundation of trust or wobble on a weak foundation of mistrust. How can you ever get on with anything – working, looking after children, making a home, running a business, playing sport, being creative – if you are worried about your partner and what they might be getting up to?

True transparency and honest accountability make for a peaceful mind and a relaxed body. Otherwise, your internal radar is likely to be on high alert, monitoring hyper-vigilantly, scanning for signs of inconsistency, deception or betrayal. How can love flourish in that sort of environment? The primary elements of trust are:

- Honesty
- Accountability
- Transparency
- Respect
- Reliability and dependability
- Consistency
- Straightforwardness
- Genuineness
- Contrition
- Care
- Fidelity both sexually and to the spirit of the relationship

These elements are interrelated but each is worth cultivating in itself, and also worth practicing individually and together as part of your relationship. While doubt may be unavoidable, and some degree of faith is a part of trust, the elements above, if practiced diligently, engender a firm feeling of trust.

Being manifestly trustworthy by embodying all of the elements, without ambiguity, promotes trust. Otherwise, you place your partner in the quandary of having to trust you only on faith.

If you keep parts of yourself split off and private from your partner, this perpetuates doubt and so limits the degree to which you can be known and, hence, loved. Transparency allows you to be seen and seen through. Then your partner doesn't have to give you the benefit of the doubt.

That said, you don't have to be an open book in every respect and all of the time. Transparency is called for where it is needed.

> Manfred loved his wife Maggie and frequently referred to her as the most perfect being in creation. She loved him too with an unwavering devotion.
>
> However, Manfred came from a horrendously traumatizing family. His father was sadistic and his mother could be hateful. He felt this left him prone to negative thoughts and sometimes extremely violent fantasies.
>
> He could imagine himself plunging a kitchen knife into Maggie's back. He might imagine drowning her in the bath or strangling her in her sleep. Sometimes he wondered if he should leave her to protect her from himself.
>
> He did not, however, struggle with impulse control. He knew rationally he would never act on these thoughts. He knew they arose as a defense against his vulnerability and his fear of being hurt. He knew that he might be overcome by such intrusive and hostile thoughts if he was even a little angry at Maggie. He also knew that his job was to manage his own mind, contain his thoughts and conduct himself in

a manner consistent with his truest and deepest feelings of love, respect and admiration for his partner.

Manfred never voiced a word of these thoughts to Maggie but brought them to therapy instead. She was not completely unaware. She knew he wrestled with inner demons. She could feel his hostility at times, but she also respected his privacy and his right to deal with his inner life in his own way. And so she was able to hold faith in trusting him.

So long as Manfred can control himself, this strategy makes sense and fortifies the foundation of trust between them.

Fidelity, both sexually and to the spirit of the relationship, is crucial to trust. Fidelity literally means to be true and to have faith. Love relationships require each partner to have faith in the other's ability to remain true, to protect each other's hearts and to preserve the exclusive field of the relationship, if that is your agreement.

> *Faith in each other grows through the feeling of trust and mutual trustworthiness.*

The meaning of 'the spirit of the relationship' is often implicit. If it is not negotiated and agreed upon explicitly through discussions, then it may take the form of an understanding that is unspoken or assumed.

Darla had given Ben financial support while he finished his studies. She had never imagined that Ben would accept an offer of six months sailing on a yacht before entering employment and making a meaningful financial contribution to their mortgage.

From his point of view, having struggled, applied himself and completed his studies, Ben felt he deserved a break.

He felt it was a stroke of good fortune that his friend needed more people to crew his boat and had invited him. However, he had accepted his friend's offer *without any discussion* about it with Darla. This meant she felt he had violated *the spirit* of their relationship. She regarded it as a form of infidelity that he took for granted that she would feel okay about his decision.

She may even have agreed – had he considered that her feelings mattered enough to raise going away as a question for their relationship. In this example we see one partner functioning as an individual, not as a member of a couple, an issue discussed in the Introduction.

○○○

Declan had cared for Carrie for two years following her diagnosis of breast cancer, and her subsequent mastectomy and chemotherapy. He had done the lion's share of the work both at home with their kids and earning money to support the family, which he continued to do for a further two years while she recovered from the effects of the chemotherapy.

Carrie had 'chemo brain' and couldn't function very well. Her memory was compromised and her cognitive functioning quite impaired. She felt like she had brain damage.

Declan then had an accident and broke his arm, making it harder for him to cook their meals. Carrie had improved considerably by this point, and he asked her to take over responsibility for the cooking. Carrie hated cooking and refused, but said she would organize takeaway (which he hated) and buy microwave-ready meals (which he hated more) but she didn't want to agree to cook all the time.

Having made a monumental effort to look after everyone for more than four years, Declan was aggrieved that Carrie now felt that cooking for a few weeks was such a terrible imposition. He felt 'short-changed' and disappointed. He couldn't help feelings of resentment welling up. It was only at this juncture that he experienced it as a breach of his sense of natural justice and, hence, a breach of his understanding of the spirit of the relationship.

Part of being faithful is being fair.

○○○

Ian and Kevin had an open relationship. They had an explicit agreement that it was okay to have sex with other people. They didn't even need to tell each other.

One day, Kevin had sex with Ian's ex. Ian was furious. He had shared many times how traumatized he had been by his former partner. He considered it an extremely abusive relationship in which he had been used and exploited in many ways. Ian had told Kevin that he had a deep well of emotional hurt as a result of that relationship.

Kevin couldn't understand what the problem was. How could his behavior be wrong when they had an explicitly open relationship?

The sexual infidelity was not the infidelity that mattered to Ian. It was the choice of sexual partner. This betrayed fidelity to the spirit of the relationship and specifically to Ian's feelings.

It was as if his feelings about his ex didn't matter – feelings that had been spoken about many times. Ian felt Kevin should know that his ex was the only person Ian would mind him being sexual with.

> *'True to the spirit of the relationship' means privileging the union between you over self-interest.*

My wife Cath has some useful thoughts on trust:
- Sexual infidelity often begins with coffee. Seemingly innocent interactions lead incrementally to not-so-innocent ones over time, often unfolding in a sequence such as coffee, then lunch, then drinks, then dinner, then a kiss ...
- Respect means speaking and acting just as you would if your partner was standing next to you.
- Trust flourishes when you avoid indulging in ambiguity such as pretending to be single when not. True fidelity involves wearing the 'unavailable' sign so other people know you are in a committed relationship and not open to anything else.
- If you're not happy in your relationship, and it can't be 'fixed' (repaired, redeemed, retrieved) then get out before you act-out.

Gifting each other reciprocal trust and respect means you can each move freely through the world and your lives without feeling limited or self-conscious as a consequence of fidelity.

> *Trust promotes freedom whereas mistrust promotes restrictions.*

The dance of love

While some people approach relating to a potential lover as a matter of conquest, love has more to do with receptiveness. But how can you elicit receptiveness from the object of your affection so they meet your interest and emerging feelings? Perhaps the answer – when it goes well – is like a dance of love.

You step toward the other and then you step back. You step forward to be noticed. You step back to create room for them to come forward to meet you. If you only step forward then the other must step back or else you will bowl them over. If you only step back, they will tire of following you. If you come on too strong, you risk driving your love interest away. If you don't come forward strongly enough, you risk not being noticed, or you fail to elicit enough interest.

There is a rhythm and a movement that helps put you in sync with each other. You want to connect and most often this needs to be a gradual, gentle process.

Part of this practice is learning how to dance with *this* love interest, *because each partner will dance with you differently.* How you dance depends on who you are and how you are feeling in the moment. How you dance also depends on who your counterpart is and how they are feeling in the moment.

> Eleana became insecure and had thoughts of calling it off with Jimmy when his mood became low and appeared a little sour. He was hot for her initially so why was he like this now? Eleana surmised that Jimmy probably didn't feel as much for her anymore; *he's cooled down,* she thought, *what should she do?* I simply suggested: *ask him.*

> She did and he explained that he had a condition like chronic fatigue syndrome. When he was unwell and lacking in energy, it affected him badly and he became a little depressed. He wondered if he would ever be well again. It had nothing to do with her. Actually, he felt as hot for her as before and, if anything, part of his depression was that he lacked the energy to express his desire.

If he is indifferent it could mean that he is preoccupied with something else that has nothing to do with you. *It doesn't have to mean that he is not interested in you.* If she is discouraging it could mean that she is just finishing up another relationship and isn't quite ready for you – yet. *It doesn't have to mean that she is not interested in you.* In both cases, if you can keep a clear mind and a pure heart – that is, you retain your emotional self-sufficiency – then the signs that you perceive in the other's reactions to you provide indications. Be perceptive but don't read too much into it; assumptions can turn out to be wrong. The indications here are to slow down and take a step back. Being in too much of a hurry can ruin a good initial contact. This indicates neediness, as discussed before. Love and haste do not go well together.

Dance slowly, or dance fast if your partner is right there with you, but don't dance completely differently to the other. The idea is to improvise your dance with each other and this should be fun. If it worries you unduly, that spoils the fun and the dance becomes more of a drag than play. Dancing well together is a precursor to co-sexuality. It can be the before-play of foreplay.

By 'play' I don't mean that this is not serious. It could become serious. This person could turn out to be the love of your life. *That's serious.* You may go on to have children and spend the rest of your lives together. *That's serious too!* Remember: love is a life and death matter and life is a love and death matter.

Let's explore the metaphor of play; there is a paradox in play that reflects a paradox in love. Playing sport is most enjoyable when we take it seriously. It isn't important but it can feel that we have everything to lose, that everything is at stake in the outcome. When we play music, the more serious the practice, the better is the performance. We might perform as if our life depends on it but it is just playing. Once performed, the live performance is gone forever. When we see a play, if it's done well, it is compelling. Yet, it's all an act. These contradictions reflect the paradoxical nature of play.

You may have lived your whole life perfectly well without this new person with whom you have found love. Now you feel as if your whole life depends on this relationship working out. It means the world to you. Yet, you've only recently met and hardly know each other. Despite that, losing the possibility of a relationship feels unbearable.

The love you have with *this* person can never be the same with anyone else, yet you still have to be okay without it (there's emotional self-sufficiency again). This may be easier said than felt.

Romeo could not live without Juliet just as Juliet could not live without Romeo. Strong attachment can be this tragic.

A light touch in matters of love means that you are okay without it even though you feel invested. A light touch gives the other space and time to see how they feel and to want to move closer toward you, or not. It is okay either way. Even though it is the most serious thing, the most important thing, you still have to be able to live without it. That is the paradox.

Let's face it: you have already been living without this person who you love and want to love you. If you really cannot live without them now, this places a highly questionable loading upon what is being called 'love'. Is it your concept of love, a story akin to a fairy tale? How did you become so dependent so quickly? Is it love or your need for a particular outcome? Are you desperately hooked or desperate to do the hooking?

There really are other fish in the sea.

So, dance well, dance lightly, dance freely, dance perceptively and dance receptively. Learn the steps, the moves, and the gestures that work and reach your partner. Learn to dance in step with your partner's way of dancing with you. Learn the dance that they want to dance, and then enjoy dancing together and enjoy dancing apart.

> An English woman named Karen was in love with Kojo, an African-American man. They had been friends, then they had been lovers. In fact, they worked well as lovers. But Kojo had come out of a long marriage and had no interest in getting into another one, at least not yet.
>
> Kojo was about to embark on a long adventure in the Himalayas and through Nepal and India and across to Southeast Asia, Indonesia, and then back home. He planned to travel alone and take time out from his usual life, friendships, work and even his children.

Kojo was independent and there was a feeling between him and Karen that with such a long break she shouldn't wait for him. He didn't want to pair up with anyone and he thought that probably when he returned the casual sexual relationship would have expired: Karen was bound to find someone else. They would probably just be friends again.

Karen wrote regular emails to Kojo while he was abroad. She did not expect him to reply and she did not demand anything from him. Kojo liked hearing from Karen, to her surprise. He appreciated her willingness to keep the connection going, and he liked being connected to her even though he was happy to be off traveling alone.

He felt that she was truly in touch with him, fully attuned. It was not too much and not too little. The emails were loving but not overpowering.

Kojo began to make a point of finding an internet café even in quite remote places, and he specifically looked for emails from Karen. He noticed how uplifting it was to have one from her. He noticed that he missed her more as time passed.

When he returned, he felt more connected to Karen than when he left. And to make a long story very much shorter, they eventually moved in together, married, and have continued to live happily together for more than 12 years.

○○○

An Irish woman named Mary was attracted to Denise, an Aboriginal Australian. Denise, being straight, was only interested in romance with men. In fact, Denise often went to Mary for advice about the men she was interested in, even though Mary was lesbian and mainly told her to give them up.

Mary was attracted to Denise and though she mainly kept it to herself, Denise was aware of her attraction. Mary contained her feelings as she didn't want to make Denise feel uncomfortable or compromise their close friendship. And Denise did feel comfortable with Mary. They gave each other massages and went out to the movies, for meals sometimes and for drinks. They shared an interest in a local band and whenever the opportunity arose, they would go to gigs and dance and have a lot of fun together.

Denise grew to feel that she could never find a man that would be as attentive, understanding and empathic as her friend Mary. Mary was highly attuned to Denise; to her needs, her preferences, her moods and her feelings. She knew when to be there for Denise and when to leave her alone. She knew how to lift Denise's mood when she got a little low, and she knew how to make her laugh. She was connected but not too connected. She was attuned but not too attuned.

Even though Denise was exclusively heterosexual she had no issue with Mary's sexual preferences. Mary was attractive and had no problem finding sexual partners. But her feelings for Denise were more about love and her interest in sex with Denise reflected her desire to express the love that had grown between them.

One day Denise had been disappointed by a guy she was interested in who had become involved with someone else. She and Mary went out and had a few drinks but then Denise felt miserable and wanted to go home. She asked Mary if she would like to come in because it was still early – she just didn't want to be out any longer.

Inside the house, Mary could see that Denise was hurting and so she held her, stroking her back and her hair. In that moment, Denise felt more receptive to Mary, she felt close, and for the first time she felt a homoerotic desire. She pressed her lips against Mary's mouth, much to Mary's surprise. In that moment, there was no need for Mary to be reserved any longer. She had wanted to make love with Denise for a long time.

Before she let herself go, she hesitated as she didn't want to take advantage of her friend's vulnerability in that moment. She paused and looked Denise right in her eyes. *Are you sure?* Mary asked, checking whether this was *really* what Denise wanted. *I am sure,* she answered with an unambiguous look of appreciation that Mary cared for her sufficiently not to let her own sexual desires run away with her at Denise's expense.

Sex and love coalesced in the co-sexuality between them.

In this example, sexual orientation became less important and less determining than the feeling of love between two people. It simply didn't matter. How beautiful.

Let's lay aside the usual stereotypes. 'Looks' are not the most important thing. Age is not the most important thing. Religion is not the most important thing. Wealth or socioeconomic status is not the most important thing, nor race, ethnicity or nationality. And there are so many other differences between people that do not have to matter when it comes to love.

Between adults, when love is paramount, practically everything else is a detail. What matters is attunement and connectedness.

Attunement and connectedness are catalysts that with time may generate loving feelings in the other. Attunement and connectedness are key themes in the music that underscores the dance of love. Listen carefully. Let the music guide your movements and that of your partner, until you discover how to move together with grace and style.

The place of romance

The concept of romance has only been recorded for 800 or so years. Many scholars believe that the story of Tristan and Isolde marks one of the first references to romantic love in Western literature. This mythic story first appeared in the late 12th century, but the story is understood to have occurred in the late 5th or early 6th century.

Tristan was supposed to be fetching Isolde from Ireland for his uncle, the English King Mark, to marry. While accounts vary, consistent across all is that Tristan and Isolde fell in love with each other because they drank a love potion. Although Isolde went on to marry King Mark, she and Tristan were compelled by the strength of their love to seek one another as lovers, despite the likely calamitous consequences.

There is an implication that we fall into romantic love because of almost magical forces that originate outside ourselves. Many will attest this feels true to experience.

The term 'romance' has crossed boundaries, cultures and centuries, to evolve into modern usage. I wonder if 'romance' originally referred to how the Romans loved? The popular notion of romance now refers to intense and all-consuming love that's exciting, idealistic and heroic. It is the love of stories, novels and films.

Some people seek more romance in their lives and loves, and some positively do not want it or seek it at all. Some go to considerable lengths to avoid it.

If you are getting excited about someone other than your partner, your primary relationship is probably in need of attention. If you are not careful, the new love interest may replace the current one. If you are already in a relationship and become romantically involved with someone outside the relationship, don't be surprised if it is discovered and your world is turned upside down. Romance changes us and it is detectable despite your best efforts at concealment.

If you require romance in your relationships, take responsibility for creating it. It's no good sitting around, fantasizing about that one in the office with the hot body, or that other one who walks their dog in the park same time as you do, noticing you and making eye contact. If you've grown bored or your primary relationship is stale or stagnant, so utterly predictable that you could write the script of what happens next, breathe some life into it. It's time to do things differently or perhaps have a breathing space apart.

Love relationships are extremely personal so when deciding how to breathe life in, it has to be in your own way – a way that expresses who you are, what you feel and what you want and, of course, who your partner is. 'Date night' has become popular amongst couples as a way to carve out some time for themselves exclusively as a couple, away from the responsibilities of work, home and kids.

Many of us value romance, passion, and the personal expression of feelings. If individual pursuits take over and the relationship suffers, if your partner feels neglected, or the relationship becomes static or dull, attend to the relationship. The longer this imbalance goes on, the greater the need to take remedial action.

Sometimes the traditional clichés have value – a bunch of flowers, a candlelight dinner, a special gift, a romantic getaway for a night or weekend, a beautiful home-cooked meal, a visit to a good restaurant, a massage, jewelry, a special present such as a subscription, concert tickets, or perhaps a book on love! The actual form a gift or gesture takes is usually less important than the symbolic value of the act, especially if the act of giving is a departure from pattern. In any case, doing something says something. It says your partner matters. And that is the beginning of the romantic quality.

If you are imaginative, or creative, make the romance act unique, and that makes it all the more special. This quality of chivalry, of going all out, and also of surprise is particular to romance.

The downside of romance is that when expectations are set too high, disappointment is inevitable. Sometimes the need for romance is beyond what can be offered, perhaps by anyone. When you are indulged by wild romantic offerings, seductions, enticements and spoiling, and it winds down or stops, what then?

The ensuing vacuum will be felt as intensely painful as the previous romantic gestures were rewarding.

If a relationship begins romantically, it may need to transition to a more practical, less intense *modus vivendi*, through a gradual downshift of expectation and romance. If the pace is smooth and the adjustment is sensitive, it can happen without undue pain or disappointment. It can even be a relief. This does not mean that romance is dead or never needs to be renewed.

One of the most difficult scenarios occurs when one partner requires romance and the other doesn't, or when one feels romantic and has a drive to express it, and the other is unmoved or disinterested. Each needs to take a step toward the other.

For many of us, there is something delightful about romance. Done well, we find romance a thrill, a rush, and something to look forward to. It can be uplifting, intoxicating and erotic. Maybe romance is our best natural anti-depressant. It brings a charge of electricity to the mundane.

Romance prior to sex builds both emotional and physical arousal, heightening the sense of excitement. It can be a soul high, a whole being turn-on, a new source of eros. As such, romance is conducive to intimacy which is generative of love and sexual fulfillment. Then, consider how to keep it alive and lasting. Romance has a place in love, if you want it to, but is not the same thing as love. It is a distinctive way of relating to someone special.

> *Romance dances on the stage of eros in the making and re-making of love.*

CHAPTER 3
Is This the One?

> *"Love is the child of illusion
> and the parent of disillusion."*
> — **Miguel de Unamuno**

How do you know?

How do you know anything? How do you really know with conviction what you want? There are inconsequential decisions such as what you want for dinner and there are issues that will affect your entire future depending upon what you decide. How do you know who you want as a life partner? The underlying basis of knowing, as an expression of your personal subjectivity, is how you feel. At the same time, feelings have no meaning without thinking.

Pure sensation is a different experience from feeling your feelings. When you put your hand under the boiling hot water faucet, the burning sensation is OWWW! That is pure sensation and doesn't require thought. If you feel anything of an emotional nature, then thought is an essential adjunct in order to know what it means. Thoughts and feelings need to accompany each other. They are partners in experiencing.

Feeling and thinking may or may not be congruent. You might feel like fast food but think that a salad would be better for you. You might feel like having sex with this new person and then you think that would be a good way to wreck your current relationship. Then, what you feel and what you think is incongruent. You have a choice.

When feelings and thinking are congruent, it is much easier to know. When we know, we know. We know because we know ourselves. We know because we know how we feel and what that means to us. If the mental and emotional channels are open, integrated and informing each other, then the question doesn't arise. It is a given; self-evident. There is no question when the 'answer' manifests.

If you have to ask the question: *is this the one?* then the answer is not already there, or not clear to you. Further questions arise.

- What is getting in the way of feeling clearly what this person means to you?
- Is there a gap between your concept, a concept infused with desire, and your perception of this 'one'?
- Are your feelings not yet fully formed? (When feelings are formed they become signified, that means symbolized by being formulated in language. When unformed but in process, this is called 'unformulated experience'.[6])

> *Feelings formulated in language become available to consciousness as a 'knowing'.*

If feelings are not in focus, then the question arises prematurely. Perhaps you feel impatient. You want to know because you don't like the uncertainty of not knowing. Are you ready to know?

Love takes time. Knowing if this is the one, or how long this will last, or whether you should commit to the exclusion of all others, are all questions that need time. Time for the feelings and

---

6. Donnel Stern has written an important book of this title *Unformulated Experience* but my introduction to this idea comes from an earlier text by Donald Winnicott: *Playing and Reality*.

corresponding thinking-through to crystallize. It can be hard to wait but love is a fruit that has to ripen to achieve its maximum sweetness, or as Shakespeare famously put it in *Romeo and Juliet:*

> "This bud of love,
> by summer's ripening breath,
> May prove a beauteous flower
> when next we meet."

Feelings are signposts of experience and point in particular directions, agreeably or disagreeably. Feelings inform our judgments and, as such, become a basis for subjective knowing. The question of knowing if this is the one is much like the very questions of love:

- Do I love you?
- How much do you love me?
- Is this the best love we could have right now?

How can we answer? It depends on how we feel.

What do feelings depend on? They depend on what happens between us. Feelings also depend on what we want, and how we are disposed, which is largely a function of our histories. However well we understand the historical influences, it is not always easy to know exactly how we feel.

> In one moment, we are together, and it feels so right. In the next, we are apart, and then I'm not so sure. I don't know what I feel. I don't even know if I feel anything.
>
> Then we are together and we go out to dinner. We are on the same page. The connection is so strong. We make love. We orgasm together at the same time. Sheer bliss. Yes, I know. I'm sure. You are the one. I'm certain of it.
>
> The next day, I don't feel the same. I'm not so happy. I'm a little bit cranky. I feel uncertain, I'm not so sure. Maybe we should call the whole thing off? (Surely I could do better.)

Feelings can be deceptive, confusing, contradictory. Feelings can oscillate, vacillate, obfuscate. How many times have I heard someone being so definite, marry even, and then feel maybe it was a mistake?

Feelings need to mature like a fine wine. And like a fine wine, feelings can go off, become sour and unpalatable.

Feelings can be elusive, cryptic, obscure and mystifying. Feelings can require reflection, discussion, translation, or unpacking, illuminating and decoding. Feelings lose their sense without being thought-through. We can also over think them and question them out of existence. Analysis paralysis.

Feelings can mislead, betray and deceive. Be very careful if someone says: *it depends on how you feel*. Feelings can lead you up the garden path, down the slippery slope, plunge you down the bottomless pit, to the darkest of places. Do mind your feelings; clichés exist for a reason.

Where is the place of rationality in all this? Think carefully through all of the ramifications of this person 'being the one', or not. Surely you should bring thought to the matter, bring the matter to mind, be mindful of what matters. Surely you should weigh up the pros and cons, what is for and against, the pluses and minuses. Put logic through its paces: induction, deduction and reduction. Synthesize the dialectic. Extract the heat from our emotions and see what is left.

The question: *how do I know if this is the one?* is answered through the interplay of head and heart, thinking and feeling.

You may need to know the other person better than you already do, through shared experiences over time. In the process, be mindful of the above and practice reflective self-awareness: feel with thought and think with feeling.

> Gabby and Dean consulted me because, having found him flirting with a girl online, Gabby was losing trust in him. He confessed and promised to 'clean up his act'. I urged him to practice a much fuller sense of accountability and transparency. He understood, seemed sincere and gave assurances.

However, the next session Gabby was more anxious and distressed. It turned out that certain representations Dean had made about himself, namely that he had been a law student and was soon to commence his articles, were not true. She had been convinced by his use of words like *exculpatory* and *jurisprudence* that gave credibility but there was now an emerging sense that the Dean that Gabby was dating was not who he made himself out to be.

They were both in their late twenties and ready to commit to a future together; they had spoken of buying a house and moving forward. She *felt* close to him, loved him deeply and believed he was going to be her life partner – 'the one'. All of this left her very confused.

Dean had indicated that he was soon to be in receipt of a substantial insurance payout. When he spent all of her money in their joint account on acquisitions for himself *without discussing this with her*, it was the last straw. Gabby started to panic.

Her inquiries revealed that almost nothing Dean had said was true. He had never been a law student, there was no position lined up to do articles, there was no insurance claim, and he had no real prospect of earning an income.

Her parents had suspected from the start and now wanted nothing more to do with him. They advised her to cut her losses. (Sometimes, parents are right!)

Dean protested that he was a good person despite the evidence, he did love her, he did want a future together, and he would 'work on himself' and make amends. He revealed a traumatic past of abuse and exploitation and begged her to forgive him, to understand, to give him another chance to prove himself.

Now Gabby was even more confused. Her faith in Dean had been completely rocked. But the feeling of being together, sexual intimacy, their dreams for the future, and his contrition and pleadings for compassion all struck her deeply. What should she do?

Gabby was split between how she felt toward Dean and what she thought about his conduct. She still wanted it to work out; she *loved* him.

She was still attached to her idea of how they could share a future together, despite the lies and misrepresentations. His earnest assertions moved her. But she had believed him before; he had demonstrated beyond doubt that he could not be trusted. Should she abandon her hopes and desires and discount her feelings?

After much soul searching, Gabby decided that she had to separate out how she wanted it to be – that she was ready for a life partner and was attached to the idea of a future with Dean – from the truth of the present situation.

She asked him to move out, even though it broke her heart.

Therapists help clients make their own choices, sometimes pivotal life decisions, for themselves. Often, it is abundantly clear that they have made the right one. Of course, I hope Dean will realize the need to take responsibility for the hurt he has caused, see the need to work on himself and address his traumatic history, and the consequences of his actions.

For a time, rationalization organized Gabby's thinking to construct things the way she most wanted, fulfilling her agenda. She could only see what she wanted to see. 'Knowing' was built according to her own design; like holding in mind an architect's blueprint of her ideal partner before really knowing Dean. The more she grew to know him, the more the answer emerged though it was not the answer she wanted.

> *There is no objective mind that stands outside of the relationship being assessed.*

Gaining objectivity in love is a challenge. You cannot be outside of the relationship you are in, in order to make objective judgments about it. Still, the clarity and definiteness you seek requires a certain sense of objectivity. So while you cannot step out of a relationship to judge whether or not it is right for you, you can aim to see your investments and desires. You can be aware of your agendas. You can work at separating out the way you want it to be from what is, as Gabby did, above.

You need to get this right, your future depends on it. The more you can process disappointment, and the more you can face what is there, the quicker you can cut your losses – if this is what needs to be done.

When I saw Gabby again some time after she split from Dean, she was still pained by what had happened. Despite that, she felt sure she had done the right thing. She knew he was not the one. She felt disappointed and ripped off, but also freer and relieved to be moving on. I was supportive without reservation.

Being objective, subjectively

> Sarah knew that Christopher was an asshole, as she put it to me. Privately, she laughed with her friends about his idiotic habits, like counting the cutlery to ensure that the cleaner hadn't stolen anything. She mocked his obsessional tendencies; always having to go back into the house to check the windows were locked and the stove turned off. He was forever straightening the wall hangings and the furniture.
>
> She derided his need to spend more time beautifying himself in front of the mirror than she did. And she was contemptuous of his 'kill-or-be-killed' attitude in his job

as a financial advisor. He not only lured elderly people into buying products that would give him a fat commission, even though he knew the product would not benefit them, but also laughed at how easy it was to convince them.

Most of all, she loathed his selfish attitude in bed. He was out for himself and not concerned about her having a 'happy ending'. He was an asshole, no two ways about it.

Sarah rationalized her decision to marry Christopher. She convinced herself that deep down he was a good man and kidded herself that she could overlook the aspects of Christopher she didn't like. *There are always some things we have to live with*, she said. *True*, I responded skeptically.

Besides he was incredibly good-looking; the classic tall, dark-haired, slim and strongly built handsomely featured alpha male. When they went out, she could feel the envy of other women.

He came from a wealthy family, and he earned truckloads of money, too. He bought her expensive jewelry that she loved to show off. When Christopher got that cheeky smile and pulled another little box out of his suit jacket pocket, her heart soared with excitement. Even if she didn't really love Christopher, she really loved that!

Where is the heart in this example?

Thought is needed in the service of emotions to prevent rationalizations from blinding you to what you prefer not to see. There is a difference between being blind and knowing it, and being blind and not knowing it; we can be blind to our own blindness. Kidding yourself that you can make a marriage work because your partner is good-looking, and you like jewelry, or thinking 'it's a lifestyle choice', is a form of self-deception based on rationalization. You can convince yourself that loving a person for 'who they are' isn't all that important.

Maybe Sarah and Christopher can make good 'use' of being married to each other for a time, but it has all the hallmarks of leading to an unhappy conclusion. Such relationships tend to produce loneliness and disaffection. Her duplicity, for example, is likely to be uncovered eventually, and the jewelry, presents and other material possessions will grow stale over time if that is all there is. Possibly the void of love will prompt the search for it elsewhere.

Working toward objectivity requires thinking and feeling to inform one another, though we must acknowledge their unavoidably subjective nature. This is not scientific objectivity but rather a highly personal mode of objectivity that cannot be proven by research.

When our perceptions and judgements are on the mark, the conclusions that are borne out of that 'objective subjectivity' tend to work better (as they did for Gabby). A feeling of objectivity prevails when we have assessed the situation accurately and not been unduly swayed by our emotions.

> *When a personal truth feels objective it stands the test of time.*

ooo

If what you want most is to find an ideal love – a love so glorious in its perfection that there is no doubt – then anything less cannot be the one. Even if you feel your current relationship is the best you have ever experienced, you might wonder if there is more. Should you pursue that? But what if you are hoping for something so impossibly amazing, romantic and beautiful that you deny yourself the experience of having a relationship as good as this one? On the other hand, what if you are settling for something less than it could be? No one can tell you.

These are pivotal questions, and their answers will shape how things unfold. You need to be able to see the future in order to judge what to do in the present, impossible as that is.

Some young women, in particular, feel a tremendous pressure to be married and start a family by 25 years old, or even younger. It sounds almost more important to be married than who they are married to!

It is as if self-esteem depends on having it all. It seems more important to obtain this particular life – 'the package' ideally including owning your own home and car, and living a certain lifestyle – than to have grown up enough emotionally to make possible a loving relationship that works. This involves rationalizing the deficiencies to protect the concept of a complete package. But the appearance of 'having love' or having 'it all' doesn't feel satisfying or fulfilling over time; it wears off. Obtaining 'the package' is no substitute for actively renewing a more deeply felt connection. The complete package looks like getting the one who also gets you as their one but if esteem is based mainly on appearances and there is little inside the packaging then all that has been purchased is a veneer of love. Without content, it will be hard to feel content.

Developing emotional self-sufficiency enables you to resist the pressure of cultural traditions or (imagined?) societal expectations to enter marriage prematurely. It is better to develop yourself individually so that you can enjoy a loving relationship when the time comes than to use a relationship to compensate for deficiencies in yourself. Then you also don't have to settle for a relationship that is not quite right. You don't have to rationalize what is or idealize what could be. If you don't feel pressured, your perspective will be more realistic and will balance toward objective assessments.

The question: *is this the one?* is such a difficult one. What if it is impossible to answer? How can you ever know if you would have been better off with another partner? Or going down a different path? We can think of films like *Sliding Doors* where the butterfly effect of one event or choice changes the entire course of what happens in the future.

Consider questions such as:
- What if there is no 'one'?
- What if there is more than one 'one'?
- What if life turns out to be a series of different 'ones' that are right or, at least good enough, for a period of time?

Similarly, the question: *how do you know?* is one of the most difficult questions to answer. Some people say they 'just know' – great! If not, you have to reconcile that while this relationship may not be perfect it has enough going for it to commit. Then, dedicate yourself to making it the best it can be. Or sometimes you have to make the hard decision that no, it is not good enough, and attempts to improve it do not achieve enough. You must free yourself, as Gabby did, however painful the consequences, for the sake of making a potential space for a better love. And grieving the loss enables us to move on.

Maybe the next one will be *the* one or, at very least, a one that is worth investing in.

The in-love feeling

The in-love feeling is one of the best feelings there is. When in love, we are preoccupied with the other, the object of our in-loveness. We think about them all the time. There is high esteem, admiration, respect and often some idealization. There is desire – desire to be sexual and desire to be wanted in return. And desire for our love to be received, valued and requited. The in-love feeling could be called a 'hypnoid' state.

A hypnoid state is one that resembles being hypnotized. You are mesmerized by the other. You are entranced. You are taken over, consumed, devoured. Love infuses you like a drug. You are euphoric with it. You are miserable with it. You have electricity running through your body, a current that is informed by your sense of the other, your beloved. Some people love this feeling, some become addicted to it and crave it or chase it and some people never experience it.

> *The word 'passion' literally means 'to suffer'.*

Is being in love a good thing or a bad thing? Is it a state to be sought, to be pursued and encouraged? Or is it something we should resist and avoid? Freud regarded it as something akin to an illness.

I see no point in judging it at all. Most people who describe to me how they feel being in love are ecstatic when the feeling is requited. When Denise eventually requited Mary's feelings, she was overjoyed. When one is in love and the other is not, it can feel wretched. Unrequited love is intensely painful. Some feel too exposed, too vulnerable. The feeling of rejection is unbearable. When feeling in love is requited, the dance goes well and happily. But when there is a step back, any sign of cooling in the other, it quickly becomes worrying. You may ruminate: why? What does it mean? What if this or that. It is challenging to cope with the uncertainty and difficult to know what to do about it.

When in love you are whisked up and down the roller-coaster of feelings, hanging on through the peaks and troughs. You can enjoy the ride or suffer it, but it is not possible to control it. Feeling out of control, exposed, and at risk when subject to the swings and roundabouts of love is one of the primary difficulties of in-love states – it is hard to remain centered and calm.

What if I am being played? Am I being toyed or trifled with? What if he isn't sincere? What if she isn't genuine? She only loves him for his money, his looks, his status, his family. He is mainly seeking a mother for his children, a housekeeper, a sex toy, a trophy.

> One 32-year-old woman told me that after some years of marriage she realized: her husband *only* married her because he needed a wife to present at various business functions. He was a rising star at his company and bosses expected executives to be partnered. (Shortly after, she was secretly packing her things.)

○ ○ ○

Is feeling in love the best basis for a healthy and enduring relationship? While feeling in love is a powerful state for lovemaking, sometimes we can lose ourselves in it. What if we can't find ourselves again?

While the in-love feeling can last for a long time, there are no guarantees. If these feelings expire, what are the implications for your relationship? Can it continue to function and feel right without you feeling as in love as you did at the beginning?

While these are highly personal questions, I think it is desirable to renew the in-love feelings, as far as possible. At the same time, I think few relationships sustain the in-love feelings all the time over the long term.

Could feeling in love be a basis for an unhealthy relationship? As an outsider, you may look at a couple's relationship with concern. You can see the risk, and the likelihood of emotional injury. You might see it as a disaster waiting to happen, a trauma in the making.

You might feel a duty to talk the in-love person out of it. While well meant, this endeavor is not only doomed to fail but may alienate that person against you. The in-love person hates to have their feelings invalidated, and their dreams undermined. But you can be there to catch them if they fall.

Just as we can fall in love, we can also fall out of love. When in it, that seems inconceivable. When out of it, it is hard to understand how we could have been in it in the first place. What were we thinking? What did we see in that person?

Idealization easily becomes de-idealization. The positive idea becomes negative. We go from being in love to feeling disdain – a painful place for the formerly beloved to find themselves, sometimes through no fault of their own. Sometimes, the love dynamic involves projecting what is best in ourselves on to the other, but living up to this adoration can be difficult for them.

What is happening here? Why does this change occur? It can be for many reasons. With ongoing experience, one day the idealized one is likely to behave in a way that disappoints, that challenges the idealization. Sometimes, idealization seems to wear off. Over time, ordinariness prevails. Sometimes the need to idealize fades. In this context, the metaphor of falling is interesting:

- What are we falling from?
- What are we falling to, or into?
- Where do we go when we fall?
- Is falling desirable or undesirable?
- Can we fall too far?
- Can we hold back and not fall at all?
- If we fall in, can we then fall out?

If you fall too far away from yourself, can you really be all there in a love relationship? Psychologically, you may be merged or fused or in a de-differentiated state with your partner. In other words, you have lost your sense of separateness, of being a separate person. A relationship is between two separate people who are connected. There is a bond of love, a tie, a connection, and an attachment. If there is no separateness, can there be a relationship in the true sense?

Picture two eggs – each rests on its own, encased in a shell. If fertilized and the mother hen nested these two eggs until they hatched, they would produce two individual chicks. They may have a relationship with each other like brother and sister. However, if we beat the two eggs together in a bowl, there is no relationship. There is no separateness and no 'between'. There is just the making of an omelet.

When two people merge in a psychological sense, there is an incorporation of each into the other. With this assimilation, one plus one still equals one. There is a scrambling of selves.

The space between us is the potential space of connection; a space that opens the possibility for relationship. The 'falling' may be a falling into a merger and out of a separate identity from which to connect. The falling may feel like love – a falling in love – but could be more akin to a surrender of self. The risk here is of falling into adoration and away from loving; adoration and loving are not the same thing. There may be a difference between how we feel about someone and having a love relationship between us.

The underlying psychology of love and the corresponding mental states that accompany it is an immensely complex subject. There are no absolute self-contained positions that may be called separate or merged. A person is not an isolated sphere like an egg unaffected by another. And we are never so 'married' as to be indistinguishable from one another. Terms such as separate and merged refer to psychological tendencies in the shifting sands of our relation to each other. But the greater our understanding of what these positions mean in practice, the more we reduce the risk of finding ourselves sinking in quicksand. The example of Andrew to follow further illustrates this point.

○○○

The feeling of love comes over you. You find yourself immersed. You don't choose to be in love; it's not a decision, not even an intention. Correspondingly, you cannot turn it off like a light switch or turn it on again if you lose it. It is not an act of will; you can no more will to feel it than will not to. But losing the power of will does not mean you have to lose your head completely.

For some, when in love, there is no doubt that this one must be the one. Sometimes they turn out to be right, sometimes not. The *feeling* of being in love does not necessarily mean that the other is 'the one', even if it *feels* like they must be in that moment.

To be with the one – to know this beyond doubt – is something that can only be proven by the test of time. You can look back knowingly, but not forward, with certainty.

Crazy love

'Crazy love' is the pathological extension of the tendency toward extreme idealization. Global idealization or totalizing idealization usually brings disastrous consequences. The best example I know is of a friend whose fall off a 'love cliff' saw him land a long way down.

Andrew met a Spanish girl Aleta in a bar. Aleta was dancing in a cage. She looked amazing; Andrew thought she was the 'hottest' girl he had ever seen. I think he fell in love with her before they even had a conversation.

He chatted with Aleta during her breaks from dancing. He asked for her phone number, but she refused saying she never gave out her number when working.

Andrew pursued Aleta, returning to the bar and chatting during breaks until finally she relented and gave him her number. The next day he arranged a dinner date. She wouldn't allow him to come to her home after dinner, so he drove her to the train station in his flashy sports car.

Things developed. Much to Andrew's delight, they became lovers and his love for her grew. He told me that he had found 'the one'. *Definitely!* He had never felt like this before.

Formerly, Andrew had always been a 'semi' kind of guy, semi-invested, one foot in and one foot out of his relationships. This time it was different. He was so excited he could barely contain himself. He was head over heels, out of his mind, off-the-planet in love. His former reserve had evaporated; he had well and truly 'fallen'.

I was happy for him despite feeling a noticeable disquiet.

He bought her expensive gifts. He could afford it. They went away for a weekend, and Andrew seemed to me to be more and more 'gone'. I kept asking: *does she feel the same about you?* He assured me she did.

Andrew described how they would gaze into each other's eyes, and he felt completely at one with Aleta. I detected signs of merging.

After a few months, something started to change. Aleta became withdrawn and was not as willing to see Andrew frequently. Then I heard that a former boyfriend was coming to visit from Spain. It would be hard for her to see Andrew while her ex was around, she explained.

Andrew got distressed. He couldn't understand what had changed. He couldn't keep away from her, but she said she needed some space during her friend's visit.

One day Andrew asked me to drive him to her house. He wanted to see what was happening. I was worried but reluctantly gave in. Andrew was so urgent about it I thought that maybe this would shift something.

We drove to her place and parked far enough away so as not to be seen. We were stalking.

After a time, a tall, swarthy man with long black hair appeared. He was unshaven and had a guitar slung over his shoulder. Aleta met him at the front of her house, and they embraced. It was clear that this was not an ex but a current boyfriend. Andrew started to melt down.

Andrew moved into my house because he couldn't cope. I gave him a lot of support. He seemed regressed and in pieces; shattered, devastated.

He phoned Aleta and demanded that she meet him. When she did, Andrew confronted her about 'guitar man'. She admitted that he was her boyfriend but claimed she was going to end it and really loved Andrew.

Time passed and Aleta didn't end it. Guitar man stayed on with her over some weeks.

Andrew became increasingly desperate to re-engage Aleta in the in-love relationship that he felt and still believed in, despite all. To me, it looked increasingly like she was 'playing' him but I couldn't understand why. I decided to have a 'deep and meaningful' with my friend, a heart-to-heart, a man-to-man discussion. I interrogated Andrew and here is what I discovered.

Aleta had enlisted financial support from Andrew. He was giving her $2,000 per week. She claimed that she had debts and that working hard to clear them was more than she could handle. Andrew believed that they were on the way to becoming engaged and so was eager to help her.

Then there was a new story. Her mother in Spain had fallen ill. Her kidneys were failing, and she needed an expensive operation. She had fallen behind on her mortgage payments because she couldn't work and was about to lose her house. Aleta had been sending her money but couldn't keep up with it. Her mother now needed $50,000. The situation was desperate. She promised she was genuine about her feelings toward Andrew and please could he help her.

Andrew transferred the money. Guitar man stayed. Aleta still didn't spend any time with Andrew. He still believed she loved him.

I was distraught. I could see what was happening. But it was impossible for my friend to see it. I pleaded with him to stop giving her money, to see things for what they were and to cut his losses. He didn't like my saying this. Previously, I wrote that trying to talk an in-love person out of it is futile and alienates the friendship, and yet I felt a compelling moral responsibility to try.

Sometimes those outside of the relationship can see more clearly than those immersed in 'love'. The story of Andrew is an extreme example of a hypnoid state.

I asked Andrew how he could be so certain that she really did love him when her actions clearly indicated otherwise.

He claimed that the feeling he had when they looked into each other's eyes made him know beyond a shadow of a doubt that the love between them was real, more real than anything he had ever known. He was sure.

This is the problem with only relying on feelings and crazy love characterized by global, totalizing idealization. We can idealize a person, or a feeling or even an idea – the dream of a magical loving relationship. Andrew refused to believe his experience when it contradicted what he had felt in that melting moment, even though he *knew* better. To him, their souls were merged into one. The One.

When he realized Aleta was living up to her name – which means 'winged' in Spanish – and this love was not what he had believed and wanted it to be, she had taken flight.

Quicksand.

Andrew had given her about $100,000 but, what was worse, he alternated between grief and depression for more than three years. He was left doubting himself and was unable to put himself back together again in quite the same way. He had fallen to pieces.

Thankfully, this story has a happy epilogue. Now, more than 15 years on, Andrew has enjoyed a beautiful, loving and reciprocal relationship for more than 10 years with his current partner who is a delightful and genuine person. Ironically, they moved to Spain!

Crazy love can be an overwhelming experience – it is compelling like the most powerful drug. It feels like a basis for knowing with complete certainty. Yet, you can turn out to be completely wrong.

In the simplest summation, knowing how you feel and what you think is primary. It is essential to know your counterpart in love as well as possible. And the perspective of others – who are free from the hypnoid spell of the in-love charm – can contribute to this knowing. Whatever you think you know (conception) and whatever you want or feel, it is worth considering the evidence of actions, for ultimately, it is the interactions between you that constitute a loving relationship.

At the end of the day, you make choices and live and die by the benefits and consequences.

CHAPTER 4

Love and Desire

> *"Tell me who admires you and loves you,
> and I will tell you who you are."*
> — **Antoine de Saint-Exupéry**

What is love? What is desire? And what is the relation between them? Love and desire can be inextricably intertwined, or they can be quite separate. Let's begin by looking at each separately.

Love as esteem

Love and esteem have something important in common. To esteem a person (or thing) is to endow that person (or object) with value. If I say: *I love you*, I am also saying that I value you.

Is it the same as saying: *I love the flowers in my garden?* Or *I value my favorite painting*, or *I love my new car?* Of course not. We struggle to express in words the love we feel for a person. We reach for metaphors and similes in our attempt to capture a special quality of meaning and of valuing that is personal and specific.

> *My love is like a red red rose.*

> *You are my sun and moon.*

> *I wish I could be like the ocean
> to touch every part of you at once.*

Whatever words you choose, it is important to allow yourself to love in your own way. There is no single right way to love though there are certainly many wrong ones.

Love is relational; it doesn't usually work well for love to be felt only in isolation. For love to be relational, there needs to be interaction between the two of you through your shared experience. Then, your way of being-in-relation to your partner, which includes your way of speaking, needs to be expressive of the love you feel.

As such, love is best expressed openly, freely and honestly. In practice, this means expressing in the right balance and measure – not too much but not too little, not too theatrical or too understated. If you want to reach your partner meaningfully and to be received in the way you intend, ensure your expressions of love are emotionally honest and genuine. You enhance your prospects of being met with understanding and a feeling of connection.

Know that you dwell within me all of the time. When I am working, when I am speaking to other people, when I play sport, even when I sleep – you are there in my psyche. Even when I am not specifically thinking of you, you are there. You are always with me.

I have tried to express love without using the word 'love'. Some of us are good with words and some find words lacking or don't find them at all, but most would agree that doing justice to expressions of love with words is hard. Expressions of love are communicated most directly through your way of being: gestures, eye contact, facial expressions that give care or affirmation, doing for and doing with, looking after, giving – there are all kinds of ways to express how you feel toward your beloved. The way we share a gaze can speak volumes and using this unspoken language can say more than a verbal flood. How you look at your partner can also express the opposite. One client said his wife couldn't bear it when he gave her 'the death stare'. He complained of her coldness but she could be frozen stiff by this look. Imagine how affectionate eyes might warm her up and engender a more loving interaction. The wonders of love can be inspired by a look of warmth and the glow of approval.

> *Expressions of love need to communicate both feeling for and recognition of the other person.*

Expressions of love must fit the person to whom they are addressed. For example, if my beloved hates roses but loves chocolates, it would be mad to give her a huge bunch of red roses, even though traditionally this is a deeply romantic gesture. A nice box of chocolates will certainly be better received.

If my love hates football, then it would be mad to throw a football match on the TV after a lovely evening out together …

The way you express love conveys a feeling of how much or little you esteem your partner. And the feeling of being esteemed underpins the desire to remain invested in a love relationship and committed to a partner.

Know thy partner

Love involves esteem, and esteem involves knowing. Without knowing your partner well, you couldn't reasonably value them. What would you be valuing?

Love can begin as fantasy, which is not necessarily wrong or undesirable. But it is worth remembering that fantasy is *your* creation. You go off on a trip in your mind about your beloved – what it could be like to be together, what it could be like to love this person, to be loved by them, to hold them, kiss them, have a passionate sexual union, and so on. You are free to indulge in such flights of desire. Fantasy is not love, however, even if it *feels* like love and you so want it to be.

The path toward true love is a journey of learning, sharing and experiencing. How do you get to know someone? They can tell you their life story but that doesn't mean you really know them. You might know a lot about someone, that is part of the story, but knowing more fully involves shared experience.

There is a knowing that arises out of a certain quality of togetherness that is not about any particular fact or feature of the other person. There is the type of knowing that understands that they like chocolates but not roses, or love roses but dislike irises. And there is the type of knowing that understands what things mean to that person, that feels in touch with the inner world of the other and that enjoys being in the same space. I know when your mother phones that you will be upset within about 10 minutes. She knows that when the stockmarket falls hard, I get depressed. I know that if I give her a hug and comfort her when she has had a rough day at work, she settles down and feels calmer. She knows that pouring me a glass of my favorite wine is uplifting and eases the pain of my football team losing (again).

Being emotionally engaged with each other makes the passage of time together time well spent. But you don't necessarily have to be *doing* something with or for your partner when you have established a harmonious equilibrium in the relationship. The togetherness is sufficient in itself.

There is the type of knowing that is based in feelings rather than the data of experience. Being together might make you feel happy, good inside, uplifted and alive. For my friend Andrew, who we met in Chapter 3, being with Aleta made him feel euphoric, but it didn't allow the time needed to know her well enough. The quality of true 'felt-knowing' is borne out of constancy over time.

It doesn't have to be romantic or poetic or intense. It can be more like a tranquil sense of balance or peace. At other times, it can be filled with sexual charge, like plugging your whole self into the electric socket, desire coursing through your nervous system. The ensuing sexuality between you can be a source of profound knowing unique to the two of you.

Felt-knowing is a 'whole-being' experience that embodies love. It is not a story that we tell ourselves, a discourse or narrative. It does not require interpretation as it is not an enigma that needs decrypting to make sense. Of course, this also makes it hard to express in language. It is for this reason that poetry is the classical medium of love. Metaphor and simile invite the ineffable to reveal itself. Though it can never be fully revealed, poetics point indirectly to our felt-experience of love.

Desire: an introduction

Desire refers to what you want. What you want for yourself is not the same as what it means to love another person. What you want for the one you love is still what *you* want.

There is nothing wrong with desire just as there is nothing wrong with fantasy. Indeed, they often go together and fantasy may be a vehicle for desire. But if we confuse desire and love, there are consequences. Cutting through the confusion of desire and love helps bring clarity to the practice of love.

Desire can be a part of love, and it seems rare to find love – in ourselves or the world – that is completely free from desire. It's hard to imagine what this would look like. For love to be completely free from desire would mean that you have no personal investment in gaining anything for yourself from the experience of loving. The experience exists for its own sake. This would involve approaching love with this kind of attitude: I love you, and I want nothing from you. I love you, and I have no agenda for anything, in particular, to come of it. I love you and want nothing for myself, only what is right and best for you.

It sounds noble. More often than not, digging a little deeper, the lover *sans désir* wants to be seen as the bearer of such nobility. So there is an implicit desire. Heroics tend to reveal a desire to be a hero though noble deeds may occur as well.

Love without sexual desire is called platonic love; an example is friendship (that is, friends without benefits). Mary moved away from platonic love to join Denise who was already feeling sexual love for her (as we saw in Chapter 2).

Originally, the term platonic love referred to the ideal of a passionate love where sexuality was not acted upon. Transforming sexual energy into spiritual experience was thought to be the virtue at the heart of the platonic. Its purpose was to bring platonic lovers closer to wisdom and beauty rather than sexual intimacy and fulfillment.[7]

What does love really mean if you desire something for yourself from it at the same time? How can it be love for another person if it is self-serving? Yet, love and desire are inextricably intertwined.

Desire doesn't have to be limited to sexual desire. It could mean:
- We desire to spend our lives together.
- I desire for you to love me as I love you.
- I desire for you to be receptive to my love and to return it.
- I desire to make you happy and for you to desire to make me happy.

Desire may be part of love, and intertwined with love, but is, of itself, not the same thing as love. It helps to differentiate between desire and love, to clear a space in which love may be revealed as to what it is and what it means. Knowing the difference helps to keep your balance and know where you are, know what you are doing and what is being done to you.

The dialectic of desire[8]

Dialectic refers to a thesis, a principle or a position and its relation to its opposite, its antithesis, with the intent to arrive at a synthesis of the two, a resolution. This may sound complicated and rather academic, but it has relevance in its application to contemporary love relationships.

Dialectic, when applied to desire, means you want what you do not have. Want implies a lack and therefore you cannot want

---

7. See Plato's *Phaedrus* and also the very important text on love *Symposium* for further insight into platonic love. In the *Phaedrus* love is said to be a form of divine madness that is a gift from the gods, and that its proper expression is rewarded by the gods in the afterlife; the *Symposium* details the method by which love takes one to the form of wisdom and beauty.

8. There are references to 'the dialectic of desire' in Hegel and also in Lacan, and elsewhere, but I am treating this subject in my own way here. Some people may find this discussion difficult to understand. You will find further elaboration on this, and other concepts from the book, by going to: meaningful.life You can also leave questions for me or examples of your own.

what you already have. You might enjoy what you have, you might value what you have, you might love what you have, but you cannot really want it. Wanting tends to emerge as the feeling of having recedes. Relationships have to navigate the oscillations of feelings generated by this movement between wanting and having (and back).

You may want and want and want. You may love someone intensely and want to get together with them. You may love someone and want them to notice you, and to love you, in return. What changes when this actually happens? What happens when you 'get' the beloved, the object of your desire? Many of us find that with time we no longer want them, especially with the same intensity of our earlier desire. Sometimes we don't want them at all anymore. Other times, we do still want them but the wanting that pertains to being together changes from the wanting of pursuit.

The dialectic of desire refers to how that desire is affected as its object is obtained. The more you have 'it', the less you want it. The more you want it, the less you have it. The less you have it, the more you want it. This is the paradoxical nature of desire. Dialectics refers to these different and varying positions of desire.

Desire is a critical issue for 'how two love' and for relationships that work and last. This discussion aims to shed light on how to navigate your way through the paradox. If your brain is starting to feel like scrambled eggs, don't worry. It becomes much easier and clearer to understand when applied to an everyday example. Many readers will have their own experiences where these principles come into view.

> Lauren and her fiancé Neil had lived together for two years and were due to marry in 10 months. They had spoken of having children together.
>
> Neil, who was eight years Lauren's senior, already had three children from his first marriage and the children stayed with

them every other weekend. Neil worked hard as a welder, doing long hours that stretched into part of the weekend.

Neil's previous marriage ended badly. His wife of 15 years had cheated on him. In their settlement agreement, Neil had to sign over his home plus significant weekly payments as his ex-wife had never been employed and had the children most of the time. He felt aggrieved that the relationship had ended because of her infidelity but despite that, he lost the home that he had brought into the relationship and was financially compromised as well.

Meanwhile, his ex had a casual relationship with a lover but denied this so as not to lose her entitlements from Neil.

Perhaps his experience had been playing on his mind when he announced to Lauren, out of the blue, that he no longer wanted to have more children. She was upset and angry. As it sank in, she felt devastated.

Why not? Nothing had happened so why the change of heart? Didn't he realize what he said was a deal-breaker for her?

Neil not only changed his attitude about children, but changed in other ways, too. He was irritable, snappy and confrontational. As far as Lauren could see, she hadn't done anything to aggravate him and she couldn't understand his aggression toward her.

Lauren pushed the issue for a few days, but Neil would not move. He didn't want any more children. He didn't want to have very young children in his forties. He didn't want more responsibility or expense. So she moved out. She felt her whole life had collapsed. She felt disappointed and depressed.

Lauren didn't want to move in with her mother because her mother indulged with illicit drugs, and Lauren didn't want to be tempted herself. (She told me she tried to be a good model for her mother!) So, perhaps strangely, she moved in with Neil's mother.

Lauren decided she would stop hassling Neil. She would look after herself and fill her time with things she enjoyed. She worked at becoming more emotionally self-sufficient. She started going to dancing classes and enrolled in a photography course, something she had always wanted to do. And she started going out with her friends, going to parties and having fun.

Neil noticed. The more 'okay' Lauren was without him, the unhappier he grew. He started texting her. His children missed her, and he wanted her to come over when the children were there. He missed her, too.

His attitude changed again, and this time for the better. He asked her out on a date. There was no discussion of marriage or having children together, but they had fun. They enjoyed each other's company like they used to.

After one date, she went home with him, and they made love. The sex had much more of their former passion. Lauren told me that they hadn't had sex like that in months; it was just like before, maybe even better.

Previously, Neil often complained that he was tired from work and seemed boring, like a grumpy old man. Now, he was more like the Neil she had fallen in love with – happier and more agreeable.

He wanted her back. He implored her to move back home with him again. She said she wanted to but what about their wedding plans? What about having children? He said that anything was possible as long as the relationship was like this.

She said that he needed to realize that she was not like his ex; she would never cheat on him, or cheat him financially.

As an example of the dialectic of desire, Neil was able to rekindle his desire for Lauren when he didn't 'have' her. From this position, he could re-open the question of Lauren's wish for children. Lauren developed her emotional self-sufficiency when she wasn't cocooned in the chrysalis of coupledom with Neil, and so sexual intimacy and passion between them became charged up again, naturally.

Awareness of the dialectic of desire helps couples to manage the transitions between closeness and distance, between separateness and togetherness, and back. To understand this as a dance of love, of desire, or of romance enables us to move more fluidly and in harmony with each other, and supports a love relationship to stay dynamic and alive.

The romantic ideal, while compelling, with time sometimes wears thin, or dilutes to the point of non-existence. Have you ever heard: *the honeymoon phase is over?* Then, what follows is the hard task of developing a cooperative and collaborative relationship. Cooperation involves 'co-operating'; operating together in a unified partnership.

> *It is easier to become addicted to desiring, and to the pursuit of love, than loving.*

Paradoxically, when romance and the intensity of sexual desire has worn thin, a golden opportunity arises to know each other in a different way, one that may be more informed by love than the earlier wanting. Some relationships fall apart at this juncture; maybe they were only about desire. Some relationships evolve into something different, something akin to a partnership, which is a good basis for having and raising children. But this does not mean that a relationship ultimately has to wind up free from desire or romance. Desire and romance and love are not mutually exclusive, especially when we understand how the dialectic can be used to promote renewal.

The dialectic of desire can be a crisis or an opportunity.[9]

As a love relationship matures, there can be a waxing and waning of sexual interest and activity and romance. When the tide is out and the energy is on the wane, we need to make an effort. When the moon is full and energy naturally high, sexual interest and activity happen effortlessly. And sometimes we have to wait for the tide to roll in again. This is a dialectical rhythm; it oscillates until it synthesizes.

Relationships need to be enlivened in much the same way as gardens need to be tended. If we want our veggies and flowers to survive, we need to water them, weed them, debug them and fertilize them. Nature requires this of us. But sometimes we get caught up with work, with kids, with sport, and with other distractions – and then the weeds grow and the bugs move in. It is easy to draw an analogy with relationships. Do we tend the gardens of our love relationships with the necessary commitment, regularity and attention?

That said, there are times when you need to let the soil be, and not force it to be more productive. This laying fallow is as essential to relationship culture as it is to horticulture. And this too has its own dialectical movement that reaches toward synthesis when the soil is fertile and the conditions are right for growth.

Forcing love is more likely to destroy its roots than to generate growth. There are times when we need to give it space, to be quiet and still. And wait. These are times for doing nothing, to let space and time to do their work; we are required to hold faith.

There is a time for discussing issues and a time for suspending such discussions. While not enough discussion reflects denial or avoidance, too much discussion becomes a tedious rehashing. Ignoring what needs attending – a form of ignorance – is not the same as a deliberate suspension, as Lauren did in the example earlier this chapter. Given time, you or your partner may feel

---

9. This point about crisis being an opportunity has been cited by American political figures including John Kennedy, Nixon, Gore and Rice, and some business consultants and speakers who claim that the Chinese ideogram for each term is the same. That is not the case though there is a relation between the Chinese characters for danger and opportunity.

different and you can approach issues with a fresh perspective, and one that is more likely to reach a satisfactory resolution. The synthesis of the dialectic occurs at the right time.

○ ○ ○

Let's return to our original definition of dialectic as a thesis, a principle or a position and its relation to its opposite, its antithesis, which aims to arrive at a synthesis of the two, a resolution. Lauren wanted to marry Neil and know that they would (try to) have children together (or, at least one child, she later told me). 'Her desire' is Position A.

Then Neil decided he didn't want more children – 'his desire' is Position B. These are opposites. The relation of these two positions can be called *no*.

As is often the case, there is no compromise with these opposite desires; no give or room to move. Either you have kids or you don't. How can they cooperate and achieve a synthesis or resolution?

There is an internal logic to the movement of love that the dialectic of desire elaborates. From a position of being together, being united, being 'one', the opposition inherent in such opposite positions melts. From a position of being two separate, individual people and being opposed – the combative position of 'my way or the highway' – they are caught up in a competition for dominance. Each seeks the acquiescence of the other for their position to prevail.

Once Lauren and Neil renewed the feeling of love between them, and their sense of being a couple, Neil felt more relaxed in his opposition to her desire, Position A. His opposition was mediated by his renewed desire for re-connection. He had expressed how he felt (I'm too old, having more children is too expensive, and so on) but then he could say: *Okay, let's see where we get to. It's not impossible.* That was all she needed. She didn't require a guarantee cast in stone. She was happy with that. She could let go of her 'deal-breaker' attitude.

They had arrived organically at Position C, a synthesis

or resolution of their differences. They had shifted out of the uncompromising positions of no-give; the position of *no*.

> Lauren and Neil dropped out. They missed appointments and didn't reply to my communications. I was puzzled and concerned because I had been pleased with how they had overcome their impasse and thought our work had helped.
>
> Time passed.
>
> Then, they resumed their regular sessions out of the blue 15 months later and announced they had a wedding date in three months' time. They were planning to try for a baby after that. Most amazing was that Neil was so excited about it! He was like a different person.

Desire has tidal rhythms. It ebbs and flows. When you are 'in each other's pockets' it tends to wane over time. You may need some separateness, possibly in the form of time apart, and then desire tends to wax, to intensify. From the position of separateness, you don't 'have' each other and so the possibility of desire is renewed.

When apart, hold faith in what exists between you, the invisible tie that binds you together. Emotional self-sufficiency helps to overcome insecurities and anxieties.

Synthesis occurs through an active process of moving together, then moving apart and moving together again. The energy in this dynamic movement is emotionally alive. When you are in 'the flow', desire's movement follows internal rhythms, as love calls the tune.

In this play between dependence and independence, there is a tension between the coupling process and the disentangling back into two individuals. The fusion of the two into one, and then reversion to consolidation of the self for each individual, is also a dialectical movement.

Desire is an improvisational art that you make up as you go along. Are you in sync or out of step with each other? What kind of movement can you improvise together, as you go? Can you come together and remain separate, at once?

The synthesis you achieve is the product of the interplay of freedom and captivation you bring to each other in the relationship bond. This synthesis needs to generate bonding, not bondage.

The matrix of desire

Consider your relation to desire in the following way:

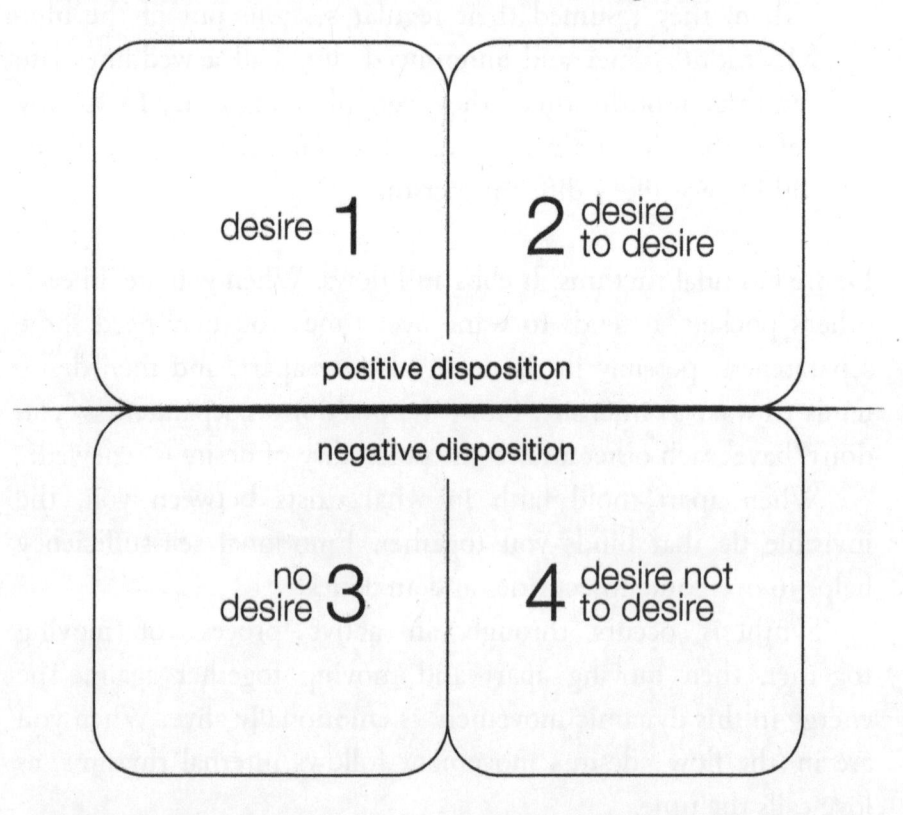

desire **1**	**2** desire to desire
positive disposition	
negative disposition	
no desire **3**	**4** desire not to desire

1. desire – *the presence of desire, without complication.*

2. desire to desire – *there may or may not be desire but whether there is or not, there is a desire for desire to exist.*

3. no desire – *the absence of it.*

4. desire not to desire – *there is a refusal to allow desire; it is a blocking of desire, a negation. Even if desire were present, it would be neutralized or countered.*

For some, desire is not complicated; either it is there or it isn't. It is pretty clear much of the time. It is what it is, as in quadrant 1, or what it isn't, as in quadrant 3.

Quadrant 2 – *desire to desire* – encompasses situations where you do not feel desire, but are not turned off to the possibility of feeling it. There is a positive relation to desire even if desire is not felt. There are many possible reasons why you might feel this way – illness, the side effects of medication, or the pressure of work or child care. This might also apply when you are tired and want to fall asleep but your partner strokes you, and you begin to feel aroused. You might feel happy to be left alone but the arousal is not unwelcome, and you are moved to respond. At least, nothing negative is elicited. Desire not only refers to sexual desire, but can also refer to wanting:

- to feel closer
- to spend time together
- to have fun together
- to hold and be held by each other.

Quadrant 4 – *desire not to desire* – is the most grave. It pertains to when you are aggrieved with your partner, hostile, resentful or angry. You might even feel punishing. Even if your body wants to be sexual, you shut this down because you don't want to give your partner your desire for them. You are in a state of obstinate refusal.

In this state, there is withholding or withdrawal, and stubborn resistance. Your negative disposition toward your partner negates the possibility of desire. This is a radically negative position and reflects a significant breach in your togetherness as a couple. There is a deliberate unwillingness to join in a unity of togetherness.

When desire becomes consigned to quadrant 4 something needs to happen to improve things. There is an issue to be addressed, an injury to be healed or damage to be repaired to reposition above the line to a more positive disposition. A change of attitude is required.

○○○

French psychoanalyst Jacques Lacan said: *man's desire is the desire of the Other.* Despite his typical ambiguity, this also points to the way that we (not just 'man') often desire the other to desire us and to desire our desire. We chase the desire of our partners. It is not just a unidirectional dynamic. In other words, it is not just that I desire you, I do desire you and also desire you to desire me. Thus, in relationships, many of us find ourselves in a bind. We desire, we desire to desire and we also desire the other's desire, and hope the other, at very least, desires to desire us and our desire.

When you have your partner's desire, do you continue to want it? Or does the dialectic turn things around?

As shown in the matrix, the dialectic of desire can swing us from above the line, with a positive disposition, to below the line to negative disposition, as happened for Neil and Lauren. Over time, there can be a seesawing oscillation from one position to another.

It is important not to get stuck in a negative relation to desire. The sedimentation of a negative relation to desire is one of the most demoralizing feelings that relationships produce. Conversely, renewal of desire and the re-establishment of connection, or the creation of an entirely new form of intimacy, is the far better operating principle and practice. Overturning relationship malaise produces joyful, uplifting feelings, as we saw with Lauren and Neil. Lauren could have become stuck but got on with her life separately in a positive way and so – as a couple – they crossed back above the line into an improved relation to desire and to each other.

> *Mutual desire is one of our best sources of fun!*

CHAPTER 5

Making Love and Making Sex

> *"I'm selfish, impatient and a little insecure. I make mistakes, I am out of control and at times hard to handle. But if you can't handle me at my worst, then you sure as hell don't deserve me at my best."*
> — **Marilyn Monroe**

Understanding the difference

Making love is making sex but making sex isn't necessarily making love. From the point of view of a fly on the wall, they look the same. From the inside, how it feels and what it means, the experience is radically different.

The challenge is to know the difference and to learn what you value in each kind of experience. Know what you want and what you are offering. When you have your own sense of this difference, you are in a good position to begin to negotiate a workable sexual relationship.

Making love expresses love sexually; each person gives and receives love in and through the sexual act. When making love goes well, we feel closeness and satisfaction, and the satisfaction is emotional as well as physical.

In making love, the language of love is spoken through the body and its senses. Look, touch, smell, caress, kiss, lick, suck; you enter your partner's body with parts of your own and allow them into yours. In the heat of it, it is hard to know where one body ends and the other begins.

Making love is one of the most beautiful things in human experience, yet many people find it complicated and difficult. All manner of things go on in our heads and bodies that prevent us from being wholly in it. It works best when we are fully absorbed in the act, 'in' the other person and the sexual experience; that is, in the co-sexuality we are creating as lovers.

Making love occurs for both parties through enjoying the pleasures of embodied sexuality together. When desire and love generate a co-sexual reverie, when you relinquish separateness in favor of a loving sexual union that you become 'lost' in, then nothing is lost and everything that can be gained from love is won.

For this to be possible, conditions of emotional safety and trust are non-negotiable. If you feel the need to be vigilant – if you have to think about what is happening to protect yourself – you are pulled out of your body and into cognitive functioning. This defensive withdrawal might be because you're feeling fear, or it could be a sign that something is not quite right about what is happening or who you are with. Perhaps you are making love and your partner is making sex?

> *Being naked is not the same as being mentally free or emotionally unguarded.*

Assuming you feel safe and comfortable – that is, you are congruent with what is happening – sex is not a time for thinking too much (though many people do fantasize). Cognitive functioning is not the best place to be for good sex or love. Getting pulled into your head may also be a habitual tendency. If you can, center yourself in your body as you involve yourself with your partner's body.

Sex for sex's sake can be gratifying and fulfilling as far as it goes. Most of us need it. Many want it. And when two consenting adults want sex with each other, it's up to them. Sex, when free from conflicts, restraints and prohibitions, is healthy. As embodied beings, our bodies may feel the need for sex. Our 'souls' can feel the need for sex too, or sexual intimacy, sensual contact or physical care.

To reiterate: making love is about love even though it includes sex and making sex is about sex, even if it is with someone we love. In making love, the aim of sex is love whereas in making sex, the aim of sex is giving and receiving a heightened experience of sensual pleasure, reaching toward sexual satisfaction and possibly orgasm. The difference makes a difference though the two are not exclusive. It helps to know which territory you are traveling in.

The ideal is when you and your lover co-create a mutually agreeable balance between making love and making sex.

The function of sexual activity

Sex can have many functions; it can be a:
- relief of tension
- relief of sexual frustration (horniness or randiness)
- relief of anxiety
- an aid to sleep
- a happy pill that makes us feel good and gives a sense of well-being
- something that bring us closer together
- a source of playfulness, lightheartedness and fun
- a deep and meaningful communication
- an attempt to get rid of sex from the body, or the need for sex
- and much more.

Of course, sex can also serve procreation, though many of us spend much of our efforts avoiding that function.

> One chap needed sex to resolve his headaches. One lass needed sex to improve her skin rashes, and the health of her skin in general (maybe these two should get together?).
>
> One client claimed sex was the only thing that cured his anxiety and depression. Another claimed that sex gave her anxiety and depression (these two should not get together).
>
> Another client still sought sex to bolster his self-esteem while a different client suffered a loss of self-esteem following sex.

It is worth considering the function of sexual activity in order to pre-empt the tremendous potential for hurt, frustration, rejection, emotional injury, disappointment or transgression *so it can be prevented*.

> Alex and Annabelle had been together for 14 years and had three children. Alex had previously been married for 18 years and said he had hardly been single in his adult life. He missed the 'sex, drugs and rock and roll' many of his contemporaries enjoyed in their youth, but had no regrets – he sought only long-term love relationships.
>
> Annabelle was, in Alex's words, fiercely intelligent. She had a PhD and was engaged in high-level biomedical research. Sexually, she was somewhat passive and therefore happy for Alex to take the lead and she would generally try whatever he wanted. She never felt like initiating; somehow the idea of seeking sex was alien to her. While she never specifically wanted sex, she enjoyed the feeling of closeness and love that they created through sex.
>
> Alex, however, was not satisfied; he wanted to experiment. He said he wanted to be fucked as well as made love to. He wanted to stretch the boundaries of what they did, discovering new possibilities for their sexuality together. He wanted to be passive sometimes, and for Annabelle to talk in a sexy way; he wanted her to be cruder than she wanted to be.

She went along with this to a point. They tried anal intercourse and that was enjoyable for both. But when he suggested it, she wasn't inclined to get involved with his anus. She didn't want to 'talk dirty' and she felt at the limit of her willingness to comply.

She accepted Alex totally and loved him dearly, but she was becoming annoyed by all this and also felt quite hurt. He clearly didn't accept her in the same way that she accepted him.

She wanted their sexual life to be primarily about love whereas he felt an urgency to pursue an erotic agenda, one that had eluded him in his previous experience. Attempts to feel okay without this hadn't worked. He wasn't happy unless they generated a stronger, more powerful sexual experience to make up for what he had missed. Perhaps she was content with the way they made love but he was not content with the way they made sex.

They were at an impasse. I advocated a compromise where she tried to meet him as far as she could and he relaxed his demand for something beyond what she felt she could comfortably offer. Neither were happy with that – the gap between their needs felt too great.

Here the function of sexual activity was different for each of them. I don't think Alex was any less interested in making love than Annabelle, but he was not satisfied with the pattern of sexuality that had become established between them. He was seeking something more powerful. He also wanted her to feel more intensely sexual than she did. She said that she always had mild orgasms.

One of the greatest challenges of long-term relationships is to accept your partner in the entirety of their being – their imperfect body, their less-than-acute mind, and the limits of their sexuality.

Suggesting sex

Many people incorporate talk into sex – it can be sexy. But talking *about* sex, especially making verbal hints, innuendos or comments that aim to suggest sex in order to put it on the agenda, is not sexy.

What do you feel like? I know what I feel like.

You're not sleepy, are you?

After the kids go to bed, I've got a plan.

Are you as horny as I am?

What shall we do tonight? I've got an idea!

Are you up for it later?

When you bend over like that, it makes me hard.

You look like you are in need of a good shagging.

The doctor said I won't get better without sex.

Or the hook-up line: d t f ?

Why make these cheesy comments?

When you live with someone long term and have a busy life including work, children and other commitments, it can be difficult to initiate sex without some form of verbal communication. But verbal gestures that attempt to evoke the possibility of sex can be a turn-off, even if you were vaguely in the mood for it before hearing them. What to do?

> Her partner complained that she never initiated sex. Actually, she did feel like initiating from time to time but whenever she was about to, he preempted it by making a sexually suggestive comment which turned her off. Her initiating never happened because he never let it happen in her own time.

ooo

Nita and Ryan had gone away for a long weekend and stayed in a private chalet. Their relationship could be volatile but this weekend they had enjoyed a fun time together, getting on beautifully, and making love every day. All went well until they were planning their last afternoon.

They were packing a picnic to eat on the beach. Ryan said: *let's take a blanket so we can have sex there.* Nita reacted badly to this. She felt he was prompting her, giving her a cue or turning sex into a plan. She felt irritated that Ryan couldn't just trust that maybe sex would happen if the moment was right and they both felt like it. From her point of view, if they continued to feel as close as they had all weekend, it might well have gone that way, but she felt that Ryan was anxious that it wouldn't happen unless he put her on notice.

Why do you have to spoil it? she said.

Ryan felt taken aback and didn't understand what he had done. He had a low tolerance for guilt and so reacted defensively: *I'm not spoiling it, you are. What's the problem? Everything is fine. Why are you getting upset?*

Nita didn't like his aggressive tone of voice. They fought, then withdrew into an angry, sulky mood for the rest of the day and the whole journey home. Their long weekend didn't have a happy ending.

○○○

Many people feel uncomfortable about the prospect of rejection, especially if they have become accustomed to it and so expect it. Some need to avoid it at all costs. Many of us would rather say: *fancy a root tonight?* (or shag, screw, roll in the hay, bonk, boink, legover, one client calls it "tang-tang") than to open up the possibility of being rejected when 'coming on' through more direct, physical acts. If you say: *no, not tonight darling, I have a headache* that feels less rejecting than if you turn away from me, turn to stone or have that cold look of refusal.

If you don't want me, then I won't bother. Just tell me now. If you don't feel like it, then I know where I stand and can manage my expectations accordingly. Many would rather not harbor the idea of being sexual if it was definitely not on the cards for the other.

> *Asking for sex is a question that requires a cognitive answer; it appeals to thought, not feeling.*

Cognition is a passion killer and unlikely to stimulate arousal. What is the alternative? If the sexual feeling is also going to be an experience of love, we need to become centered both physically (in our bodies) and relationally (in the connection between us) at the same time.

To center relationally requires us to synchronize to each other. If we are too far from being synchronized, we must work out what is needed for each of us to move toward the other. This reciprocal movement is the dance of co-sexuality choreographed by our emerging attunement.

If the sexual feelings are devoid of love, arousal is reduced to its bare physical minimum. Maybe it is just that your hot body turns me on. Maybe that makes you feel good; there is narcissistic gratification in being admired and affecting me that way. However, you may well grow to feel that it is only your body that affects me, and so the feeling is more one of use than esteem, or at best, a very partial esteem. You feel missed as a person. While it might be sexy for a time, this dynamic can grow stale, and love never has to come into it. If I make out that I am feeling love when what is really happening is only sexual attraction, you may well not experience it as love.

In that event, the sexual dynamic becomes reduced to a physical need: my body needs your body (or your desire), my genitals have an impulse, a yearning or a craving. Tension is urgent for relief. When a sexual comment is voiced and there is no love in it, it can feel unwelcome, and possibly offensive.

If there is love between us as well as sexual attraction, and we are in sync and attuned – even if I am 'on fire' – then the same sexual comment may be welcome and arousing. Such comments can go well or badly, there is a risk – expressed beautifully by Shakespeare: *As soon go kindle fire with snow, as seek to quench the fire of love with words.*

If you and your partner need to have a discussion about sex, such as why it isn't happening or working, this is a different matter. Choose a suitable time to talk about it fully, frankly and in detail. This is a cognitive task. Sex needs to be the subject for both your minds to engage with and confront together. Put your heads together first in order to put your bodies together later.

○○○

Long-term couples often have familiar ways of referring to sex where they test the water to check if the other is so inclined or not. It is up to each couple to see how and if this works.

A different approach involves seduction. This is a way to breathe new life into initiating sex, especially when you have been together a long time and know each other well. By seduction, I mean activities that draw your partner into feeling sexual and eliciting desire.

Seduction of a partner who is open to it draws them into their body and the feeling of sexual arousal. If done well being seduced can be delightful, uplifting, playful and fun, and very rewarding. Making your partner feel desired and desirable is exciting.

Of course, not every sexual encounter must be a seduction.

If too strong or your seductive actions push the other person into feeling sexual when they don't want to feel that way, or aren't ready, seduction can have the opposite effect. When not done at the right time or in the right way, it can be a turn-off or create conflict. Through drawing the body toward arousal when the mind does not desire it, a split can be created – internal conflict becomes external conflict, thus affecting the relationship.

> *Causing a split between body and mind in a partner will soon effect a split between the two of you.*

The practice of seduction depends on context, opportunity, mood and timing as well as what kind of person you are, what kind of a person your partner is and what kind of relationship you have.

Part of the pleasure lies in discovering what turns your partner on. Experiment: What floats his boat? What lights her fuse? What rocks their world? How can you do it differently from time to time? How can you ignite fireworks between you? The time to use your mind is before foreplay. Be creative.

> On a trip to Rottnest, a small island a short boat ride from where we live, my wife Cath and I found ourselves alone on a secluded beach (context). It was a warm, balmy afternoon. There are no cars on Rottnest, and our kids, who were off on bikes exploring the island were quite safe. We relaxed, knowing we didn't have to worry about them.
>
> We waded into the ocean realizing that a rare moment of being alone together had presented itself (opportunity). I stroked her back sensuously, we kissed, and there wasn't much need for more seduction than that. We embraced standing in water up to our ribs, arousal building (mood).
>
> Before too long (timing), we were out of our swim suits and starting to make love in the water. People could have appeared at any moment but something about the possibility of being discovered made it more exciting (context again).
>
> We were getting into it, half exposed but not feeling self-conscious at all when suddenly, a head popped up out of the water, right alongside us. Looking us straight in the face was a curious sea lion. The voyeuristic creature dropped down under the water and had a good look. Despite the

shock, we couldn't stop laughing. Then, the sea lion popped up again with an expression as if to say: *oh! so that's how humans do it!*

Perhaps this is more of an example of spontaneity than seduction. Especially with children around, there are too few opportunities where sexual feelings can emerge of their own accord. But then, we have to make our own opportunities.

Sometimes it is better to hold off so the right moment can present itself. We miss some of these special moments when we can't wait. Do you ever get caught in the feeling of needing to make sex happen? Sure, you feel something in your body – something like an itch that wants to be scratched, a tension that wants relief – but do you have to push for it? It can easily become forced and turn into a power struggle, or a matter of persuasion and neither is very loving. What about dwelling in the discomfort zone for a bit?

If you can't hold the sexual feeling in yourself and live with the discomfort, you might push your partner too intensely toward sex, not mindful that they are not yet feeling sexual. This can easily put you off side with your partner (like Nita and Ryan earlier in this chapter).

There is value in holding an uncomfortable feeling without having to act on it, and while feeling sexually needy can be intense, changing the context can help you to quieten your arousal. One of the best ways is to remove yourself from the source, your partner's body, and engage your attention elsewhere. If you hear your partner's breathing become heavier, infused with sleep, stop running your hands along their body.

Sometimes, you may want sex to happen, or feel that it should be happening, when neither of you actually feel sexual. There is some kind of pressure, as if you should feel sexual or want to feel sexual, but actually, you don't. You don't *have to* feel sexual. Of course, it can be frustrating if a rare opportunity presents itself and one of you isn't experiencing the same sexual feeling as the other.

Sometimes it's worth making an effort – seize the moment and get into it. You will feel better together for doing so. Some other times making sex happen with a push can turn it into an obligation and that is not the best feeling, and again not particularly loving. This runs counter to intimacy and becomes more about meeting the need of one. And the relationship winds up feeling worse for it.

There can be value for the relationship, and specifically for your co-sexuality, in being patient, holding off for optimum conditions, and resisting the urge to push for sex. You may have fewer sexual releases but make up for that in quality of contact. Those sexual experiences you do have are likely to be more powerful for the benefit of waiting.

Emotional safety

Emotional safety is paramount in matters of sex, as it is in matters of love. Many people have been traumatized by some terrible past sexual experiences or by criticisms, negative attention, degrading treatment, or derogative, unsympathetic or derisory comments. It only takes a parent to make a fuss about a child's weight. A good number of adults remember these comments, sometimes forever. Many of us at various ages and stages have heard from a physical education teacher that we're getting flabby, or from a friend that they wouldn't be caught dead in those clothes, or a past lover saying that we've lost our mojo. Such comments can induce a high degree of self-consciousness that lingers, leading to the development of an inner critic. Many people have a negative view of themselves fuelled by these past critical comments.

If he doesn't like that dress then maybe you can take it off and put on another one. But once you take off all your clothes, what if he doesn't like what he sees? What if she takes issue with the spare tyre around your middle? Or the size of your manhood?

Once a 70-year-old patient told me that a girl he had hooked up with for one night told him that he was too gentle for her. He had never forgotten that comment even though it had been made some 50 years earlier. It hurt but telling him was a gift because it freed him from his overprotectiveness. He didn't become the opposite, too rough, but he understood that his lovers wouldn't break if he was more passionate in sex. This is an example of how powerfully we can be affected by just a couple of words, in this instance with a positive outcome.

Generally, we need to feel safe with each other and we need to feel safe with ourselves. We need to feel safe in a social context but we *really* need to feel safe with a sexual partner in private. It can take a long time with a partner before we grow to feel safe enough to be uninhibited.

Safety goes beyond the physical: if she decides to go ahead and make love with him, then what will it mean to him? What if it means more to her? What if it means nothing to him? What if she falls in love with him but the feeling isn't mutual? What if she wants to see him again but he doesn't want to see her? *What if she wants a relationship?* If it isn't going to mean that much to him then maybe she would rather not have sex with him. She'd like to know in advance.

Men too express hurt and disappointment that sex didn't mean more to their female counterparts.

> After they became lovers, his feelings for his friend grew. She had many lovers, both women and men, and though she was loving, she was also a free spirit.
>
> Once, after they had made love together, he felt close with her and had powerful feelings of love arise in a new way. He thought she felt that too but as she got up from his bed and walked away, she said: *that was a nice bit of fucking...*

Maybe she was threatened by the potential of the sex to mean more? Maybe it's fair enough if it turns out to mean less to one than the other. Maybe sex is a gamble, and you have to take your chances and hope for a good outcome. In any case, the feeling of being unsafe is highly likely to inhibit sexuality. If you really are unsafe, it is better not to risk too much, as healing from an emotional injury can be tough, sometimes even harder than from a physical injury.

We may be safer with our partner than we are with ourselves. Ironically, the harshest of critics are often internal ones. If you look in the mirror and think: *yuk!*, if you examine yourself in fine detail and notice every imperfection with disgust, it is hard to bring yourself to your partner openly, freely and receptively.

In our culture, women have extreme pressure to look perfect, or better than is humanly possible. I hear about it constantly in therapy. Men have pressure too but much less than exists for women. This pressure makes it incredibly hard to be accepting of self and relaxed about appearance, face, shape, body image, aging, weight, skin, hair or anything. *OMG! What is that spot doing there!*

Ask a woman what she sees when she stands naked in front of the mirror. It is irrelevant what anyone else sees. Expressions of extreme distress are notable but not unusual. Sometimes there is horror, repulsion, and a refusal to accept the image she sees. This can be the result of the slightest detail, like the spot above. The shape of a nipple, cellulite on the thigh, eyebrows too full, a skin tag on her back, a crooked tooth, an abdominal patch of dark hair, a new mole – anything can be a reason for a loss of confidence or worse, a breakdown.

> A young woman in her twenties told me she feels 'disgusted' by her genitals, and by female genitalia in general.

Where does this come from?

As a culture, we seem hell-bent on creating nervous, self-conscious, harshly self-deprecating critics out of our women. Perhaps this is so they will buy more products – a common understanding – but at what personal cost?

> *How is a woman ever to feel safe in her raw and naked sexuality with a lover if she cannot feel safe with her own mirror in private?*

While discussing specific trauma is outside our scope here, it must be referred to briefly. There are people who have been traumatized by an earlier sexual or emotional experience. It is a frequent reason for sexual inhibition – or sometimes its opposite, uninhibited promiscuity – or possibly other defensive sexual manifestations. These may include being closed, dissociated or switched-off, lacking in libido, being anorgasmic, feeling frightened about sex or during it, breaking down and crying, feeling anxious, depressed or mentally preoccupied before, during or after sex, and having distorted or out-of-place sexual feelings. The effects of past trauma may create a feeling of lack of safety in sexual experience in the present. Trauma-informed therapy can be enormously helpful, especially if undertaken over time.

From a general perspective, the best way to encourage uninhibited sexual freedom of expression is to cultivate a convincing feeling of safety in the total environment surrounding sexual experiences. Acceptance is key and can unlock the safety catch for the spark of passion. Loving the person – warts and all, whatever happens, whether sex works well or not at all – contributes to present and future emotional safety.

Passion

The word passion derives from the Ancient Greek verb πάσχω (paskho) meaning 'to suffer'. In our modern world, passion can be synonymous with love. It can refer to an intense desire, a compelling feeling, enthusiasm or excitement about something or someone. How did we get from 'to suffer' in Ancient Greece to something that sounds more like its opposite – intense pleasure and excitement?

To feel intensely can be experienced as suffering. Even pleasure felt in the extreme can hurt. When the feeling is strong enough, there is a curious crossover (a fine line) between pleasure and pain.

I love you so much it hurts.

When passion is intense, we are taken over by it, consumed. We can lose ourselves in passion, or be driven by it. We might find it hard to control ourselves, and to remain composed and balanced. There is pain in this pleasure, a suffering in the intensity of our enjoyment.

○ ○ ○

In traditional thought, there has been a dichotomy between reason and passion. Reason was regarded as the higher, more noble virtue while passion was considered base, originating in the body, the instincts and the drives. Reason was associated with the head and passion with bodily urges and impulses.

More recently, this understanding has changed. We know that even though emotions and passions can dramatically affect the cognitive processes of reasoning, the absence of emotion is also damaging for cognition. Feelings are now regarded as essential for rationality and we need emotion, in balance, for our reasoning faculties to function optimally. The whole range of passions unavoidably influences brain function and all our cognitive faculties.[10]

The idea of marriage as the culmination of a love relationship, and *only* marrying someone we love, regard as a soul mate, and aim to stay together with over the long term, is taken for granted in a modern Western context. But it has not always been so. The classic text by the prolific Swiss writer Denis de Rougement[11] shows how passion and marriage have been regarded as being in tension or, more specifically, in opposition for about 1000 years of Western history. It is only relatively recently, since the 18th century, that love has even been prescribed as a part of marriage.

---

10. See the work of Antonio Damasio for a more detailed and erudite treatment of these ideas.
11. Originally published in 1939 and then revised and translated in 1972 as *Love in the Western World*.

Many of us associate passion with physical or sexual passion and seek a passionately sexual engagement with a partner, and then hope and expect this to continue. Sometimes it wanes over time. When lovers have an ability to rekindle the passion between them, they often have fewer arguments, and, if they do argue, they get over it more quickly.

Therapists often hear that a relationship is struggling because it started off passionately and then, over time, the passion has diminished, fizzled out or dried up completely and hasn't been renewed. Sexual frustrations, if built up for too long, create tensions, generate resentment and fuel arguments. Conversely, unresolved issues also prevent passion. Resentments detract from the sexual relations of the couple, and sexual frustration causes more resentments to develop, creating a negative spiral.

In this example, there is a specific cause to the loss of passion.

> Tyrone and Taylor had been together for some years and had consistently enjoyed a passionate sexual relationship. Indeed, Taylor had always been passionate about Tyrone and thought of him as a rare prize, as he was physically strong, well-built and virile. And he wasn't just good-looking but had a lovely spirit, was rarely grumpy or unpleasant and was also intelligent and creative. Plus, he was tough and could stand up for her – in her words: *he wasn't a pussy*. She felt lucky to be with him.
>
> It was puzzling and distressing when her passion dried up. She not only didn't feel passion but also didn't feel like having sex with Tyrone at all which was most unusual. From Tyrone's point of view, things had been going well on the whole and they should be happy and on track. He didn't understand what had changed for her.
>
> And neither did I – at first.
>
> It was her second long-term relationship and his first. She had two sons from her previous partner. The two boys –

aged 13 and 10 – lived with Taylor and Tyrone almost full-time excepting alternate weekends spent with their bio-dad. The boys liked Tyrone and appreciated his willingness to do activities with them, buy them things, play sport and take them to the movies. He was a great step-dad.

The only real problem was Tyrone's attitude to discipline. A stint in the army had seen him trained by the Special Forces, an elite of the military; highly trained and used for dangerous assignments. Tyrone had valued his training and embraced Special Forces' values of discipline, hard work, compliance and the sometimes extreme application of mind and body to meet challenges and reach a high level of endurance.

Though he left the Special Forces for a change of career direction, Tyrone applied a somewhat military attitude to Taylor's boys in his approach to step-parenting. Des, the 13 year old, found Tyrone too hard on him and often complained. Des would say: *is this boot camp, or what?* Mostly, Taylor appreciated Tyrone's input and valued his strong fathering contribution; that was until Des became distressed and overwhelmed.

In their father's home, the two boys shared a room but it was regarded as theirs to do what they wanted. It was usually a tip, with all their belongings, toys, books, games and music strewn about. Their father expected them to be tidy in the rest of the house, but they could keep their room as they liked.

Tyrone had a completely different attitude. He did not subscribe to the 'floor-drobe' idea. He was a stickler for order – everything in its place. He expected them to keep their rooms presentable.

Des had his own room at home. One day, Des made a mess and just left it. He had a water polo match and ran out of time for cleaning up. When Tyrone got home and saw the mess, he was not impressed and grounded Des.

The grounding meant Des was not allowed to go to his friend's party over the weekend. He was furious – he felt it was unfair and unjust. Instead of complying, he refused to clear up his room. He said that it was his room to do with as he pleased. Tyrone, not accustomed to defiance, made Des stand at attention in the corner until he thought better of his attitude. It was an impasse. Des got more and more distressed until finally, Taylor intervened.

Usually, her attitude was one of solidarity with Tyrone. She had seen the benefits of adopting a strong hand of discipline with the two boys. With Tyrone, she was much stronger in her authority with her sons than when she had been on her own. But this was too much. Des had been pushed beyond what he could cope with.

She felt that Tyrone had gone too far and that this had become harmful to Des. She felt that sometimes flexibility and a willingness to negotiate might be a better approach, especially as the boys got older. She tried to talk to Tyrone, but he was insistent that if they gave in, it would send the wrong message to Des. It would mean Des had won.

Taylor started to feel that both Des and Tyrone were acting like children, both too proud to give in, each battling it out in a competition of wills. This was a no-win situation and she started to feel angry and resentful toward Tyrone.

Eventually, she told Tyrone that she never thought she would say this, but if it came down to a choice between him and her children, she would always choose her children. He was quite shocked, and disappointed in her. He thought their united front was unassailable.

Resentment acted like a fire extinguisher to Taylor's libido.

In therapy, when we trace things back and arrive at the point where passion has dried up, sometimes the reason is abundantly clear. Taylor's passion for Tyrone was temporarily derailed at precisely the juncture where she started to feel that his attitude to discipline had gone too far and could be harmful. At the very least, it was too distressing for Des and so she could not support it. It put her in an untenable conflict between her devotion and commitment to her son as his mother and her devotion and commitment to her de facto, as his partner.

These were the most important allegiances in her life. They were different, but she felt a sense of unity with each. She never thought she would be forced to choose, but she needed to defend her son. Her passion for Tyrone was the casualty – not by choice, but as a direct by-product of this conflict.

My contribution was, first, to discover the reason for the change in her passion for Tyrone and, second, to help them understand that the consequence for their relationship was more important than the battle over Des cleaning up his room. I know it was a matter of principle for Tyrone but, more than that, I could see that he suffered the loss of Taylor's love expressed passionately and sexually.

> He got it; Tyrone softened (a bit). And Des agreed to clear up his room if he could go to the party.

Once the heat of conflict subsided, we could undertake therapeutic repair for this couple. It didn't take much for these two to fire up again, but it helped to understand what had happened, how Taylor's passion had temporarily died. Her resentment of Tyrone and her maternal empathy for Des created a barrier that turned her off sexually toward Tyrone. Therapeutic repair involves overcoming the reasons that cause such barriers to be erected and sustained. Therapeutic repair can be effected without a therapist if, on your own, you can uncover those reasons that cause resentments and loss of libido or the build-up of barriers between you.

○○○

Some people are not inclined toward outward demonstrations of passion. What matters more is how deeply and intensely the *feeling* of passion is experienced 'inside'. They may be incredibly passionate but do not show it; they may not have orgasms where it feels like the whole world shakes, or dramatic exhibitions of emotion. They might even be quite reserved and restrained in their responses. But some people's emotional lives are like rivers that run deeply, deeper than the calm surface suggests. Underneath the serene exterior, currents of deep feeling, intense emotion, and a powerful sexuality can be even greater than that of outwardly expressive people.

You see what someone shows, but it can be hard to know what they really feel. The more connected you are, the more you can sense it, especially if they are outwardly reserved.

Of course, if you are feeling passionately about your partner, it can be an incredible gift to show this with the fullest possible expression. Exchanging this gift reciprocally not only generates and sustains passion, but helps to recover it when it wanes.

Vanilla sex and unconventional sexual practices

Vanilla sex refers to what is considered standard or conventional physical intimacy in our culture. It tends to mean sex without any kinkiness, domination, sadism or masochism, without fetishes, dressing up, or adventurous or unusual activities. Some might describe vanilla sex as lovey-dovey; for many it is just simple or tender lovemaking.

The term 'vanilla'[12] has a connotation of being boring. Its current usage, originating in the 1970s, is derived from the whiteness of commonly available vanilla ice cream.

All of the preceding discussion of sex and love in this chapter could be seen as vanilla and yet what I mean is not boring at all.

---

12. Interestingly, the word 'vanilla' came to English from the Spanish word *vainilla* literally meaning 'little pod' and referring to the vanilla plant. But the diminutive *vaina* or 'sheath' originally derives from the Latin word *vagina*.

Sex does not have to be anything other than how two people express their desire – as in making sex – or express their love – as in making love. Neither is exclusive of unconventional practices that can be used for either sex or love or both at once. Vanilla sex can be passionate and satisfying and unconventional practices can be boring, or vice versa.

More and more I hear unconventional sexual practices discussed in my therapy practice, which is why it is included here. I suppose the unconventional can become conventional.

Unconventional sexual practices aim to heighten and intensify sexual experience (what Alex was seeking, who we met earlier). For example, sadomasochistic practices are more an exercise of power than an expression of love. Playing with dynamics of power in sexuality can make for powerful sex. Often, an experience from childhood was erotically charged. A child was handled in an arousing way that set up a power differential or a child was exposed to a sexually-charged event that is then re-enacted in their adult sexual life. Perhaps being washed in the bath, or going to the toilet, has become an intensely charged sexual experience. There are also cultural fashions that influence sexual trends, and this may be the case with sadomasochistic practices.

It is not hard to find perverse or deviant sex, domination, bondage and submission, cross-dressing, latex, rubber and other costumes, whips, toys, ropes, handcuffs, role-playing, cross-identification, transgender tendencies, transsexualism, and fetishes. The use of dildos and vibrators can hardly be called unconventional now. There are also threesomes, partner swapping, swinging, orgies, sex parties and clubs.

What makes sex perverse or deviant? The way we look at such questions depends upon our cultural assumptions and values on what is normal or abnormal, what is natural or unnatural, what is permissible or forbidden. Deviation assumes there is a norm from which to depart. I would argue: there is no normal.

Perversion depends upon the context. Some argue that any sexual act other than for the purpose of procreation in the context of marriage is a perversion. From that perspective, the majority of the population of the Western world are perverts. These judgments are spurious and unhelpful, more often used to persecute than enlighten.[13]

Speaking as a therapist, I don't care what adults do sexually with each other if it is consensual and doesn't cause harm. When I hear about such practices causing emotional pain, physical pain, misery, subordination and suffering, I care a lot.

With bondage and submission, some people find it powerful to be made helpless, hostage or enslaved to another. Some feel an overwhelming need to be punished, spanked like a naughty child, whipped, beaten, or imprisoned in a small space. Some find it sexually exciting to be humiliated, degraded, or urinated on, and more.

Some people argue that we should put a stop to such practices, that they shouldn't be allowed. My view is that repression, restriction and prohibition do not tend to stop the feelings that underlie these practices. Over time, this builds a tension that increases and makes the drive to experience the forbidden activity more powerful. And, of course, we cannot assume that those who do it want to change their behavior. Regulatory suppression is itself another form of bondage dressed up as law. If we dress up in latex, rubber or any costume and it enhances sexual experience, then I fail to see the harm in it.

Cross-dressing can be done for a range of reasons including sexual gratification, but also fun and performance, and it does not necessarily indicate transgender identity. People with transgender identities feel that they should not have been born a man because they identify as a woman or vice versa. These days, surgery and hormonal treatment are more widely available to help transgender people transition to the gender they identify with.

Cross-identification is when two people imaginatively swap gender roles, in the stereotypical sense. One client described how she straps on a dildo and penetrates her male partner anally, who experiences himself being penetrated more 'like a woman', as he

---

13. Leonard Cohen once said that 'enlightenment' means to *lighten up*.

sees it. Both find it sexually exciting and something not otherwise reached in more conventional sex.

Role-playing might involve assuming paired character roles in sexual play. Dressing up as a police officer and a criminal, or playing doctors or nurses and patients, teachers and students, naughty children and scolding parents, army officers and soldiers, animals and their keepers, and so on, can all take on an erotic quality.

Fetishes, and other so-called paraphilias, tend to be classed as unconventional. A sexual fetish attributes a high level of sexual arousal to a particular object, class of objects or part of the body, also called partialism. The most common objects of fetishes are clothing, rubber items, footwear, leather, and body parts.

Some theorists believe that fetishes tend to originate from childhood or even infantile experience in which a particular object has been endowed with an erotic charge or a function such as soothing or tension relief (a nipple, for example). An object can substitute or symbolize a part of mother's body, for example a soft toy for the breast. The object becomes endowed with the power to excite and satisfy, and this experience persists into adult sexuality.

In some cases, a fetish may function like a synecdoche. A synecdoche is a figure of speech in which a part stands for the whole. If I say: *the crown has declared*, then 'crown' stands for the king or queen. If we take the example of a sexual fetish for a lady's shoe, then the idea of synecdoche is that the shoe stands for the whole woman. Similarly, a lady's ankle or foot can stand for her entire sexuality or, fetishistically, her genitals.

We only need to enter a sex shop to find all manner of toys and devices for the purposes of sexual stimulation.

At a professional workshop, I met the incredibly dull presenter, named Mortimer. Afterwards, a few of us went out to dinner together, and my head nearly nodded forward into my soup out of boredom. Walking back to the car, we passed a sex shop, and Morty said that he was also a certified sex therapist and knew about every item in the shop. *Shall I give you a tour?* he offered meekly. *Absolutely!*

We went in, and he lit up like a Christmas tree. Suddenly, Morty was in his element; he became animated and energized, describing in detail every single device, toy and article of clothing. It was quite an education. *What's this metal thing for, Morty?* I enquired. *Oh, you insert that into your anus, and the curvy end stimulates the prostate and that intensifies your orgasm.*

Thanks, mate, this is the stuff you should be teaching at the workshop!

CHAPTER 6

Co-sexuality

"Human life is only dust and ashes without love."
— **R. D. Laing**

What is co-sexuality?

Co-sexuality[14] is the unique relational quality of sexuality for each couple. In the context of a primary love relationship co-sexuality expresses reciprocal love through a given couple's sexual intimacy. It belongs to each love relationship alone and characterizes it.

It is not a sexuality that is imposed by one upon the other or vice versa. It is not what one needs to be satisfied. It also doesn't exclude individual preferences or what one needs to reach orgasm; co-sexuality is not restricted to such preferences.

The term 'co-sexuality' could be applied to a loveless but fully sexual relationship though that is not my focus. I have nothing against sex for its own sake or sex between consenting strangers. Sex can be uplifting, rewarding, enjoyable and a welcome relief for the tensions that our bodies collect through living. The idea of co-sexuality conceptualizes sexuality differently for the purpose of

---

14. My use of co-sexuality has a completely different connotation than co-dependency, which refers, in its colloquial usage, to symbiotic emotional need, and is usually seen as a sign of emotional pathology. As co-sexuality is a new term, you can find further elaboration on this and other concepts from the book by going to: meaningful.life

a discussion about love relationships. Here, I am referring to the way that the unique sexual union of two people who love each other is expressed.

| *Co-sexuality is how two love sexually.*

If we speak of *a field of co-sexuality,* we can begin by thinking of a literal field that has a fence around it. That fenced-off field becomes a metaphor for the frame of a relationship that is exclusive and monogamous. The field is our home ground – even though sex can happen almost anywhere – and that home ground provides the environment for sexual love.

Does co-sexuality require exclusivity and monogamy or can sex with other people outside the relationship be a part of how two people conduct their relationship? Can they bring others into their relationship sexually without damage to their co-sexuality? Without monogamy, there is still co-sexuality that belongs uniquely to the primary couple. In my experience, love relationships work best when the fence is strong, and the sexuality of the couple is contained within it, to the exclusion of all others. Many have experimented with open relationships, and many have failed. But I would not like to say it's impossible. Some people are not prone to jealousy or possessiveness. Some can treat this issue with casual disregard or even experience joy when their loved one takes pleasure from another romantic or sexual relationship while others are driven insane to the point of murderousness. Echoing the Preface, polyamory may appear attractive in principle but exclusivity seems to be the most usual orientation for lovers in coupledom.

For the purposes of this discussion of co-sexuality, it works better to draw a boundary around a love relationship that is definite, not fuzzy, wishy-washy or ambiguous. Defining this boundary involves asking questions such as: *What is permissible? What is not?* It helps a relationship work when its partners have a clear understanding of the answers; this is an important function of co-sexuality.

> *Co-sexuality is an agreement and moral commitment to live in good faith through unwavering loyalty.*

The gauntlet is thrown down. Many of us find this challenge unfolds as a battle first within ourselves, and then continues in a world full of temptations. Successful, enduring love relationships usually dwell within the enclosure of fidelity. The agreement is the fence and the fence defines the environment. The idea of environment applied to relationships is developed more fully in Chapter 9 – 'The Ecology of Successful Relationships'.

What about: *don't fence me in?* By shifting the imagery from a fence to a plant pot, the meaning becomes clearer. If a plant finds its pot too small, it is stifled. If the frame of the relationship is too constrictive, it is not the best condition for growth, sexual emergence, and satisfaction.

Plants grow well without any pot at all, but they become unwieldy and can overpower other plants in proximity. They need pruning back for optimum yield. Without a limit that you determine for yourselves, without a mutually agreed container for the relationship, you don't know where you stand. Some feel anxious, insecure or even paranoid. You do not share a solid frame for your relationship and an understanding of the environment in which co-sexuality can flourish. Thus, the context for eros – the life-giving principle – is weakened.

The frame or fence that contains your relationship is not meant to restrict unduly, or function as a device of power, possessiveness or control. That is the opposite of eros. The fence is a self-limiting factor to serve the love in your relationship and demonstrate respect for your partner. Within that frame, your co-sexuality can emerge and form, strengthen its roots and develop. You create a context and a process for the ripening and deepening of sexuality, so that the longer you are together, the richer it gets. This is the antidote to what long-term partners commonly complain of: sexual expression becoming boring, predictable or stale, if it survives at all. From within the safety of the frame, we can open our hearts more freely and so create a meaningful co-sexuality that evolves over time and matures in its sexual intensity.[15]

It is possible, sometimes even easy, to have a passionate sexual encounter with someone you have just met. The sex can be amazingly exciting. Not knowing each other makes it even more charged. But without knowing each other what does sex mean? You are playing the role of lover rather than making love. You might 'know' each other in the Biblical sense but you don't really know each other.

Sometimes people have such powerful sexual experiences with a new person that love grows between them. Other times, we might mistake sexual intensity for love when it has little or nothing to do with it.

> *Co-sexuality is a mutual creation between two people who love each other and express that erotically.*

The eros in eroticism is what makes for sexual arousal and excitement. It needs to crystallize not just in one, not just in the other, but also between the two. It is not solely a bodily function. It is also not solely a flight of mental fantasy or an emotion. It refers to sexual energy without having to be an act of sex. In a broad sense, 'eros' means life-energy, but here I am using it relationally, in a more intimately interpersonal sense.

Eros manifests organically between two people when they bring their whole selves to love and sex, and are open to the feelings of arousal as they emerge. Eros refers to the chemistry of a mutually loving sexuality; it is the source of electricity felt at a personal bodily level. Because it means something, it is not only physical.

---

15. Safety in co-sexuality might appear to contradict the notion of *vulnerability as the ground of love* but I believe that safety within the frame of co-sexuality makes vulnerability possible, and a risk worth taking.

Turning eros into a relational concept gives us the term 'inter-eros' which is then synonymous with co-sexuality. Inter-eros is 'the erotic between' – what is co-created by our erotic interactions. It is not just me turning you on. It is not just you turning me on. The 'turn-on' grows out of what happens between us, in the interplay, the touch, the looks, the speech, and the movement that develops naturally as we go.

Co-sexuality is not an idea about sexual technique. Rather, it refers to the co-creation of sexual love in and through the intercourse of our way of being together. Intercourse is the to-ing and fro-ing of our communications, the quality of exchange, the interplay of meaningful touch and touching meanings. Of course, intercourse can refer to sexual intercourse but is also part of a larger whole-being activity that is a function of loving each other, erotically.

Inter-eros refers to an erotic exchange. Here, the sex is not just a thing-in-itself but is a special thread in a fabric woven by love. Then sex is dynamic love expressed passionately. Co-sexuality integrates sex and love, the physical and the emotional, self and other. You transcend your individual separateness in favor of a spiritual union that creates something new. In this vein, you can make love for the thousandth time and feel that you have never been *here* before.

Co-sexuality is a loving sexual closeness – an erotic absorption in the body and person of each other, at once.

> *A healthy co-sexuality is at the heart of happiness and makes love work and last.*

Co-sexuality involves a shift from an I-centred, one-person sexuality – what one wants, what one needs, what turns one of you on – to a two-person sexuality; how the two of you make sexual love with each other. It is a relational sexuality where the felt-experience is both generative and restorative of the love between you at the same time as being fuelled by it. Thus, profound sexual satisfaction is created.

This sense of co-sexuality is the opposite of what can happen in long-term relationships where the sexuality dries up or becomes routine or perfunctory. If sex happens at all, or as is often the case, happens a few times and far between, it is reduced to a bodily function. It becomes a bit like going to the toilet, physically necessary but not particularly meaningful or loving.

> In one session, a client said: *We made love last night, I don't remember the last time we did, I think we both just felt a physical need for it, but I didn't feel anything. There was no closeness. As a man, I have looked to sex for the feeling of closeness but it wasn't there. Do you think that means I should leave?*

> It's hard to respond to a direct question with life-changing ramifications, especially on the strength of only one person's account. I said: *I wouldn't like to signal the end of 16 years of marriage from one unsatisfactory lovemaking experience but it does sound like the relationship is in need of some remedial attention.*

What I consider to be 'remedial attention' is a deeper communication with each other than perhaps occurs normally. If you can address your partner openly about sex, and the ensuing discussions bring changes and inject life into your lovemaking, you don't need couples therapy. Therapy often begins at the limit of couples' own communication. If I ask a question in a couple session such as: *when your partner is bringing you to orgasm, do you feel he or she is doing it right or do you wish they were doing it differently?* – sometimes it seems easier to answer me directly than for a couple to address a highly personal question like this on their own.

Sometimes, such conversations happen between friends over coffee, and people are shocked to discover how different their friends' sexual relations are from their own.

Many people feel shy talking about their sex life in therapy in depth or detail. But approached in a matter-of-fact way, the subject opens up and often brings insights, even revelations, partly because previously it hasn't been talked about enough.

When couples are ready for a fresh experience of inter-eros, sometimes a third person can be helpful. (And I'm not talking about having a threesome.) In therapy, exploration of sexuality occurs through reflection and discussion, in a forum that is safe but frank. When people open up in therapy, and reveal what they have always kept to themselves – when they discuss their sexuality freely, fully and candidly – they start to know themselves in a new way. When their partner is included, knowing each other is enhanced. This often helps bring couples to a more conducive place to develop and improve their co-sexuality.

Foreplay and before-play

A common problem in relationships occurs when one wants sex and the other doesn't or when one wants sex more often than the other. Ronald and Donna have a good relationship but have never been able to agree about sex. Much of the time, he wants sex, and she doesn't. Can they negotiate and resolve this difference?

> Ronald would like sex at least once a day whereas Donna would be happy with once or twice a week – a big difference.
>
> Ronald likes quickie sex at the kitchen sink, as he described it. But more than that, he wants to make love for hours. Once, he said he wanted to make love for eight hours.
>
> I said I'd never heard of a couple with small children making love for eight hours. Donna said she would never want sex for eight hours, kids or no kids!
>
> When they went on holiday without the children and had a long sexual session in their hotel room with private spa, Donna said she felt that Ronald *still* wasn't really happy.
>
> When I asked him about it during one couple session, he said: *it was all right, but it could have been better.* Donna

was quite hurt and offended by this comment. She said she didn't know what it would take to satisfy him.

The principle difficulty was that he could 'do sex' at the drop of a hat but she needed to be warmed up to get into it. She didn't feel ready without some contact and a feeling of closeness. He said he always feels close and always feels ready.

I try to avoid generalizations. Not all women are the same nor are all men the same but despite that, this generalization does have currency:

> *Women need to feel close before they feel sexual and men need to be sexual before they feel close.*

This may not apply to every heterosexual couple, or be consistent across genders, but it certainly applied to Donna and Ronald.

> With that in mind, I said to them: *Foreplay begins when we wake up in the morning. I don't mean sexual foreplay, I mean the way we treat each other can function as foreplay, or perhaps more accurately 'before-play', if it brings us closer. Then, when an opportunity to be sexual presents itself, it is more likely that both parties will feel like it. Also, Donna might be more responsive if she doesn't feel that she is obligated, or being used like a sex toy.*

She is also more likely to be responsive if he was able to feel satisfied by what was possible, sexually, between them.

It is easy to regard sexual contact as a discreet event that happens in private when you're alone together and under the covers. It might work better to regard sexual contact as something that can happen anytime and in many different ways. A look, a caress, an intimate word, a quiet moment of connecting, all can have a sexual quality, without specifically being sex. In other words, there is eros in our interactions, inter-eros.

Eros is not an attempt to induce the other person into feeling sexual per se, or into doing anything. It is not a seduction. There is no plan, no agenda. You don't always have to be going somewhere, or have an intent or end goal in mind.

A kiss is but a kiss.

If I smile at you lovingly, it doesn't have to be because I want something in return. If something is truly given, it doesn't incur a debt, a burden of obligation or an expectation of reciprocity.

These ways of interacting that have a subtle sexual quality can be characterized by a sense of play. The word 'play' is critical in 'foreplay'. Play is something done for its own sake. The pleasure in playing is its own reward. And in this kind of play, it is not a competition and there are no winners or losers. There is no training to play well, no competencies to be assessed or techniques to be mastered. Eros can be embodied in play because play expresses love without there being anything at stake.

> *When eros is at play, there is nothing to lose and nothing to fear.*

In a playful mode, and when our sexuality is contained within our own relationship (as we said previously), there is no risk of loss. In a more general way, we are vulnerable in love and so have everything at stake. But being sexually playful in a particular moment holds no risk *because it is just play*. Playing in our own backyard, our home field, is both safe and holds great potential for intimacy. But when our sexuality is uncontained and threatens someone else's relationship or our own, it can feel like everything is on the line.

This contradiction points to the power of the erotic element in play, and the need to be aware of its power and, hence, be careful. Because before-play is the antecedent of foreplay, because there is an inherent ambiguity in the boundary line between what is sexual and what is not, and because such play can be generative of bonding in love, it can easily get out of control. Playing with a single flickering flame might appear innocent but that same match can also ignite a conflagration causing devastating burns and destruction.

Belinda and Tony had another couple over for dinner. At the end of the evening, Claude, one of their guests, gave Belinda a good night kiss as he left. They were not observed by Tony, who was in the kitchen, or Claude's girlfriend who had gone to the bathroom before getting in the car.

It might have appeared to be an innocent kiss-on-the-cheek good night but it was not. He had looked at her penetratingly, sexual sparkles in his eyes. His left arm circled her back as he held her neck with the other, gently but firmly. He stroked her body as he withdrew. She shuddered and briefly felt a sense of surrender.

Eros.

In that moment, Belinda felt her relationship with Tony was over. She knew what she had been missing. She had known for a long time it wasn't quite right and had thought of leaving before. She knew Claude was just playing. He had a girlfriend and wasn't making a full-on pass at her. If anything, he was probably retaliating for something Tony had said at dinner. She knew all of that.

But it affected her. He had touched her in a place that had been yearning for loving sexual contact and that had gone unfulfilled for too long. Because of that sensual contact, her whole mood changed. When she went back into the house, Tony could see it instantly. *What's wrong?* he enquired. *What happened?*

She couldn't explain it to him then and there. She didn't know what to say, but she couldn't hide it either. Something in her had broken; her commitment to stay together with Tony had collapsed in that moment. She didn't say anything, but she knew she was going to have to deal with this. And soon.

I started by discussing foreplay and before-play in the context of a relationship and have arrived at what can happen when a kind of erotic before-play occurs outside a relationship. This is powerful stuff. It can be innocent or lethal, depending upon how it happens.

In the context of a relationship, foreplay and before-play can be a delightful expression of loving energy transacted between couples as an expression of co-sexuality. Then, when it's possible and you want to take it there, loving sex can evolve seamlessly.

A sexual tension may be generated in the process. It can be frustrating to wait; too frustrating if you have to wait for long. But the waiting period of sexual tension can allow the feelings to grow and intensify, so that when it finally happens, you are both ready. Maybe you are more than ready, bursting, but then the sex is powerful and fulfilling, and you are much more likely to feel satisfied. And then it builds again.

Or this season of eros has gone cold. Maybe you aren't feeling very playful, sexually or otherwise. If there is no feeling for foreplay or before-play then remembering the dialectic of desire, you might need to take some space from each other. If no sexual tension can be generated, if your co-sexuality is lying fallow, wait for winter's snows to thaw before the new growth of spring. Hold faith in the love between you and just as the seasons turn, the re-emergence of inter-eros will return when it is time.

Being a good lover

How many times have I heard: *I love my partner dearly but they are not a good lover. Everything else is just right, couldn't be better. They are my best friend but I wish we could generate some heat in the bedroom.*

It can be awkward to talk about problems. Such discussions need to happen to deal with what doesn't work in the relationship. Much can be improved in sexual interaction if it is addressed with honesty and sincerity. Talking about it may not be sexy in itself but if a new understanding promotes changes in sexual behaviors it can lead to an enhanced sexual experience. And sometimes the process of sharing can bring you closer, even without a full resolution of problems.

> Jacinta's relationship with her partner was perfect except for the sexual part of it. She positively disliked the way he made love.
>
> I suggested spelling out for her partner the fine detail of how she liked to be touched – where, when, how hard or soft – how she liked to be kissed, and how to be sexual with her *precisely*.
>
> Jacinta came back saying she had done what we discussed. She had thrown off all caution and told her partner in every detail how to make love with her; what she liked and wanted, what she didn't like, what worked for her and what didn't. He was receptive, thanked her, and seemed to understand.
>
> Then they had the best sex ever. She was rapt. She thought we had cracked it. Problem solved.
>
> Unfortunately, he had forgotten everything the very next time, and was right back at square one. Why? What happened? She was bitterly disappointed.
>
> I didn't know what to say. This suggested the problem was deeper. By her account, his forgetting had a dissociative quality. It was hard to understand. Didn't he want to be a good lover for her? He seemed to, but he couldn't hold what she had told him in his mind. He reverted to his prior pattern, and sex was awful again.
>
> The bad sex was now compounded with disappointment, and Jacinta felt worse. Now she knew it could be better, but there was some block to sustaining the improvements. While there were probably reasons why her partner couldn't hold in his memory what she had taken pains to communicate, his failure limited the feeling of connection for her.

Jacinta didn't want to keep insisting he change. She didn't want him to feel attacked and so risk traumatizing him (again?); she feared making it harder for him to function sexually as a consequence.

Generally, we shy away from what needs to be said out of protectiveness for our partner.

Sexuality is at the core of our sense of who we are. If we are made to feel inadequate or lacking in some way, there can be global ramifications to our feeling of worth. We can become self-conscious about our performance in sex, which can make that performance worse, and then it becomes even harder to be absorbed in lovemaking. When criticized sexually, we can feel terribly diminished and this creates further obstacles to talking about it. Jacinta was aware of this.

Perception is critical here: read your lover's body, zero in on what they feel, what they respond to, what works, what is stimulating, exciting and arousing, and what isn't. Focus on breathing, or any sounds, feel your partner's body tense, writhe, quiver – is this pleasurable or not? Is this enjoyable or irritating or indifferent? Is it enough or do they want more?

Everyone is unique. Some people like to be pleasured gently and some much more strongly. Some like a sensual, whole body experience, while others prefer a focus on genitals or breasts or bottoms. There may be a time for one focus and another time for something different.

Sexual experience can be a great adventure of discovery if you can be open and attentive. It is better to make love with your 'L plates' on (Learner's Permit for Lovers) than to make love as if you're an 'expert'. The attitude of learning enables you to be open to where the other person is at. How does your lover feel? What do they want in this moment? Explore with your hands, notice what they respond to, and what you feel in the process.

On the receiving end, let your body speak to your lover in a way that communicates pleasure or displeasure or whatever you feel in response to every gesture. Use your hands. Use your voice.

The image of dance comes to mind again. Making love is like a dance where you move together, or one takes the lead, and the other follows. Take turns taking the lead. Try to avoid predictable patterns. Sex is less likely to get stale if done differently from time to time. Improvisation brings fresh results.

Alternatively, if you both like the way you are sexual together and have no desire for anything different, then why change it? There is no 'best-before date' if your way of making love still has plenty of life in it. You don't have to swing upside down from the chandeliers or get into some yogic or tantric contortion. The best approach to sex is to love the person through their body by the use of your body.

We are not required to have perfect physiques. It is wonderful to look great but looking great is no guarantee of being a good lover or feeling intensely sexual. It is more important to give love and to allow yourself to receive love in a sexual way.

> One client told me he had the good fortune to wind up in bed with a gorgeous woman. She was so physically stunning he felt nervous about being sexual with her.
>
> But she turned out to be about as sexual as a glass of ice water. It would have been better to admire her like a beautiful piece of art rather than to try to generate a sexual feeling of intimacy and excitement.
>
> She said she was like that with everyone, much to his relief!

Physical beauty is not necessarily the most important ingredient. In loving your partner sexually, you have to love their body as it is, as it changes, with all the wounds and scars that we accumulate with age on the battlefield of living. If you are connected to each other, such physical defects are but a detail and do not have to detract from passionate sex and an ultimately satisfying experience.

Nevertheless some people are inhibited sexually – they won't make love except in total darkness, won't allow themselves to be seen, and feel self-conscious and uncomfortable *because they are not physically perfect*. This even occurs for people who are nearly physically perfect in the eyes of others but do not see themselves that way. It is far better for sex and for being a good lover to throw off all fears and doubts, if you possibly can, to accept yourself as you are, and say: *this is me, I can only give love and receive love as I am.*

Communicating sexual needs and preferences

How is your partner supposed to know what you want if you don't tell them? We have spoken about being attentive, about reading your partner's body, and about perception and attunement. Communicating about sexual needs and preferences begins from there.

Jacinta told her partner in detail how to make love with her. It made all the difference. They went from sub-zero to sizzling sex. Once. Then he forgot. He didn't hold in his memory the most important communication on which his most valued love relationship depended. He loved her dearly, but he couldn't remember what she had said. (This may have been a consequence of past trauma but it is not fair to diagnose someone from a distance or based on second-hand information.)

I ran into Jacinta at a friend's party a few years later. She was with a new partner (perhaps not surprisingly) who was noticeably preoccupied with sex. He kept bringing the conversation around to the subject of sex. Maybe he knows what he's doing in the bedroom (or what she liked) better than the last one?

What your lover does not pick up about you sexually may need to be addressed in a straightforward and explicit manner. If you want it to improve: spell it out, don't omit the details. Be specific, while explaining with tact and love. There is an essential balance between protecting your lover's feelings and getting through to them with enough information to make a difference. If you are not explicit enough, then how will this ever improve?

You can tell or show your partner 'how to make love' in a way that is right for you and if your partner gets it, they never need to be told again. This can be transformative for the quality of mutual sexual enjoyment and plays a vital role in making a relationship work and last; this is key for how two love.

When you rub my clitoris, the pressure you apply is too hard. It hurts and that makes me shut down sexually. I'm extremely sensitive down there. What works for me is a gentle, light touch. Please don't be too heavy-handed.

It is better to take ownership of your sensitivities than to sound like you are accusing your partner of being clumsy or stupid. It is better to claim preferences – *I don't know what other people are like but when you suck my nipples hard it turns me on so much.*

Darling, it is the underside of the penis that is the sensitive part, that is what makes me hard when you touch me right there. Once hard, you can really squeeze me – don't hold back, you won't hurt me – it feels amazing!

Running your fingers around my anus sends sexual shock waves through my whole nervous system. That is what makes me orgasmic.

It may be uncomfortable to say these things but if you don't, how is anyone supposed to know?

- Some people love you to stick your tongue in their ear, and others find it disagreeable.
- Some people love you to insert your finger in their anus, and others find it disgusting.
- Some people love a big, sloppy, open-mouthed kiss, and others find it too messy.
- Some women prefer vaginal penetration, and some prefer clitoral stimulation and some prefer both at once.
- Some men love oral sex. Some hate to do it and some love to.
- Some can't wait to get inside their partner's vagina and some can't wait to get inside their partner's anus.
- Some like to be on top and some on the bottom. Some like to face each other, and others like to face away. Some like to be lying down and others are standing up, or on all fours.

- Some like to make love in the morning, some in the afternoon, some in the evening and some in the middle of the night.
- Some people like to change it, mix it up, and make it different every time and some like it just the same way as they have done for years. Why change what works?
- Some like to make love for hours and some for minutes.

The degree to which these kinds of themes need to be spoken about will vary from one couple to the next.

Many people find the arousal of their partner the biggest of all turn-ons. Therefore, it helps to show it, to give voice or expression to your arousal. To fully hear your partner, you have to listen actively and attentively. What you're listening for may not be expressed in words.

A sexual relationship is likely to require communication about needs, preferences, moods, fantasies, feelings, and other desires from time to time. And this may require words spoken separately from your sexual interactions. Often the following formulation works: the more communication, the better the sex, and the better the sex, the greater the love, and the greater the love, the more durable the relationship. It works in reverse as well. The more durable the relationship, the greater the love, which makes sex better and communication easier.

Sex can precede love and love can precede sex. Either way, sexuality is one motivational driver that compels us toward another person in the pursuit of a love relationship. In that pursuit, words are a medium of communication and sex is a medium of communication. Both modes of communication inform your co-sexuality which facilitates love's evolution and the development of relationship.

Sex as a barometer

Not every love relationship has to be actively sexual, but for many the sexual relationship is a barometer of the overall health of the relationship and its prospects for durability and longevity.

Often, at least one person in the couple is not happy without regular sex. When couples consult me and their sexual relationship has died, sometimes for months or years, the prognosis for restoring the relationship is poor unless the sexual relationship can be revived.

> Vince consulted me on his own. He told me that he and his wife Victoria had grown apart. They had been married for 17 years and had an 11-year-old son. They led different lives, had different interests, and even had different friends. There had been a gradual drift apart over some years.
>
> He wanted to hang in for his son's sake for another five or six years, ideally until he finished high school. Vince was the primary carer as he was home-based. Victoria worked full-time, and then some, in her own business. She was often away as her business involved travel abroad.
>
> He wanted to have a sexual relationship with Victoria. She wasn't interested and they slept in separate bedrooms.
>
> She indicated that she felt they should call it a day; the relationship had run its course. Resentments had grown. They were often irritable with each other. It seemed pointless to continue.
>
> Vince felt gutted for a week and wondered if there was any chance his marriage could be saved. He had serious doubts; they hadn't had sex in eight years. He found himself calculating the value of their joint estate and what he thought would be a fair split in a settlement agreement.
>
> I suggested it might be worth my having a single session with Victoria, sounding her out, and then meeting with them together to see how they wanted to proceed, if that was agreeable to both. Victoria turned out to be keen to see me and discuss the situation.

Victoria said that Vince constantly criticized her; she felt he was always sulking and had nothing positive to say about her, even though she was the primary earner.

While Victoria was very social and often out with friends, Vince was more of a homebody. Though he didn't like to socialize, he also complained that he felt excluded but she didn't want him along because of his negativity.

She felt like she'd been walking on eggshells because of his moods and easily-triggered irritability. He plays on his computer; she's not sure doing what. She does all the cooking and all the homework with their son. She wondered if Vince was depressed.

I asked her what she felt the issues were. What was the main problem between them? She answered that there were two areas that had become untenable for her. The first was respect. She felt his criticisms were undermining, devaluing and degrading. The second was resentment. A reservoir of resentments had grown over many years and was now spilling over. She wanted a happy partner or no partner at all. (Happy husband, happy life?)

They never went out together, for a meal, a show or a movie. She would love to have some romance in her life. When they went on holiday together, they didn't get along. She felt that Vince could be a bully to her, and her friends had commented on this. He got frustrated with her and had no patience. When he recently went away for a couple of weeks she realized how peaceful she felt, and on his return asked him to move out.

We arranged a joint session. I wondered whether they would decide that the relationship had truly expired. I accepted that sometimes people just have to come to terms with a long relationship ending, then grieve and clear the air so they can move on. I prepared myself to support them in making this kind of adjustment.

During their joint session, I asked each of them what it would take for the relationship to work. Victoria reiterated what she had told me; she wanted respect and to resolve the resentments. She admitted that she decided eight years ago that the intimacy would stop *for these reasons.*

Vince said that a lot of his frustrations and resentments had built up because the intimacy had ceased. He had been expressing his frustrations about her refusal to be intimate directly through being critical, and indirectly, through being irritable and moody. (How circular.)

I asked what the relationship had been like in the beginning, during better days – what had they liked about each other, what had they valued in each other? They were each quite enthusiastic about the positives while acknowledging it seemed a distant memory.

The strange thing about this session was that the more we spoke of their relationship, feelings, and perceptions of each other and how each was being affected by the other, the more each seemed surprised at what they were hearing. I wondered if this couple had communicated at all in a meaningful way for nearly a decade.

The session ended inconclusively. It was agreed that Vince would try to rein in his tendency to be critical and negative toward Victoria. She would try to be more inclusive of him, and they would try to get along better.

Victoria was more open to make things better with Vince than I had expected. She wasn't following through with her request for him to move out, yet. He was relieved and seemed willing to make an effort to improve his treatment of her and the atmosphere in general.

We spoke about sex. I encouraged them to spend some time together on their own, maybe go out for a meal, see if they could re-connect and then if they felt like it, consider resuming sexual relations. Obviously, there is no scope for being fully sexual together after such a long gap unless the right feelings are there.

We agreed to meet again in two weeks.

At the next session, I anticipated that they would have reverted to the previous pattern, as this is often what happens. Generally, therapists know not to be overly optimistic when a relationship has broken down.

It was a shock when Vince and Victoria came in again. They had experienced the most dramatic turnaround. They realized they had been 'stupid'. Each had started to treat the other completely differently – with respect, care and affection.

They had been out. They had been sexual. Once they started being sexual again they found it hard to stop; they had spent much of the two weeks in a sexual reverie. Remembering what they loved about each other, and loved about being together, they had fallen in love again!

They were going to phone me and cancel the session because they didn't need it, but they wanted to tell me in person what had happened and say thanks!

I was blown away.

Eight years or more of hostilities were overcome through one couple therapy session, an hour of meaningful communication triggering all the change that was needed. For me, this was delightful and unexpected. They were like a couple of lovebirds. Most therapists have their own collection of dramatic successes. Occasionally, the rewards of the job are beyond expression.

Here, the prognosis was poor and I thought it was 'game over'. Let's fight over the settlement, if we must, and be done with it. Relationships usually need an hour of good quality communication on a regular basis. If you start with a single consultation, then you just might be able to take that experience home and practice it yourselves, on your own. Maybe Victoria and Vince will be back if they hit a wall but hearing from them 18 months later, they are still going strong.

A good sexual relationship is essential as part of the overall emotional health of a primary love relationship. Where this is not the case, we need to find out what is in the way. Commonly, we find two classic dilemmas:
1. The lover is great 'in bed', but not suitable as a life partner.
2. The reverse: one feels the other is just right as a life partner but not right sexually as a lover.

The challenge is to get both, in one.

When achievable, the loving sex of co-sexuality is a source of intimacy and happiness. It is one of the most powerful experiences, and one that makes life feel worth living. Once 'there', we don't want to go anywhere else.

CHAPTER 7

The Lifespan of Love

> *"... he who cannot reveal himself cannot love, and he who cannot love is the most unhappy man of all."*
> — **Søren Kierkegaard**

Many of us enter a relationship imagining an open-ended future. *Let's stay together forever* we say, and this sentiment remains while the relationship goes well. So, how can you keep your relationship going well?

Extending the lifespan of love requires a willingness and capacity to address issues that come between you. If you are coasting along swimmingly, then maybe this need hasn't arisen, but rarely does it remain this way.

When problems arise it can be easy to look at the other person and place blame – you see where they are going wrong, and the ways it is their fault. You believe you are right and want to address the issues. But your partner could be harboring similar feelings toward you and feel the need to address the issues from their point of view. Sounds like a recipe for a stand-off.

You probably want your partner to take responsibility for the issues you raise while your partner wants you to take responsibility for the issues they raise. It's much easier to see what the other person needs to do. But the durability of the relationship depends upon both of you taking responsibility for your contribution to the issues. Even when one acts-out and has to take responsibility for their actions, the underlying reasons for acting-out can be shared and often require both to assume some accountability.

Beyond that, there is much we have to live with. Relationships that last involve a high level of mutual acceptance by each party. Acceptance requires a working understanding and practice of forbearance, tolerance and forgiveness.

The length of time a relationship flourishes depends a great deal on these attitudes and capacities, which are worth cultivating together as your relationship develops. And it's not just the lifespan of love that will be affected; studies have even suggested that life expectancy can be impacted by an individual's success in preserving love in their primary relationship.

Addressing issues

The operating principle in the endeavor to preserve love is that when something comes between you, you have to address it. **Have to!**

Does that mean you have to sit down and have a heart-to-heart meeting about every little thing that arises between you? No. The commonly experienced little annoyances can be brushed aside like dust on the floor boards, forgotten without a second thought.

The 'have to address it' principle refers to issues that have sufficient substance to undermine the relationship or that threaten its continuation. Often such issues are recurring, cumulative and patterned. They tend to create resentments, anger, fear, guilt, shame, anxiety or other negative emotions.

In couples therapy, the relationships that have the worst prospects for improvement and durability are the ones between people who have the most difficulty communicating about their issues. Therapeutic work is needed to identify issues, to articulate feelings, to initiate communication and to reach an understanding that promotes necessary changes and improvements.

Love requires maintenance to keep it running smoothly. Just as we service our cars to ensure we get good mileage out of them, we need to service our relationships to make sure love can go the distance. We think nothing of getting our cars serviced, accepting it as a normal part of owning and running a vehicle. We do it regularly, and we are willing to pay for it. Many people will not hesitate to buy expensive accessories and parts, cleaning and polishing, gadgets and embellishments, for their cars and bikes. After all, our cars are the vehicles that move us and our significant others around the place and get us where we want to go.

The same can be said about a love relationship: it is the vehicle that moves you through life, holds and transports you, safely and securely or not, comfortably or not, happily or not. It might seem desirable to have a partner who does not require a high level of maintenance, however:

> *Low maintenance does not mean no maintenance.*

Obviously, relationships are not exactly the same as cars but the analogy works to a point. Just as we can look after our cars, we can look after our relationships by addressing the issues that prevent running smoothly together as a partnership in love. Relationships need inspecting and checking out, maintaining and renewing on a regular basis. This begins with addressing the issues that most need attention.

Therapy is the garage to restore run-down relationships, or simply those in need of a regular check-up or tune-up. Some people balk at spending money on therapy. *It's so intangible* they say, but there is nothing intangible about a miserable relationship. One patient's friend said to him: *therapy is sooo expensive.* Without hesitation, he quipped back: *it's a lot cheaper than divorce!*

When we maintain our vehicles well, they often need fewer costly repairs. In the same way, therapy can not only repair damage but can also prevent damage in the first place, so we incur less personal cost. We cannot measure the exact savings from proactive or early interventional therapy, but the change in the quality of living is noticeable.

One of the benefits of couples therapy done well is that couples who do not know how to address issues on their own gain experience in how to identify issues, unpack them, give examples, demonstrate the emotional impact and consider solutions. A therapist functions as a facilitator and mediator. Once they have been walked through it, couples learn the territory of addressing issues with more effective communication. The roadmap becomes notated with an emotional vocabulary to help point the way.

Chapter 11 on couples therapy provides a more detailed account of the process.

Mutual responsibility

By design we look outward, so it is easy to see what our partner is doing 'wrong'. The much harder task is to look inward, to see yourself from a position as if outside of yourself, as you are seen by others, especially from your partner's view.

Generally, we raise our concerns with our partners. We feel justified. We know we are right. We know what we are talking about. Why can it be so hard to get through? Why doesn't our partner see what we see? It's so obvious. So clear.

Our partners have concerns about us, too, about what we are doing. They counter our communications with points they want us to take up from their point of view. They know they are right. They know what they are talking about. Why is it so hard to get through to us? Why can't we see what they see? It's so obvious. So clear.

We can go around and around, until we are worn out with it. It produces feelings of futility, hopelessness and frustration. Perhaps we get exasperated and might start to think about getting out of the relationship. *Surely, being on my own couldn't be worse than this. Why am I hanging around? This is not what I signed up for.*

The *modus operandi* of being a couple involves each taking responsibility for their part in what happens. It requires us to be reflective and to cultivate a perspective that considers the other's position. It doesn't mean that the other is necessarily right, rather that there is value in considering their point of view. It may be possible, and beneficial for the relationship, for us to take responsibility without even agreeing with the other's position.

> He complained she was always going out with male friends and having fun without him.

It would be easy to point a finger at her and judge her to be neglectful of her partner.

> She explained that he never wants to go out. He comes home from work tired and wants to watch TV; they don't even like the same programs. He doesn't want to make love with her and she feels ignored most of the time.

It would be easy to judge him as the cause, leaving her little choice but to go out with others.

> But he doesn't want to make love with her because he doesn't trust her. Some of her male friends were lovers in the past.

Maybe he's right, and she's the cause.

> She explains that being lovers happened over 10 years ago and has nothing to do with the current friendships that are more like brother–sister relationships. She is hurt that he doesn't trust her when she's gone to great lengths to be faithful and always stopped guys at the first hint of them 'hitting' on her.

Maybe she's right, and he's the cause ...

And so it goes. Each sees the cause in the other but neither looks inward and takes responsibility for themselves. Many couples spiral forward in this blame game of critical judgments and causal attributions toward the other, coupled with blindness toward themselves. Each feels justified and fortified in their respective positions and neither is willing to give ground.

Stalemate = stale mates.

| *No one ever wins in the blame game.*

This pattern of action and reaction, followed by reactions to the reactions, and further counter-reactions needs to be arrested and reorganized. It is like two people pulling on a rope. One pulls and the other lurches forward. The other pulls back and the first lurches forward. If each pulls back at the same time, they remain in a tense but static state. Each needs to take a step toward the other and give their partner some rope, and be on the same team instead of pulling in constant opposition.

I told the story earlier about how I prompted a fight with my wife Cath after a night out together because I turned on the football once we got home. The next morning she said sorry for being angry. I was ready to keep fighting, still feeling touchy. She gave me a hug while taking responsibility for her part in what transpired *even though her position was probably more justified than mine*. Her generous attitude and willingness to take some responsibility cut through my combativeness. It made me want to take off the boxing gloves, melting my steely resolve to fight on for some imaginary sense of moral victory. By taking responsibility, she pointed me in the direction of taking some responsibility also. Instead of pursuing the conflict, I apologized for being selfish and felt better. Feeling good together was able to be restored.

Mutual responsibility is rewarding. It is a relief to hear that the other has thought better of their actions, that they have understood their affect upon us. When your partner takes responsibility it is an expression of empathy, borne out of love. It is also regenerative of love. If you embrace responsibility at the earliest opportunity, it is much easier to feel giving and forgiving.

You let go of grievances and this prevents filling up an internal reservoir of resentments.

A useful way of understanding the word 'responsibility' is by de-coupling and inverting the word as 'the ability to respond'. It doesn't mean you always have to put your hand up and say: *guilty, I'm at fault, I got it wrong* or that you have to carry the weight of the world on your shoulders. It means that when some responsibility belongs to you, a meaningful response is needed.

> *Being responsible involves an ability to respond.*

Cath was quicker to respond to the need for our relationship to repair than to her original need, as an individual, to be right. She was not attached to her feeling of anger at my disregard of her.

Thinking of responsibility in terms of responsiveness also gives a sense of two people in an active emotional partnership where each takes the other's feelings seriously and makes them a priority. In this way, we focus more on the consequences of our own actions and less on the consequences of our partner's actions. When both can do this, we travel on a two-way street, with a balanced flow of self-awareness and responsiveness. And the distance covered over the course of love's journey is lengthened.

Acceptance, and its limits – Part 1

Acceptance as a non-judgmental attitude is simple until we reach the limit of what we are prepared to accept, or worse: when confronted by what we regard as unacceptable. Then the attitude of acceptance becomes a conundrum that needs addressing.

How can we accept the unacceptable, or should we?

'Acceptance' is a term that is used and defined in a multitude of ways, and is a central psycho-spiritual concept for most of the Abrahamic religions. Of interest, the Jewish mystical school of thought Kabbalah can be translated as 'acceptance' (it also means 'tradition' or 'receiving') and the term Islam can also be translated as 'acceptance' (and also means 'surrender'). Acceptance is close to the meaning of Buddhist 'mindfulness' and counter to the psychoanalytic term 'resistance'. The acceptance of Jesus as Messiah or Christ is central to Christianity, where acceptance also refers to forgiveness. And acceptance of Torah, the commandments and the covenant with God all feature generally in Judaism. Psychotherapy sometimes encourages acceptance, especially self-acceptance, in some moments, while discouraging acceptance in others – for example, in situations of mistreatment, disrespect or abuse.

I distinguish between the principle of acceptance and the practice of acceptance. While the principle of acceptance means accepting things as they are, the practice of acceptance requires thought and emotional processing. It is not a matter of accepting anything and everything at all costs, and without question, but to know the difference between what is acceptable and what is not in your love relationship.

Each of us must decide for ourselves what is *unacceptable*. In doing so, pay attention to the reasons why this is the case for you; is it really more than you can bear or are you being inflexible? Are you determined to be controlling or is this a behavior that is disrespectful and shouldn't be tolerated? There is a critical difference.

If you are being treated in a contemptuous, degrading or, worse, abusive way – then don't put up with it. If it is extreme, get out. Or, if getting out doesn't feel right, at least make a stand. Otherwise you set a precedent whereby mistreatment becomes accepted and, therefore, acceptable. Abuse is not love and has no place in a loving relationship.

> *Acceptance does not mean accepting anything without question.*

Remember: while a *feeling* of love may overlook 'bad' behavior, a relationship of love is not unconditional, nor should it be.

> *Acceptance begins at the limit of the negotiability of desire.*

You may find yourself in a relationship with a person who is 'good', well-behaved, well-mannered and, for the most part, respectful. Occasionally there is a lapse, and the lapse is an aberration from their usual conduct. Should you run a mile? Or should you be forgiving? Your partner is now remorseful and contrite. It can be a hard call.

It can be incredibly difficult to decide when things have gone too far. There can be a great deal at stake, and you may want to give your partner the benefit of the doubt. Practically everyone makes mistakes or mistreats or disrespects occasionally. You will have to define where the line is for you and what it means for things to go too far. When is enough, enough? First get clear with yourself, then you can get clear with your partner.

The principle of acceptance is to accept the other as they are. It requires you to know what you want from your partner, to hold that in abeyance, so you can accept without condition or qualification the *differences* in the other person (within reason). Many people find this impossible. What you want of your partner may or may not be negotiable.

What you desire and what your partner desires may not be the same. What you desire your partner to desire and what your partner desires you to desire may not correspond. These differences can be negotiated until you reach the limit of what negotiation can achieve. The gap of difference is precisely the potential space for acceptance.

The degree to which acceptance fills that space and closes the gap of difference between your respective desires enhances love and engenders a feeling of expansiveness for the relationship. Conversely, the degree of surrender (the giving up of what you want) required to reach to acceptance, in practice, is empowering and, perhaps ironically, often brings a sense of fulfilment. While you might believe that satisfaction is achieved by *getting* what you want (and therefore you pursue that), the paradox of acceptance is that satisfaction can also be achieved by *giving up* the pursuit of what you want. Notice the word 'giving' in that formulation.

Cultivate a capacity for satisfaction through giving as well as getting.

As an individual, you may feel satisfied by giving or receiving. As a couple, satisfaction is best achieved by giving what your beloved wants as well as getting from them what you want – ideally in a fair balance.

Acceptance does not mean you have to agree with what your partner is saying or doing. It is not complicity, compliance, or overlooking your disapproval. Acceptance does not mean that you must let everything pass tacitly without comment.

The principle of acceptance is based on understanding that the other is as they are or acts as they do, without undue criticism, intervention, contradiction, argument or opposition. The practice of acceptance exercises the conditions. A line that cannot be crossed is drawn between what is acceptable and what is not. The line represents your acceptance limit. When that limit is exceeded, a vocal protest is called for. One client said: *I'm extremely tolerant until I'm not. Then I become extremely intolerant.*

You may fear your partner will be out of control if you don't control them. You may fear they will become undisciplined, or lazy, or loose, or objectionable. You may fear they will leave. You may also fear your partner will not do their best and lapse into irresponsibility. There are many things to fear that *could happen* if you become accepting.

- If your partner only does what you want because you keep the pressure on them – what does this say?

- How meaningful is your partner's fidelity,
  loyalty or respect if they exist only because you
  remind, insist and threaten consequences?

What part of love means that you have to 'risk manage' your partner? How loving and how loved are you if your partner is only being 'good' out of fear?

Acceptance gives space for the other to grow into their own sense of duty, responsibility, care and appreciation. It enables them to develop their own qualities of esteem and love, faith and commitment. The question arises: if these qualities are absent from your partner and you need them, how do you cope? Much of this book is about how to navigate this very position.

The first step is to give expression to how you feel and about how what happens affects you, without demands, hostility, threat or punishment, because acceptance involves relinquishing control and manipulation.

> *To get the best out of your partner, give up control and manipulation.*

Giving and receiving love is a practice. With repetition, it becomes part of who you are without self-conscious monitoring. Similarly, a relationship is a practice and so is the disposition of acceptance.

For example, when your impulse is to criticize, it is easy to comment on what your partner does that is less than perfect (which is practically everything). Probably most things could be done better. You can choose to focus on the gap, the margin in which things miss perfection – it is there to be found if that is your focus. If you want to make your partner feel small, then keep hammering away at the shortfall between how they do what they do, and how it could be done better. Watch them shrink. Alternatively, try commenting affirmatively on the best of what they do and watch the change in their response. Your partner will not only be happier but happier with you.

Commonly, people justify their critical attitude by saying that they are only trying to help, that it is constructive and their intention is to help their partner be a better person. But is this really what is achieved?

When criticism is unwanted and unsolicited, it tends to create a siege mentality that can include withdrawal into a private space and an armoring against attack. When someone who is critical re-orients to an attitude of acceptance then their partner's relief is palpable. It's like being able to dance after you're let out of a straitjacket.

When the person you love is not performing or succeeding and you can see their greater potential, it can be hard to live with. In these instances, encouragement works better than negativity.

Acceptance, and its limits – Part 2

The principle of acceptance is my way to speak about 'unconditional love'. But remember that the feeling of unconditional love is not the same thing as a love relationship. The practice of acceptance in a relationship is not unconditional but does involve allowing the other person to be who they are, with all of their shortcomings and imperfections, and remain wholly loved.

Acceptance is an essential prerequisite in how two love.

> Alexandra and her new boyfriend Derek had a long-distance relationship. He decided he would move across the country to live with her. From there, long discussions have ensued about his drinking and his drunkenness. She is happy with him but doesn't want to live with a partner who gets drunk on a regular basis.
>
> In his current community on the other side of the country, drinking is a way of socializing – his friends do it to let off steam and enjoy themselves when not working. And they drink a lot.

> He has accepted her point of view and cut down on his drinking. He has one week left, and he intends to say goodbye to all his mates before he moves, and this will involve drinking.
>
> Alexandra is afraid that if she doesn't take a stand, it sends her boyfriend the message that she doesn't mind his drinking anymore. What should she do?

Acceptance means there are times when you bite your tongue. This is where 'the line' must be held clearly in view. Do you hold your opposition and contain your feelings or do you lay down the law and make a stand?

In this example, goodbye week is probably not the best time to rigidly make her point. They may not have as much time to connect on the phone together but the week is about him making a break from a way of living and a community of people where he has been for over 10 years. He knows what she doesn't approve of, but being flexible doesn't say: *I don't mind anymore*. Rather, it says: *I am prepared to give you some rope and understand that you need this on this occasion.*

If he resumes heavy drinking once he's moved to be with her that might be the better time to make a stand. Then she could make her condition explicit through explaining that she loves him but doesn't feel comfortable with him in an intoxicated state, especially on a regular basis.

Deciding on your boundaries of acceptability and applying them in practice provides you with a sense of knowing where you stand. Standing firm feels immeasurably better than the feeling of being swayed by your partner's rhetoric of persuasion.

The position of acceptance can remain loving to your partner without being overly compromising to yourself. If the position you take is too personally compromising, then the love of your partner is paid for with a loss of love for yourself. If there is no flexibility or acceptance for your partner, then self-love is privileged over the love of your partner and they are compromised. Each of us have our own inner scales of justice to weigh up the best approach.

Mia and Jonny experienced financial challenges. She was training to be a yoga instructor, and he ran a café.

She had to travel interstate to attend training workshops four times a year. Jonny wanted to support her but the cost of travel, food and accommodation plus the workshop fee made it quite an expensive event for them.

For each workshop, she had to stay for two or three nights in dormitory-style accommodation. Each unit had two bedrooms and normally the training school placed participants in units without regard to gender or any preferences, meaning sometimes men and women shared a unit. The school said they never had a problem.

In the first three workshops, Mia had shared with women but in the last one she was placed to share with a man.

Though he trusted her, Jonny was uncomfortable with the idea of Mia sharing a unit with a man. She had a private bedroom, and the bathroom could be locked, but he still wasn't happy about it.

There was an option to book a unit for one but it cost twice as much.

Jonny put his foot down and said he didn't accept Mia sharing accommodation with a man. Mia felt in an awkward position. She already felt guilty about the cost of her training weekends, but Jonny assured her that he would rather wear the cost of the double unit. Mia accepted Jonny's non-acceptance even though she thought that he was a little unreasonable.

Then, she thought of something she was uncomfortable about, too.

There was a waitperson in Jonny's café named Elaine who always dressed in a sexy manner. Mia had made a few snide comments such as: *nothing like a tart served by a tart* and: *some like their meals a little saucy.* Jonny had ignored her because Elaine was a good worker, he quite liked her and felt her attire was just how some young women dressed these days.

But Mia had heard some gossip that Elaine had lost her previous job because she had sex with her former boss (who was married). While she didn't know if it was true, it was enough to make Mia feel that she didn't want to live with this situation, especially when out of town.

Mia put her foot down and said that Elaine had to go and that she would take over her shifts at work until she could be replaced. Jonny was uneasy about this because it felt unfair to dismiss Elaine in this way. But Mia insisted.

The nature of Elaine's employment contract meant it was possible legally to let her go even if some of the customers might miss her, especially some of the men.

Jonny accepted Mia's non-acceptance even though he felt uneasy about how to explain to Elaine why she was losing her job. (He managed his unease by finding her another job at a friend's café.)

This couple privileged the feelings of each other out of love. Also, they accepted the limit of what each was prepared to accept, and each accepted the non-acceptance of the other. The balance sheet of give and take was reconciled.

Cam loved his wife Patty and wanted to make love with her, but Patty's lack of acceptance of her own body prevented her from enjoying intimacy. In her twenties, she was a stunner – she was exceptionally beautiful and had a striking figure. After four children, she felt like her body had been through a war.

When she consulted me as a 40 year old, Patty was perfectly lovely looking, but she had gone from enjoying sex and finding it easy and fulfilling, to feeling largely turned-off. She preferred to not be touched at all.

Patty felt she had blown up like a balloon when pregnant. She told me that she had some stretch marks on her lower abdomen, lower back and buttocks. Her breasts had shrunk and dropped. And though she was not at all overweight, she felt as if her skin was hanging off her.

She used to be a little exhibitionistic. She had been proud of her looks and happy to be seen, clothed or not. Now she wouldn't even allow her husband to see her naked. She would not undress with the lights on, or let her husband in the bathroom when she was showering.

He found this all terribly frustrating and pointless. He couldn't understand her change of attitude. To him, she was still as beautiful and as desirable as before.

Here I am reminded of the ancient Hindu belief in the four stages of life called the Ashramas. The first stage of life is that of a student, and your mission is to learn. Students are expected to be celibate(!) and concentrate on study.

The second stage is called The Householder Stage, and focuses on family and raising children. It is a time for enjoying the sexuality of a primary relationship and perhaps a time of accumulating material wealth. It is also the time for pursuing your chosen occupation.

The third stage – which could be quite a long time later – is called Retreat or The Hermit Stage, also known as The Retirement Stage. Your children might be grown up and have children of their own. Here you move on from your usual occupations, give up material wealth and the pursuit of sexual pleasure. You are more involved in spiritual practices at this time. (Obviously, a lot happens between stages two and three.)

The fourth stage is called The Stage of Asceticism or The Wandering Recluse. You give up all of your attachments and devote yourself to spiritual concerns. Sometimes this phase is thought of as a time to merge with God and prepare for death. In this final stage, we are called upon to let go of fear and specifically fear of loss. The imminence and unavoidability of death mean that all of us have to give up everything, eventually.

> *When hard to accept, adjust or let go, consider the principle of impermanence and all your attachments are loosened.*

These are ancient beliefs, and I'm not sure how many modern Hindus still identify with these four stages of life. While our actual life paths are varied and complex, I see value in the idea that we pass from one phase to another, each time giving up what we had been immersed in before. For example, there is a shift from accumulation and acquisitiveness to divestment and a distributing of wealth to others.

What is of most value in these ancient Hindu ideas about life stages is that we need to focus on the primary aim of the phase that we are in and let go of the emphasis that consumed us previously. As we get older, we move from one stage to the next, seamlessly and gracefully, if we can. If we are centered in the correct disposition, there can be as much pleasure in giving away what we have as in accumulating it in the first place. How many of us practice this in a contemporary context?

The relevance for Patty is that she had her youthful beauty in her twenties. What is making her miserable and self-conscious now is that she cannot give up that image of herself. She clings to this image as her primary identification and she hasn't been able to adjust to what has changed. She has four healthy children and a husband who loves and desires her. He says that he doesn't care about the stretch marks or other imperfections. He accepts her as she is, but she does not accept herself. Of course, she can have cosmetic work done at vast expense and some risk, but will that change how she feels and sees herself? The practice of acceptance may have more to offer our mental state than the benefits offered by surgically re-sculpting our bodies.

Not accepting yourself can be projected onto your partner. Patty not only refuses to accept herself but also is unwilling to accept Cam's acceptance of her. She invalidates his experience of her and discounts his point of view. I sensed she couldn't really believe his expression of acceptance and desire as she couldn't hold this attitude for herself. Her negative view of herself gets mapped onto and overrides his view. She doesn't apply these same expectations to his body – she has no difficulty accepting his physical imperfections. She has a double standard that compromises herself.

Cam is grateful for all she has been through – the pregnancies and births, the breast-feeding, and for the family they have created together. It is somewhat spoiled by her not accepting herself and not receiving his acceptance or desire for her. Her attitude builds a wall between them.

Women have been anxious about their appearance for many centuries. Seventeenth century French aristocrat, Marie de Rabutin-Chantal, the marquise de Sévigné, also a celebrated figure of French literature wrote: "The heart has no wrinkles." Perhaps it is hard to bring a wrinkle-free heart to ourselves but obstinately refusing to accept our imperfections risks putting more wrinkles in the face of love.

Forbearance, tolerance and forgiveness

Forbearance is an attitude of refraining from enforcing something that is due. This could refer to a debt, a right, an obligation or a matter of principle. In a relationship, if you do something for your partner then you may well feel that your partner should do something of equal weight for you. Forbearance means we don't enforce this; it is another form of giving as giving up.

Generally, if I make dinner, you do the washing up. If you are attending to our sick child, and leave the dinner dishes, forbearance means I won't hold you to your usual obligation. I am not keeping score. Or if I am unwell and you do my share of the housework, when I feel better you won't demand I make up for it. Forbearance means that despite the principle of reciprocity in love, we let each other off the usual expectations.

> She gives him the best oral sex he has ever had. She is the only woman who has been able to make him come this way.
>
> But he refuses to go down on her, he doesn't like it, and doesn't want to. It might seem that she has a moral right to insist. It's only fair. But should she? Is there a limit to reciprocity? She likes doing it for him, but he doesn't like doing it for her.
>
> Could he reciprocate in some other way?

Like acceptance, forbearance has its limits.

> She pays for everything for the three children: school fees, clothes, medical care, books. She earns more than her ex-husband, the children's father, but he spends his money on himself, goes on expensive holidays then cries poor, and has nothing left to spend on the kids' needs.

Forbearance quickly reaches its limit when exploited.

> *Forbearance works best in an environment of fairness.*

Forbearance is a generosity of spirit that love requires in practice. While we don't have to be absolutely reciprocal, forbearance is an attitude that needs to be shared in more or less equal measure. Otherwise, we find that one person does everything, pays for everything, gives everything and the other takes.

For some reason, there is often an attitude of entitlement on the part of the taker. He is a man or she is a woman (that's reason enough for some). She is a scholar. He is a champion athlete. She is a model. He is a successful entrepreneur.

It doesn't matter who you are. The preservation of love is best served by the practice of forbearance with generosity. If forbearance happens willingly, freely, and without resentment or indebtedness, you don't need to undertake detailed accounting on the balance sheet of give and take.

The same applies to tolerance. How much should you tolerate?

I have heard women in the consulting room complain that their partner's hygiene has slipped badly. He doesn't wash enough, his bedclothes smell of urine, he doesn't brush his teeth, he smokes and his mouth is dry and breath stale. And so on.

I have heard men complain that their partners are messy, never put their clothes away, leave piles of papers to accumulate in common areas, leave their toiletries all over the bathroom, put used tampons or pads in the waste bin, leave used tissues on the bedside table. And so on.

I have heard both complain that the other burps and farts, and also snores. He picks his nose, and she chews with her mouth open. How much should we tolerate?

> Paul told Rene that her manner of chewing food and talking at the same time so that he could see the contents of her mouth being masticated was sickening to him. It made him feel nauseous so that he couldn't carry on eating his own food.
>
> She was an unselfconscious, easy-going, carefree kind of girl who wasn't bothered about putting on airs and graces. Etiquette was not her primary concern.

But she understood that her behaviors bothered him. With a small amount of effort, she could change and remember to chew with her mouth closed and speak after swallowing.

In this example, because she took his concerns on board, he didn't have to tolerate her behavior with forbearance.

Other things do have to be tolerated.

Rene also snored when she slept: not loudly but audibly enough to affect Paul.

Sometimes he lay awake listening to her. She couldn't help it but neither wanted to sleep in separate rooms.

And of course there are things that can be done.

Paul worked out that earplugs blocked out not only Rene's snoring sounds but a lot of street noise as well, and he slept better for using them. His willingness to tolerate her sleeping sounds lead him to the idea of earplugs.

Often when the blush of the in-love feeling wears a little paler, more behaviors that need tolerance come into view.

When Brad first fell in love with Jane he thought she had the most beautiful eyes in the world. Now, after some years of marriage, crow's feet are forming by the side of her eyes, and baggy sacks have appeared below them from tiredness.

Brad has struggled with his partner's aging look but can't bring himself to suggest that she think about cosmetic surgery. He knows she would feel hurt and worried by the suggestion.

Meanwhile, Jane told me privately that she used to love Brad's thick dark hair but now it has thinned out and a bald patch is growing at the crown of his head. She wondered if she should speak to him about getting a hairpiece or some hair transplanting or other treatment, but she knows this suggestion will offend him.

How will this couple accommodate the natural effects of aging? He sees her aging eyes but doesn't see reflected in them his own balding head and vice versa.

> *Your partner is a mirror of your own aging.*

Tolerance understands we do not stay the same – we are not always at our best, and don't always look as good as we can or used to. Tolerance is a gift of love. It needs to be a two-way street, practiced with fairness and reciprocity.

Forgiveness is a difficult subject and does not operate in the same ways as forbearance and tolerance, in which we have more choice. Forgiveness is not a decision; it is not an act of will. We cannot choose to forgive if we don't feel forgiving.

Forgiveness happens in its own time when it is ready. You can choose to have a favorable orientation toward forgiveness – you can *want* to forgive. But you cannot make yourself forgive if you are not yet ready. And if someone says sorry when they don't feel sorry, that is not likely to elicit forgiveness in you any sooner.

Many people love to advocate forgiveness. It is easy to say.
- *Maybe it's time to forgive your parents. They did their best.*
- *You should forgive your ex. He just wasn't ready for marriage and a family.*
- *You're better off forgiving your lover. She got taken advantage of by that predatory guy.*
- *It's time to forgive your son. He was just a kid and didn't know what he was doing.*
- *Your business partner was financially desperate. Why not forgive her?*

But it's not that simple.

Sometimes, you may well want to forgive but you aren't feeling it. Just because I say: *forgive and move on* should I expect a client to do it? Why? Because I say so? Because it is in their best interest? Because therapist knows best? Very doubtful, indeed! You may not want to forgive. You have been wronged, and some transgressions feel utterly unforgivable. Maybe you'll never be ready to forgive.

You may know you would be better off if you could forgive. What will it take to bring you around to a position of being able to? Sometimes you can work at it. You can try to understand the extenuating factors that contribute to why someone wronged you. You can explain it and rationalize it. You can make excuses, and find reasons. Sometimes that is not enough.

Sometimes it is just a matter of time. And sometimes that is not enough.

Perhaps you can think of a situation where you have been severely wronged, and you still do not forgive the culprit even if the intensity of outrage has diminished with time.

The phrases: *I apologize, I'm sorry,* and *I forgive you* are said often and sometimes lightly, but there is more to feeling it and meaning it than merely saying it. Something needs to be gone through to overcome the obstacles to true contrition and, once reached, greater success in eliciting forgiveness is likely. Deeply felt contrition expressed sincerely draws forgiveness from the most hardened victims, but there are no guarantees.

> Naomi's parents had grown up in the hippie era of the 60s and had continued in the same mode in many ways. They smoked pot openly and were so laid back and relaxed that they used to forget to feed their pets, forget to pick up their kids from school, overslept in the morning despite commitments, and passed out at parties and didn't come home until the next morning.
>
> They spoke their own hippie dialect with expressions like: *Can you dig it? It was such a gas that we crashed at Dave's pad. I have to split this scene. It is such a groovy thing, baby.* And: *it's just not my bag.*

Naomi hated all of this and found her parents an embarrassment. Her mother had inherited enough money for them to live in an upmarket suburb and send Naomi to private school, but Naomi couldn't invite friends home. She was mortified when any of her posh friends met her 'daggy' parents. She harbored intense outrage at their neglect, their lack of reliability, their selfishness and their indulgent lifestyle.

Naomi never specifically decided to forgive her parents but one day, when she was about 27 years old, she found that she had forgiven them.

She realized that they were a product of their generation and their environment. They didn't carry on like that out of any malice. There was no intention to embarrass her. They were just unconventional and so didn't fit in very well with the more conventional families of her peers. She began to see the funny side of it. A fondness and even love grew in her for her parents now that she was independent and able to live her own life.

She started to see them more like children who hadn't grown up. And she could also see how much they loved her, in their own quirky ways.

Previously, she had intense and uncontrollable emotional reactions to them, especially when something too hippie occurred. She would lash out, castigate them, mock them or ridicule them, to which they might reply: *chill out, man, that's not cool* which made her even more furious.

Even though she wasn't in a relationship, she began to want children. These longings and imaginings were new, and rather unexpected, as previously Naomi never wanted to have kids. She found herself imagining what it would be like to have them.

She could imagine her children might find her way of doing things a little old-fashioned even though she would not be like her parents. This process changed how she felt toward her parents. Her insight grew, helping mitigate the feeling that her parents came from another planet.

As her desire to become a parent grew, Naomi noticed she felt more forgiving toward her own parents.

Forgiveness happened of its own accord, when it was ready. It was a great relief to Naomi to feel forgiveness because she didn't like the person she had been – full of victimization and the corresponding accusations and recriminations. She didn't like herself when she was nasty to her parents. She had wanted to rise above all this and feel better toward her parents but couldn't reach to it until she arrived at a position of forgiveness.

> *Being ready to forgive occurs in its own time and not on demand.*

Can you forgive if you are not ready to? I don't see how.

Is there anything you can do to bring yourself to a position of readiness so that forgiveness can emerge within you? Yes, a lot.

Start by noticing if you are attached to being the victim.

- Are you getting anything out of having been wronged?
- Is there any gratification in complaining about it?
- Are you feeling sanctimonious by occupying the moral high ground?
- Are you clinging to being hard-done-by?
- Have you become addicted to self-pity or eliciting sympathy from others?

If there is even a trace of a 'yes' in response to any of these questions, you can begin to cultivate forgiveness by dealing with these tendencies in yourself. Work through them by reflecting upon your answers to the above questions and dismantling ingrained attitudes that perpetuate a lack of forgiveness. Just as you exercise the body, you need to exercise your mind.

For Naomi, a range of realizations helped her move toward forgiveness. Even though they have the same DNA, her parents are not the same as her, and therefore it was okay for them to be different. They grew up in a different world, had different values and attitudes, different outlooks.

A useful mental exercise in working toward forgiveness is to cultivate empathy[16] for the other. As Naomi moved toward the position of parenting in herself, this became easier. In addition, it helps to remember your own flaws and shortcomings.

It is often issues in ourselves that bother us most in others. Sorting this out can be a catalyst toward readiness to forgive.

> Naomi recognized that though she didn't like her parents' hippie style, what bothered her most was their tendency to be irresponsible. She noticed that when she was most scathing about her parents, the focus was on how easy it was for them to disregard a parental responsibility without any apparent discomfort.
>
> She identified a similar tendency in herself. She wasn't a parent, but she could easily 'forget' to pay a bill or she might lose track of an agreement to do something for a friend. She often missed appointments by failing to enter them in her calendar. Library books never got returned on time, and she was frequently late for work.
>
> She couldn't understand it when others didn't want to let her off the hook about minor instances of diminished responsibility.
>
> Forgiving her parents corresponded in time with her realization of the connection between her own pattern of irresponsibility and that of her parents. This insight not only created a readiness to forgive, it also created a readiness

---
16. How to cultivate empathy is detailed in Chapter 9.

to deal with her tendencies toward irresponsibility. There was a sense of growing up in arriving at a position of forgiveness and in assuming a greater sense of responsibility. Perhaps this shift also corresponds with becoming ready for the possibility of becoming a parent.

○ ○ ○

It is easy for self-interest to get the better of us. The greedy inner child holds sway, and the other may be compromised. This might apply to your beloved partner, children, parents or friends. They are beloved, but you cannot let go of a grievance or an issue. Maybe you find gratification in harboring a grudge and the accompanying feeling of empowerment and righteousness.

In this mode, you remain focused on your disappointment, nursing your emotional injury, while feeling justified in your victimized position. You find yourself nurturing hostility inwardly, while secretly blaming the other.

If we are brutally honest with ourselves, sometimes the degree to which we are unable to forgive another is in equal proportion to the degree to which we let ourselves off the hook for our own sub-standard conduct.

> *Loving feels so much better than harboring grudges against those you love and who love you.*

When unable to forgive, your mind is filled with negativity. You cannot simply decide to forgive, but you can work on decanting the negative contents of your mind. While clearing what is in the way and working out why you are attached to your injury or feeling of injustice, ask yourself: *what will it take to let it go?*

Forbearance, tolerance and forgiveness go together. Each generates and supports the others. Together, they interweave a disposition toward your beloved in a fabric that joins the two of you compassionately, enhancing and preserving love. Addressing the issues that come between you while accepting what you can and standing firm on the unavoidable limits of acceptance increases the durability of your relationship. Feeling gratitude both from and toward your partner for each other's generosity of spirit engenders emotional health and maximizes the lifespan of love.

CHAPTER 8

Partnership Unity

*"There is always some
madness in love. But there is also
always some reason in madness."*
— **Friedrich Nietzsche**

Trust and trustworthiness – revisited

One of the most common reasons that relationships founder is because trust is damaged. Let's revisit the subject since trust is fundamental in creating partnership unity.

Remember the elements of trust:
- Honesty
- Accountability
- Transparency
- Respect
- Reliability and dependability
- Consistency
- Straightforwardness
- Genuineness
- Contrition
- Care
- Fidelity both sexually and to the spirit of the relationship

Each of the elements must be lived. Credible trustworthiness breeds and fortifies trust. Doubts arise when any of the elements of trust are enacted like a performance without authenticity. A partial experience of trustworthiness detracts from credible integrity and a loss of faith eventually follows.

The 'real deal' in trustworthiness resides in how we act, and the way our representations of ourselves match our actions. If they match consistently, the need to defend ourselves or convince others doesn't arise.

> *To be credible: say what you mean and mean what you say.*

Trustworthiness becomes self-evident unless the doubter is suspicious independently of the evidence. There is always room for doubt because you can never be certain about anyone's trustworthiness or credibility. A paranoid attitude will find reasons to doubt however honest you might be. And no amount of protestations of innocence will overturn an entrenched attitude of disbelief. However, as long as paranoia isn't excessive, then to be trustworthy in word as well as in deed is usually enough to build a foundation of trust as a platform.

When trust is compromised, the foundations of the relationship become like shifting sand. It becomes difficult or impossible to know where we are with each other and hold steady. Faith has lost its bearings.

Many people are trustworthy but come unstuck because their relationship isn't right, or isn't meeting their needs – possibly because they aren't sexually satisfied or because the intimacy is diminished. In these events, in the face of deprivation, frustration, distance or disconnectedness, it can become hard to sustain integrity and honor the elements of trust. Trust and trustworthiness are not solely badges of individual character but exist in the context of a relationship.

> If Lara's partner Gil starves her of love, sex and affection, should she be entitled to seek something from someone else? Should she be forgiven?
>
> If Carl is rejected every time he makes sexual overtures to Gail, would he be justified in purchasing a sexual experience in a massage parlor or a brothel? Should his wife understand?

A loving trust and a trusting love mean privileging the interest of your partner over and above your own self-interest. But to what degree is this fair and reasonable? It works both ways and if one does all the privileging and the other does none, it risks becoming a form of masochistic self-denial for the one and exploitation by the other.

> Gail is married to Carl and looks after their two small children all day, every day. When taking Carl's overcoat to the dry cleaners, she found in the pocket a list of prostitutes with phone numbers and prices.
>
> He claimed that he did not visit any of them and didn't telephone them. Gail said that the ads in the newspaper did not list prices for their services. How could he have possibly found out prices if he never picked up the phone?
>
> Carl said that one day when he was feeling desperate with sexual frustration, he did a little research on the internet but then decided he couldn't possibly act on it.
>
> Gail didn't know whether to believe him or not.
>
> I didn't either.
>
> Carl was convincing. When he consulted me on his own, he was insistent this was the absolute truth, no bullshit. I wanted to believe him but it was hard not to be skeptical.

What people say and what people do is not necessarily the same. The trust between Carl and Gail was now called into question, as was the trust between Carl and myself.

I want to believe people, but I do not want to be 'played'. Nor do I want to be overly suspicious.

> After finding the list, Gail became more turned off Carl. She wanted to believe him, and she wanted their relationship to be better, but there was a great deal that needed to be addressed before the trust could be restored.
>
> We needed to explore why she was so shut down sexually toward him in the first place and what was turning her off. She said that he was often grumpy around the house and kids and that being part of the family seemed like a chore to him. He enjoyed his work and was happy to have his face in his laptop or phone but during the evenings and on weekends, he was either emotionally absent or flat.
>
> She wanted a happy partner, one who would step up, take leadership of the family, make suggestions about things they could do together, and be motivated to take initiative with the children – meeting their needs and participating in their activities. That would be a turn-on for her.

> *Her resentment was like a fire extinguisher on her libido!*

Trust refers to sexual fidelity, of course, but also to your role in the relationship in a broader sense. Notice the circularity of the situation. Gail is turned-off sexually because Carl appears unhappy in the relationship and family in general, and so Carl considers the services of a prostitute because his wife won't have sex with him. This creates a much larger problem, and by Carl creating mistrust, Gail is even less likely to want to be sexual.

To live up to trustworthiness, it helps to be happy in your relationship. In the example above, no one should blame Carl for *feeling* as he did. It was a real problem for him, and anyone who has felt intensely sexually frustrated might sympathize.

Gail wanted to feel sexual toward Carl and felt frustrated too. She was in quadrant two of the matrix of desire – desire to desire. She had not decided to be turned-off and didn't enjoy her diminished sexuality. She wasn't punishing him. Her feelings were a reflection of what was happening and not happening between them.

As we said in the previous chapter: when something comes between you, when an issue arises, and one is not happy with the other, or something isn't working, you have to address it. Have to! You have to address it in the relationship, instead of acting-out of the relationship. If you cannot do that effectively with each other, you need to get help to make it possible, to work at it, and, ideally, to resolve it.

> Carl and Gail came to therapy, worked hard at it, and consequently took the insights and indications of therapy home and incorporated them into their relationship. We spoke a great deal about Carl's transition of roles from managing director to father of small children and back. We spoke about what a family requires of a man emotionally. I encouraged Carl to make his role at home a form of play, to make it fun. Prior to doing this therapeutic work, he didn't seem to enjoy himself in practically any context. Gail loved to have fun with him as they once did. Carl made efforts to re-engage with the family and take pleasure in their daily activities which benefited Gail and their kids.
>
> Gail felt more forgiving. They not only repaired trust but, in the process, also overcame some major obstacles between them. They were able to re-ignite a sexual connection together and told me that their relationship had improved to be better than since they first met.

Looking after your partner in a love relationship encourages them to want to be trustworthy and to work at it – assuming they have the moral character. Trust and trustworthiness are relational qualities that are negotiated and transacted between us. While this sounds a little commercial, it refers to an emotional economy that pertains to happy relationships. When feeling wealthy with what your partner gives you, you are far less likely to breach the boundaries and limits that trust requires. If you are happy and satisfied with your relationship, what else is there to seek?

The rules of engagement

The 'rules of engagement' refer to the spirit of your involvement at any stage of relationship. They are not a book of rules; rather they clarify your intentions and expectations, guide your actions, and indicate where you are with each other.

At a certain point, the two of you regard yourselves as 'a couple' *in a relationship*. You don't have to be living together, but you are together as a unit. Coupling-up is a landmark moment for any two people who might start off by going out with each other or dating; it is the commencement of a partnership-in-love. Now that you have achieved unit status, you are a two-some and you are working toward unity, a oneness.

Many people, not only young people, like going out but don't necessarily see that as a prelude to coupling. There is nothing that says that it has to be. However, going out may be assumed to be a prelude to coupling by some and it is important to be clear. Being up front about what things mean, about where you are, and about where you are going helps avoid unnecessary pain and disappointment.

- Just because I take you out to dinner and pay for you doesn't mean we are a couple.
- Just because I tell you I love you doesn't mean that I'm not saying this to anyone else.
- Just because I gaze into your eyes with love sparkling in mine doesn't mean we will be together happily ever after.
- Just because we have sex doesn't mean we will get married.

What exactly do your actions mean? That is the guiding question of the rules of engagement.

Of course, you don't always know what your intentions are – and if that is the case, you must be clear about that too. You may not wish to plan where this will end up. You might simply feel open to what happens between you and see where it goes. This is valid. But what if you don't have an agenda but your partner does? It would be best if they were clear about it, and you, too, were clear about the differences from your position.

As things unfold, we need to develop an understanding of the meaning of being a couple; how far have intentions formed? Sometimes intentions form at a different pace for each person. Some couples have an implicit understanding between them of what their relationship means while others require it to be spelled out, explicitly. Sometimes I find that couples believe they have an understanding until one partner acts in a way that reveals a different understanding. I wonder how many couples in the early stages have the same understanding as each other. How can you achieve unity unless you both have the same understanding?

If you are going out, but not yet a couple, do you both agree to clear a space for your potential relationship in which there is no sex with anyone else, even if you're not sexual with each other yet? Maybe you're not even intimate yet. What about agreeing on no romance with anyone else even before a full-blown romance develops between you? At what point do you make such an agreement?

This tentative agreement already holds within it, implicitly, that you may well be moving toward becoming a couple, even if it remains to be seen. It is an indication but not a promise. It is a sign, but not a guarantee. It depends on what happens.

When you decide you have arrived at a point where you declare to the world that the two of you are together – in a relationship – you have achieved unit status and you are a couple, then what does that mean?

- How should that affect your conduct socially?
- How does it affect your attitude toward others?
- What is permissible and what isn't?

- How do you know what is permissible?
- How do you make the shift from functioning as an individual to functioning as a couple?
- What is involved in the transition to coupledom?
- What thoughts or conversations have you had about what this relationship means?

Typically, none of this is discussed in advance of lived situations in which these unanswered questions can become divisive issues. In other words, often there is no agreement. Nothing has been made explicit. No prior discussion – no understanding between you. Consequently, you act on assumptions.

> So, we go to a New Year's Eve party and at the stroke of midnight everyone kisses each other. You have a rather intense kiss with a guy who seems attracted to you and I have a rather intense kiss with an old female friend who identifies as lesbian. Is there a difference?
>
> I argue that my kiss is different from yours because my friend and I could never be lovers; there is no threat to our relationship. Your kiss was threatening because I'm sure that guy would have loved to take it further given half a chance.
>
> You argue that your kiss was identical to mine. There is no difference. How could I even argue there should be different rules governing each? They were exactly the same. It just happened he was right there at the stroke of midnight, and she was closer to me. It was just a kiss and didn't mean anything.
>
> Who is right?

Remember what the kiss meant to Tony's partner Belinda when she was kissed by Claude (in Chapter 6). That was not 'nothing'. His deliberately intimate gesture affected her quite dramatically.

> It put her in touch with a well of feelings about what was missing between Tony and herself. She had been harboring

such feelings for a long time. She knew in that moment that something in her had died. Her relationship was over. She was so triggered by Claude's kiss that she did go on to end her relationship with Tony.

While Belinda and Tony didn't separate because of the rules of engagement, couples commonly do become unstuck because the rules of engagement have not been thought through, discussed and agreed between them. While you cannot anticipate every possible scenario, you can consider how each of you would feel about possible situations.

The idea of having rules of engagement is to co-create a frame for your relationship that is mutually agreeable, that protects the emerging love between you, preserves trust, and guides your conduct with other people. It gives meaning to being a couple. It places love as the ultimate destination on the roadmap of social experience.

Ideally, being a 'unit' inspires unity.

> Jonny doesn't mind that Mia's male yoga teacher works closely with her body as he corrects her postures through close physical contact. *Hey, that's yoga!* he says. But he does mind her sharing accommodation with a man she has never met before.
>
> Similarly, Mia feels threatened by sexy, young Elaine sharing the workplace with her husband even though he says he isn't attracted to her and it wouldn't matter if he thought she was the 'hottest' girl in town. He would never act out of line with her or anyone else.
>
> He just wants the coffees served hot.

By embracing their own rules of engagement these two reached an understanding of what they required to feel safe and comfortable with each other. Through this process, they felt grateful for their feelings being taken seriously and respected by the other. Enacting the spirit of their understanding became an essential element of partnership unity.

The contract

Establishing a marital or de facto contract is an extension of the rules of engagement.

In some places, a de facto relationship is the same in law as a marriage once a couple has been living together for a few years. You are bound by a contract whether you know it or not, whether you have agreed to one, written one, signed one – *or not!*

The contract in a love relationship is no different from a commercial contract. When everything runs smoothly there is no need for one. But contracts exist for when things go wrong, even if this is furthest from your mind when you start out. They apply equally when you are in love and when you are not. The best time to establish a contract is when your partnership is united so that you can work collaboratively in creating your own agreement.

I'm not suggesting that you have to see a lawyer and draw up a formal contract. A contract doesn't even have to be written – though it may be better if it is. It will depend upon your circumstances, your needs, and what you feel comfortable with.

As with the rules of engagement, a contract provides a clear understanding that doesn't change with variations in the emotional climate between you. Typically, such understandings are clear when you're happy together and then change dramatically when you fall out with each other. When traveling well together, no contract is needed. When falling out with each other, you wish there was one.

> *The love contract needs to remain constant despite changes in the emotional climate.*

You can use a document to spell out your intentions toward each other moving forward and in advance of any conflict. With this documentation of your joint 'understanding', you're less likely to become subject to distortions in memory caused by changes or reversals in your or your partner's emotional state or disposition toward each other.[17]

When your relationship deteriorates, you become subject to powerful external forces, such as lawyers, other stakeholders including friends and family, and the court system. This, in turn, compounds the difficulties of remembering your original understanding and your willingness to abide by it.

What seemed fair at the outset can seem extremely unfair later. Generosity can be a product of love just as meanness can be a product of the reversal of unity, the disentangling of a partnership. And your perception of what is mean or generous can have more to do with how you are feeling about your partner than what is the case from anyone else's point of view, or from an objective standpoint.

The privileging of the other's interest in functioning as a couple can revert to the privileging of self-interest as a separate, individual person. I have seen fairness go out the window and I have also seen the opposite, a kind of bitter, self-abnegation expressed as: *I don't want to take anything with me, I just want my ex to leave me alone now.*

Journaling events and contributions along the way supports clarity about what is fair and what is real and becomes even more valuable when things go wrong or escalate to more serious conflict. It's not just about the material position though this is an important part of it. Often, settling up is the ugliest part of separation and divorce.

When you are de facto or married, a joint estate begins to grow. Sometimes, you don't have a sense of it. You just go out and buy a bed together, or a television, or a trip to Phuket. But what happens if you break up before the date of the trip? Will you still go together even though you've separated? If not, who gets the air tickets?

---

[17]. *While a written contract may seem a good idea with hindsight, it is rarely something we do, with foresight!* Con Coroneos (personal communication)

It can be hard to think it through.

If you get the tickets, then what do I get?

Anyway, I paid for the bloody plane flights with my frequent flyer points.

Oh yeah, your credit card was linked to my frequent flyer account.

And who gets the bed? You know I had trouble sleeping and chose that bed specifically.

But you paid more than half, yes, I do remember that now.

But didn't I pay for delivery?

It can be so confusing and painfully difficult to unravel.

The romantic domain and the practical domain affect one another. If the practical is in order, this often preserves space for the romantic. If the romance is over no matter how much you both wish it was otherwise, being clear about the practical domain – how the joint estate is constituted, or simply who owns what – can help preserve the friendship, or at very least, preserve civility.

Separating is hard enough emotionally. Going through it is helped if you don't have to quibble, fight, or go to war about the material possessions. This is even more important when you have children to co-parent from a position of separateness.

The purpose of such contracts is mainly to preserve and protect the unity between you. However, if the relationship comes apart, a contract also has value in preventing a falling out. Many people will testify that coming to an agreed and fair settlement is harder and more painful than even the emotional loss of the relationship.

> *Breadwinners remember: your earnings were made possible by your partner's care of your children, your home and yourself.*

The contract is also about what is permissible within both the spirit and letter of the relationship, much like the rules of engagement. Can such contracts ever be changed? Yes, of course, by mutual agreement. Are we bound to them forever? Til death do us part? This is a harder question. For some people, the answer is definitely *yes* – the contract is permanent. In this sense, it may be different from a commercial contract that can be broken or revised or that expires.

For others, the contract expresses an intention that we go on until we no longer want to. There is an awareness that many marriages and de facto relationships don't last forever. Many end before anyone dies. These days, probably the majority reach a use-by date before either of you literally expires.

The point of having a contract is to know where you stand. It is a formalization of the status of the relationship. It is a device to sustain unity and protect against discord.

Often, it states what each has brought into the joint estate, which may be very different. Then, such documents need revision, as you go, as each of you contributes in somewhat different ways and proportions over time. This is what frequently gets fought over after the partnership has ended.

A contract isn't just about quantifying the material value of what each contributes. Typical examples are:
- He earns 75 per cent of their joint income but she looks after his kids from a previous relationship, as stepmother.
- She has sold her house and moved into his, but he has invested and lost her capital.
- He has given up a lucrative career opportunity to support his partner through illness.
- She has given up the possibility of having children knowing her partner could not cope with a family on top of everything else.

Contributions to a love relationship take many forms, sometimes intangible and impossible to quantify. A 'contract' is a symbol of unity, and while there is no guarantee that it will be honored at the end of the day, it provides documentation of the understanding between you.

There are cases where it seems that one person is attempting to secure their partner into a guaranteed arrangement out of insecurity that their partner won't want to stay. This doesn't sound like it has much to do with love; more like an expression of fear, of extreme vulnerability and a tactic to prevent loss, like an insurance policy. This is not what I am advocating here. A manoeuvre such as this risks pushing your partner away. They can feel your fear in this manipulation and are bound to experience it as an expression of mistrust rather than commitment. Unity cannot be dictated or secured through tyranny, bullying or even legally binding documents.

When made in the right spirit, a contract can express your willingness to throw your whole self into it with your partner, all of what you have and will have, and all of who you are and will become. That is wholehearted commitment and a profound expression of trust and devotion; indicative of the transition from functioning as individuals to a couple in a full sense. It is total investment in the relationship, a powerful demonstration of faith in your belief in a future together and your warrant of partnership unity. On this basis, a contract can fortify love and symbolize it as a monument built to last.

CHAPTER 9

The Ecology of Successful Relationships

> *"Your task is not to seek love, but to seek and find all the barriers within yourself that you have built against it."*
> — **Rumi**

Successful relationships have their own relational ecology. Human ecology refers to the interrelation of people and organizations or institutions in our culture. A relational ecology pertains to the internal systems or patterns within your and your primary partner's way of relating. This sense of ecology may be called a relational ecosystem.

The first challenge is how to assess your relationship from a position within it, with a view to making it successful and durable. We are always a part of the environment we are assessing. When we look out on the physical environment we can see the effects of the weather, pollution and development, and make assessments of its relative health. When we look at our relationship from a position within it, assessing the environment is not quite as straightforward. Nevertheless, there are tangible signs of whether a relationship is faring well or if there is erosion or ill-health.

Do you see a look of discontent on your partner's face? Has that become the norm? Do you register moments of being disregarded? Of coldness, distance or passive-aggressive hostility? Do arguments dominate your discussions? Does it appear that your partner would rather spend time with your child beyond need? Did your partner forget your birthday or anniversary for the first time since you met? Has the sex become less frequent or more perfunctory? Does your partner seem less than enthusiastic about activities you used to enjoy together? These questions begin to assess the functioning and well-being of your relational ecology.

The investigation of relational ecology involves the examination of four interconnected elements:

- emotionally honest communication
- reciprocal attunement
- empathic negotiation
- affective compromise

These elements elaborate the principle ways you relate to each other. Their integrated functioning constitutes the ecosystem within the environment of a love relationship. In discussing relational ecology, we separate out these four elements of the relational ecosystem so they can be explored, understood and developed to enable your relationship to grow ever more successful.

What does 'successful' mean in the context of love relationships? The underlying pre-supposition of success is that you feel good with each other, that you feel in your right place and want to be there. Highly subjective personal terms such as 'right' and 'good' must be left to each of us as individuals to determine. What successful really means is what it means to you. To me, relationships are successful when couples enjoy all the benefits that being together brings and make the inevitable sacrifices feel worth it.

Emotionally honest communication

Success often begins and ends with communication. It is worth understanding that communication can be made in different modes:

one or unidimensional, two-dimensional, three-dimensional and theoretically even four-dimensional.

Briefly, examples of unidimensional communications include texts, emails or voice messages. It's amazing how often we hear about important, deeply personal communications being made by unidimensional means.

> *I won't be coming over this evening because*
> *I'm breaking up with you. Have a nice life ...*

Choosing to end a relationship by text message is an especially cruel form of rejection. Maybe it reflects a culture of expendables and disposables when someone is prepared to discard another person with no respect for what has been of value between them.

Some examples of two-dimensional communication are Skype, private internet video rooms and Facetime. In person communication is three-dimensional because there is sight, sound, smell and touch. The fourth dimension takes us into metaphysical realms that are beyond the scope of both my understanding and of this discussion, but is still worth mentioning. I will never forget this account, my best example:

> Many years ago in London, a patient described to me how when fast asleep one night she woke suddenly at 3am, sat bolt upright, broke into a sweat and felt nauseous. She was overcome with a feeling of foreboding, bordering on panic. She knew something was terribly wrong.
>
> When she phoned her husband, who was in New York on a business trip, he didn't answer.
>
> When he returned home, she had a heart to heart and begged him to tell her the truth about what he was doing at that precise moment. After much pleading, he confessed that he had been with a prostitute.
>
> He was, in fact, ejaculating at precisely 10pm New York time. He knew because his phone rang five minutes later.

The call register confirmed the missed call was from her.

There was a five hour time difference between London and New York.

Metaphysical communications can occur between people who share a strong connection. You might prefer not to be so connected at a given moment, but like it or not, that is the fourth dimension.

Communication that is emotionally honest gives weight to conveying how you feel and how you are affected by your partner without any agenda other than to convey your felt-state and without any intention to effect a pre-determined outcome. You invite your partner into an otherwise private, interior zone of felt experience that makes such communications intimately personal. They are made for their own sake.

Emotionally honest communication requires even-handedness in both saying what needs to be said and hearing the response to it. This is best achieved through three-dimensional communication – in the flesh, person to person, one on one. It works best to speak to each other directly, conveying your own personal subjective truth while being ready and open to hearing the other's own personal subjective truth. This is a primary currency in love relationships; such communications grow in value the more direct, the more articulate and the more genuine you are.

There is no substitute for speaking from the heart in your own words. Even the most sophisticated emotional vocabulary cannot replace saying what you have to say, in your own way. Don't avoid it *because it will hurt the other's feelings*. At the same time, I am not suggesting you state what you really feel in a way that will plunge a knife in the heart of the person who loves you. With tact and compassion, you can minimise hurt caused by painful truths.

Sometimes it can help to involve others such as family, friends or a therapist. Many people have disclosed information to me in front of their partner that they have been unable to say to them on their own.

Emotionally honest communication is not the same as a 'spilling of guts', an indiscriminate regurgitation of the entire contents of your private thoughts and feelings. Judge carefully what needs to be communicated and also what needs to not be communicated. Sometimes there is a good case for containment. Further, as far as possible, know what you're talking about before opening your mouth. That is not the same thing as having an agenda or aiming for a particular outcome.

Consider also the timing for emotionally honest communications. This will enhance the prospects of being well received. If you have been judicious with containment, communicating at the right time is more powerful and effective. Better to hesitate than prevaricate as true thoughtfulness gives pause to speech. Sometimes, you have to wait and sometimes there is no right moment.

> One client couldn't bring issues up first because it was Christmas, then because it was her partner's birthday, then it was New Years then her family was visiting, then she had her period and didn't feel emotionally balanced enough. Then it was their anniversary and she didn't want to spoil the mood.
>
> By then, there was no particular reason to defer raising the hard issues but she felt they had lost their relevance. Too much time had passed from when her examples had occurred.

○○○

One client told me that she found farting disgusting.

> Her partner was accustomed to letting it all hang out, burping or farting whenever – he didn't even care if other people were around. He was a free spirit; it was their problem if they didn't like it.
>
> She didn't have a lot of other complaints; it was just this farting thing that got her down and she couldn't figure out how to talk to him about it.

She was in charge of laundry and found his underclothes soiled with poo stains and sometimes even bits of fecal matter that had been farted out, which she found disgusting.

With a bit of encouragement, she told her partner how she felt. He said it was only natural, that she was neurotic and should use her therapy to help her get over it.

It is pathologizing to define the other's feelings as a symptom of a psychological condition. She was made to feel bad and wrong through this invalidation.

My client thought it over and decided that she had been contained for too long and now she would tell her partner that, natural or not, he could do his own laundry from now on and if he didn't stop farting around her (she didn't care what he did anywhere else), she was going to do a big poo on his pillow and tell him it was natural and to go to therapy if he didn't like it.

That was strong, I remarked.

She said that it worked. Her partner got the message that she didn't like it and wasn't prepared to tolerate it and he started to practice some self-control around her. And she felt respected and happier with him.

Emotionally honest communication often requires saying what you already know your partner does not want to hear. There needs to be a space for this. Find a way of talking about what is displeasing or disagreeable, otherwise nothing changes and it becomes entrenched. The longer it remains entrenched, the harder it is to shift.

> *The 'truth' you are too anxious to tell is probably already evident.*

Many people discover that when they spill the beans about something they found difficult or were afraid to divulge, their partner already had an inkling or had been wondering – possibly for quite some time. There is a difference between implicit knowing and explicit knowing. Some have dreams about what they haven't yet been told as if the truth has been dwelling in a latent psychic space.

The attitude of emotionally honest communication needs to be met by your partner with a receptiveness and a willingness to address issues. If your partner is closed, if you feel 'the phone is off the hook' and they don't want to know, that makes it harder to speak freely. If you are anticipating a big reaction, possibly anger or aggression, whenever you are even slightly critical, this is bound to inhibit communication.

You don't have to be addressing issues all the time. Perhaps you can agree on a time that works for both of you to address what needs to be addressed. It works best to be 'in the right space' or mood, open and ready, in a spirit of cooperative partnership. If you don't know if it is the right time or not, try asking: *is this a good time to bring up a disagreeable subject?*

Make a point of listening, of taking into yourself and being receptive to each other's point of view. Communication is just as much about listening as it is about speaking. Even if it is not sitting well with you initially, consider what your partner means before reacting. Give time for thought. These moments are incredibly important in preventing a build-up of ill feeling and promoting a relationship to move forward positively.

Consider what would help you to love your partner more.
- What could he do that would help you to open your heart?
- What could she do that would help you to feel more for her?
- What is in the way for you?
- Is there anything your partner can do about those things that are in the way? There may not be, but it is still worth considering.

Just as we need to spring clean or de-clutter our homes from the accumulation of useless things, working together can you clear out the issues that remain unresolved to make space for growth?

Establishing open and honest communication involves revealing what you really feel. This can be hard, and painful. It can require an adjustment. Pretending is not satisfying; it amounts to living a lie. It is better to 'put your cards on the table'.

> *This is how I really feel and I'm sorry if it is not what you thought, not what you hoped. It's not what I had hoped!*

Emotional honesty requires a balance of opposing considerations. Sometimes the honest truth is black or white, and there is nothing in between. However, it is essential to consider your partner's vulnerabilities and sensitivities. How can we balance such opposing forces in our communications? I don't want to hurt you or upset you, *and* this needs to be said. I know you won't like it *and* it is the truth all the same. You are sensitive to criticism *and* I have to point it out anyway or it won't change. Aim to balance your communications to be genuinely truthful while honoring your partner's emotional disposition and your own.

> *I'm so frightened to lose you by telling you the truth. I'm desperately hoping you can hear this without having to take flight from me.*

Ambivalence is the natural position in which two opposing values are held at once. Emotionally honest communication endeavors to give voice to both sides of ambivalence in balance while taking into account the likely affect upon your beloved.

> Craig came in for an individual session. I recognized him as a well-known actor from a successful TV series. His striking good looks and suave style made him highly noticeable. His de facto of 27 years, Marjorie, had discovered a lovey-dovey text message from Caroline, a local woman she knew.

Craig's phone was locked but the message popped up on the screen when he left the room. Marjorie wasn't snooping around his phone, she just heard a beep and glanced across.

The message was enough for her to press Craig about what was going on. He confessed that he saw Caroline regularly but they never had sex. True, they were more than friends but not lovers. Anyway, Marjorie knew that Craig couldn't get an erection and so sex wasn't something he could contemplate even if he wanted to. He and Marjorie did manage it about once a year with the assistance of medication. But Marjorie didn't like sex, didn't want it, and was happier without it.

Craig admitted to me, however, that he had been lovers with Caroline for more than six years and he didn't have a sexual problem with her. He had thought his erectile dysfunction was a medical issue – what did I think?

I said: *your penis probably reflects your wife's indifference to sex and Caroline's passion for it*, though I wasn't endorsing his affair.

Since discovering the text message, Marjorie had turned hostile toward him and so Craig wanted help from me with his marriage. Her trust was shattered; she was extremely hurt and offended and felt she didn't know him. He said she called it 'an emotional affair' and felt the responsibility was entirely his. According to Craig, Marjorie said: *if he wanted a better sexual relationship or more intimacy with her then he should be more romantic toward her.*

And would I see both of them for marital therapy to help restore her trust in him?

I said: *No, I cannot enter into marital therapy with both of you knowing that you had a full sexual relationship with Caroline when Marjorie does not know that. If I collude with you in keeping a secret from Marjorie, that puts me in an unethical relation to Marjorie. I'm in the truth business here. If she asked: I don't feel like I can trust Craig – do you think that is unreasonable? – what kind of answer could I give her?* When I said the word 'unethical', Craig looked like I was speaking a foreign language.

Craig said he didn't tell Marjorie about sex with Caroline because he didn't want to hurt her (he believed he was being emotionally honest). I replied: *I'm sorry, Craig, but that sounds like bullshit to me. If you didn't want to hurt Marjorie then you would not have had an affair with Caroline in the first place. But you are right that to tell her will hurt her more.* Craig was taken aback by my bluntness.

I wasn't saying that he must tell Marjorie the whole truth; that has to be a decision for him. It is not my place to tell her, but I won't conceal it from her either. *If you do decide to come clean with Marjorie, you need to be prepared for the possibility that your relationship could be over. I don't know if Marjorie would be willing to keep going. If nothing is kept from her and you both want to pursue marital therapy, then I have no problem working with both of you.*

At the end of the session, I suggested Craig think it over and let me know how he wanted to proceed. Apart from anything else, I was pretty sure Craig would not open himself up to negative publicity. News of his affair and marital break-up would have appeared in the press and made his emotional mess into a much bigger and more painful public relations problem, an airing of dirty laundry.

Craig had quite a portfolio of 'opposing values' to negotiate, and then the challenge of working out how to communicate with his partner. He didn't want to break up and didn't want Marjorie to leave. He and Caroline seemed to be in love even though he was trying to break off contact. He wanted Marjorie to believe that he was trustworthy but didn't want to give up having sex with other women. In the past Marjorie had looked after him domestically but this had now stopped. Now, she could not resist attacking him, something he was quick to admit he deserved. Her attacks, however, served to rationalize his infidelities in his own mind.

> Caroline was not the only instance of sexual infidelity though she was the only one with whom he had been involved for any length of time. Craig confessed to me that he had not used a condom with Caroline, or one or two other women that Caroline didn't know about, and then had sex with Marjorie, also without a condom. Marjorie had her doubts about the story of Craig not having sex with Caroline, and didn't really want to have sex with him but felt she should *because he was so unhappy*.

> Craig then revealed to me that Caroline told him that her husband had asked her how she would feel if he had sex with a man. She wondered if he already had.

Craig had no difficulty in telling me in one breath how much he loved his wife, Marjorie, and in the next how he had cheated on her for many years with multiple partners and put her at grave risk. Amongst many ethical issues at the heart of love relationships, this example also highlights the tension between honesty in communication and the need for containment in love. Here, an explosive situation has built up fuelled by Craig's acting fame and the resulting adulation he receives. It would be easy to judge him for his narcissism.

However, I see two people who are suffering in a long-term relationship where each party has fallen into roles that do not satisfy them. Communication and the willingness to address issues has been neglected on both sides. This does not exonerate his affairs or his disregard for his wife's or his lovers' health in any way, but it does underline the urgency of emotionally honest communication at the earliest opportunity. When duplicity leads, much damage follows.

○○○

Communication that is emotionally honest replaces 'you-statements' with 'I-statements'. You-statements are often accusatory: *You did this or you didn't do that. You said this and you misled me.* You-statements often carry blame.

I-statements own feelings, reactions and experiences. They articulate how we have been affected by someone. *When you ignored me, I felt like I didn't exist.*

You-statement: *You are such a slut!*
I-statement: *I feel anxious when you dress in a way that exposes yourself.*

You-statement: *You don't want to be with me. All you do is work and play golf.*
I-statement: *I feel abandoned when you divide most of your time between work and golf.*

Often, it is said that no one makes us feel anything, we choose to feel that way, but this is not true to experience. Yes, you are responsible for your feelings but you don't decide to have them or turn them on or off like a light switch. You may have some choice as to how much attention you bring to how you feel, but you don't have a choice as to what you feel. There is no volume control to adjust the intensity of how you feel though there are things you can do to attend to how you feel or direct your attention away from it.

I hear clients say they don't like the way their partner makes them feel and wish they could immunize themselves so that they weren't so affected. I understand this, but if your partner didn't affect you, what would be the point of being in a love relationship with them?

If you were my partner and had sex with my friend, I might feel enraged and accusatory. But to point my finger and charge you with the crime of infidelity is not going to communicate anything that you don't already know. The far more powerful communication is to say how your behavior made me feel.

This is expressed as an I-statement *'I feel this'* rather than the you-statement *'you did this'*. You know what you did, but you might not know what you have done to me.

If I ask you about it, I may not want all the gory details thrown in my face, but I also don't want you to fudge it and make it sound like nothing more than holding hands. Presumably, there is something you are disenchanted about as my partner. Yet, you are still here, with me, as a couple. It's late and maybe too late but we really do need to talk ...

Emotionally honest communication intends to reveal the truth; it does not set out to deceive. For the truth to be revealed *as the truth*, it depends enormously upon how it is expressed. I could say: *when you snore loudly and wake me up I feel like strangling you* (which is true). Or, I could say: *I am finding it disturbing how loudly you snore at night, and I wonder if you are aware of it. Maybe there is something you could do about it* (which is true and tactful). It takes account of how I feel about you beyond the irritation of your waking me up with your snoring.

My partner may say to me: *you eat all the food before anyone else has a chance to get to it.* On the receiving end, this feels like a completely different communication than if she says: *maybe we need to buy more food because it disappears so quickly in this household.*

Notice the accusatory tone and blame of the first communication – made as a you-statement, which is likely to invoke defensiveness (and might elicit a reply such as: *I do not eat everything, besides I buy the damn food*). The second is more subtle and less attacking. The person on the receiving end is far more likely to be receptive to it.

> *While communicating a painful truth make sure there is a place for ruth.*

Failures in communication are the most common issue that brings couples for therapy in my practice. How you communicate is the heart and soul of love relationships and often has everything to do with whether your relational ecology thrives. Resentment, blame, insinuations, sarcasm and accusations pollute love's environment over time. Then, a major clean-up operation is needed. This is why the channels of communication need to remain open between you.

Communication begins at the limit of our shared attunement.

Reciprocal attunement

Attunement in our adult relationships is probably an extension of our earliest experiences of mother-baby attunement. Here, the good-enough mother[18] knows what baby feels and needs without having to be told in words. There is an empathic identification and through attunement a mother can put herself in baby's position; she can intuit her baby's experience, at least some of the time and to some degree.

Just as mothers become attuned to their new babies' needs, babies are extremely attuned to their mothers even if not focused on meeting their mothers' needs. Yet sometimes they do. One example is when mother's breasts are engorged with milk and need emptying. Mother's and baby's needs are reciprocal and complementary. Another example is when mother and baby are both exhausted. Mother puts baby down for a nap and so gives herself a break. These needs are reciprocal and symmetrical.

There is a similar quality of attunement that carries over into adult relationships; adult needs may be symmetrical or complementary. There is a place in your psyche for the needs and feelings of the other person. Their feelings appear on your internal radar, and you have a sense of where the other is at. Sometimes this operates with extraordinary accuracy across oceans and continents, as in the example of the woman in London and her husband in New York at the beginning of this chapter. You can be separated by huge distances and still be highly attuned and strongly connected to each other.

---

18. Here, I am using the term 'mother' to refer to the role and not exclusively to a gender determination. Sometimes, men 'mother' and women 'father', in the stereotypical sense.

We speak about being on the same page or wavelength. Interdependency, vulnerability, connectedness, empathy and intimacy are all somewhat different nuances of attunement, and each is a component part of how two love.

Attunement means not having to have everything spelled out in words. You are already traveling in the same vehicle, pointing in the same direction.

Attunement is not exclusive of difference; rather it is the means through which differences can be accommodated.

> Michael used to finish the sentences of his partner Wendy when she paused searching for the right word. He was attuned. He listened. He understood where she was coming from and where she was going. He wasn't taking over her communication but facilitating it.

> Wendy would bring Michael a glass of water without him having to ask. He was astonished at how she could anticipate his need. He would say: *you read my mind.* Sometimes she was there a second before he registered himself that he even wanted a drink. She was so attuned.

There was something beautiful about the feeling of togetherness that this couple enjoyed with each other. We could say their attunement gave them a sense of 'at-one-ment'. They had different needs and desired to accommodate each other, and it worked on many levels.

> She might say: *I feel like vegetarian tonight,* and he would reply: *Perfect! I was just thinking we had been eating a lot of meat.* He might say: *I was thinking about choosing something light to watch tonight,* and she would reply: *Cool! I'm tired of the splatter platter movies.*

This carried over into their sexual life. They often wanted to be sexual at the same time and frequently recognized opportunities that were conducive to being sexual. They both loved looking after each other sexually and each was excited by the excitement of the other. They often orgasmed together, each enjoying the other's pleasure as much as their own.

| *Reciprocal attunement is bliss!*

Attunement is more likely to happen over time, and with the benefit of shared experience. It also requires feeling comfortable with inter-psychic intimacy – it can feel like the other 'person' is in your head. (Here 'person' refers to an object of mind: the thought of the other person.) Inter-psychic intimacy refers to your thought of your partner and their thought of you. Intimacy is achieved when your way of thinking about each other is congruent with your sense of yourselves.

To become attuned, orientate your attention toward and focus on your partner. Be observant and perceptive of what they like, what they don't like and what they are like. Take the time and give care to registering their feelings. And listen; active listening is hearing with your full attention.

In this endeavor, empathy is essential. Connectedness is indispensable. Vulnerability is key. Attunement contributes to empathy, connectedness and vulnerability. They are interrelated. Working together, these three qualities are the very constitution and composition of love, not just as a feeling but as a practice. The practice is the making of love; the 'how' in how two love.

Sometimes attunement means that we don't need to communicate – we both just know. But many people expect their partner to know how they feel, what they want or need, all the time without a word of communication. It is as if Wendy should be able to read Michael's mind, or simply because of the love that Michael feels for Wendy, Michael should know exactly what Wendy needs, and when. Magic! This does happen for Wendy and Michael sometimes, but it would be a mistake if they assume or expect that it always will. Love doesn't mean we should be able to read each other's minds.

Wendy also needs to communicate honestly what goes on inside her mind and heart, as well as her intentions and plans, in order for Michael to know what is happening and respond as he sees fit. Otherwise, they are in the domain of guesswork.

Sometimes, being vocal enables attunement to follow. Sometimes, non-verbal facial expressions speak volumes. There is an interrelationship between the implicit dimension of attunement and the explicit dimension of verbal or more direct modes of communication.

I urge my clients to spell things out in detail, even if they think it is unnecessary. The detailed communication that happens in the consulting situation usually clears up misunderstandings, creates closeness and is generative of love. Then, I hope my clients take this experience home.

This is what happened with Victoria and Vince (my one-session wonders in Chapter 6). All they needed was to embark on the path of open and detailed communication with each other, both positively and negatively, that started in a single session.

Reciprocal attunement and emotionally honest communication: each picks up where the other leaves off. Each can stimulate and initiate the other. Reciprocal attunement grows when emotionally honest communication addresses and resolves whatever is in the way between the two of you. This process, when operating mutually, bridges the gap of distance; it closes the margin of separateness to keep you on the same page, together and in touch.

If you start to feel offside or disconnected from each other, this assessment alerts you to a need for a greater sense of attunement. Where attunement is not happening, communication is required. Communication will assist in determining what is in the way. Without this, you risk falling too far away from each other, into a river of resentment. When such rivers become too full, they burst their banks and overflow into nit-picking, arguing, passive-aggressive behavior and fights. Flirting and other forms of acting-out often commence at this juncture as an expression of distance and alienation from each other.

The enjoyment of a harmonious relationship is largely a function of attunement and communication working in concert.

Empathic negotiation – Part 1

Combining empathy with negotiation incorporates love as the driving force toward resolving competing needs, desires and agendas. If you consider your partner's position empathically, you will move in their direction, and vice versa, toward affective compromise. Empathic negotiation is the process by which couples move from their individual positions toward great unity.

Relationships are commonly a battleground for the sexual politics of who decides what is going to happen, when, and how. Who is the boss, if there is one? Who is in charge and who is in control? These questions arise in practically every relationship, and if there isn't a clear answer or at least an amicable approach to them, then it's easy for love to be damaged.

The question arises: on whose terms do things happen between you and your partner?

- Who calls the shots?
- Who decides what happens?
- Who determines how it happens?
- Which of you steers your joint direction?
- Which of you navigates the course of events?
- Whose pace determines the timing of how activities unfold?

Competition turns love into a power struggle whereas:

| *Equality brings democracy to love.*

Who wants a relationship to be a battleground? It doesn't have to be like that, on any one person's terms. Both of you can work together as partners and be more or less equal. If you are willing to negotiate and accept the principle of equality – or, at very least, fairness – your sense of togetherness is unified and enhanced.

Decisions get made and executed, tasks are accomplished with a feeling of progress.

> Val couldn't stand it when her partner Wyatt got angry. It was okay for him to be angry with her, but she couldn't bear it when he was angry about something that had nothing to do with her.
>
> Wyatt could get angry because his motorbike wouldn't start, because he got some dirt on his trousers, because the price of his shares fell, or because they had run out of beer. He could be angry because it was raining. Wyatt could also get angry about nothing.
>
> When he got angry, he would swear and shout abuse – not at her, but as if to some imaginary source of his frustration. He would speak with a vicious, nasty tone full of scandal and persecution. *How can this be?* He could be irritable as a victim and, hence, irritating. This didn't happen often but when it did, she invariably questioned herself: *What am I doing in this relationship? I don't want to hear this. That is not the voice of someone who loves and cares for me. I don't want to be living in this sort of atmosphere.*
>
> Of course, when Wyatt was angry, Val knew that was not the time to be communicating about anything. A short while later when he calmed down, she could find a way of telling him that she wasn't the sort of person who could just adopt a 'water off a duck's back' attitude to his angry noises. It pierced her through the heart. She knew it didn't mean anything and that he was just venting, but she couldn't cope with it and didn't want to.
>
> With a little help, this couple was able to negotiate what happens between them when Wyatt got angry. They agreed that she would just walk – she would leave the house or wherever they were and take off. This could be a little

inconvenient, but it was better than remaining in a place where she suffered. She agreed to do this if he agreed to do his best to realize that his anger tipped her into despair. He did and also made efforts to contain his outbursts.

That was such a valuable negotiation.

In individual sessions, we came to understand why Val was so sensitive to anger. This realization helped her to develop a greater capacity to separate herself psychologically, to immunize herself against the effects of Wyatt's anger and thereby reduce her suffering. Despite that, she still didn't want to put up with Wyatt's anger or live with it.

The bottom line for her was that she shouldn't have to.

> *Negotiation is a key relationship skill that closes the gap between us.*

There are so many subjects where negotiation is needed. Sex is an obvious example.

> Ainsley wants sex regularly, and Aubrey does not. Aubrey wants an intimate contact before sleep but Ainsley is randy and just wants relief.
>
> In the absence of intimacy, Aubrey feels exhausted and wants to roll over and fall asleep. Sometimes, strangely, when Aubrey does feel like making love, Ainsley would rather watch TV.

In my experience, this is not always gender specific.

Another major area of difference is money.

> Beverley works long hours and Beverley's partner Blair loves to shop. Blair loves to spend money on all kinds of things, even things they don't need. Beverley doesn't mind Blair's shopping, to a point.

One day Blair came home with a large framed painting for their living room. It cost $9,000 and Beverley didn't even like it. Beverley was now seriously challenged.

○ ○ ○

Chance wants to save up to buy a house for their future, and Courtney wants to spend money on going out and having a good time. *Let's live for the present and not worry about saving.* Courtney feels bored by putting money away for a rainy day but Chance wants security based on the accumulation of appreciating assets.

Courtney claims that you cannot count on any asset appreciating these days but Chance counters by saying you can count on resources not appreciating, if they're spent!

There are as many examples as there are people to populate them. Unresolved differences – whether about sex, money or other issues – can cause a build-up of resentment that over time becomes corrosive to love. What has been made can be unmade.

As we've said before, resentment is like a fire extinguisher to the libido. It can become the source of snide comments or aggressive shots at each other, sarcasm, or cold withdrawal and sulking. When communication becomes infused with ill feeling in this way, or is a device of subordination, negotiation is strained.

Both parties need to enter into negotiation willingly. One successful businessman told me that the secret of his success was that he didn't go to the negotiating table with the intention of squeezing every last possible cent out of his counterpart. He went seeking a good deal but a fair deal. He knew that if his counterpart ended up unhappy, resentful or feeling ripped off, sooner or later, one way or another, he would pay for it.

There is much to be learned from this attitude. I think it makes for better business and better relationships.

> Dakota works long hours and comes home to a cooked meal. Darcy looks after their small children, keeps the house together and makes food for the family. After dinner, Dakota is exhausted and wants to rest, watch TV and relax.
>
> The dinner dishes still need to be cleared up, the food put away, the children bathed, read a story and put to bed plus a number of other daily chores. Darcy has been at it all day too and wants a break.
>
> Whose job is it to attend to these responsibilities at the end of the day?

This is a common scenario of families with small children where negotiation is essential to make living as a family harmonious and to preserve love.

> They talked about how they each felt. Dakota agreed to put the kids to bed and read stories if Darcy would finish up in the kitchen. Darcy felt like being finished in the kitchen but agreed in exchange for a break from the kids.
>
> They realized the importance of an automatic dishwasher and agreed to purchase one even though they couldn't afford it and had to buy it with credit.

The actual agreement reached is not what's most important; rather it is how you arrive at that agreement. It should feel fair and each party should be willing to be flexible.

> On the worst days, when Dakota is more tired than usual, and so is Darcy, but there are still kids and dishes that require attention, they decide to prioritize. The dishes can be left but kids cannot: *let's attend to the kids together.*

For negotiation to work, each party must take into account the other's position and what it feels like to be in that position. This requires empathy (elucidated in greater detail below) which draws on communication and attunement and in sharing the mutual aim to reach an agreeable compromise, often through giving ground.

The idea of giving ground might run counter for those who usually set out to get what they want for themselves. Functioning as a couple, however, means your orientation needs to shift in the service of love. Then, giving ground to make your negotiations successful can be incredibly satisfying. It has a different quality, different from the experience of satisfaction based on merely getting what you want.

Empathic negotiation – Part 2

Empathy may be defined as identification with, or the vicarious experiencing of, the feelings, thoughts, attitudes and values of another person; in general, the experience of another person. Empathy is a strange idea because, in one way of looking at it, it is impossible. You cannot actually experience the experience of another person. But you can use your perceptions, intuitions, observations, interpretations and understanding of another person to gain insight into how they feel and what their behavior means in a given moment. However:

> *Being empathic does not mean being telepathic.*

The aim of empathy is to know the experience of another person as far as possible. Through this practice, we gain valuable information about another's experience; a constructed inference of how another person feels.

Here is a brief guide to the practice of empathy. Consider:

Present knowledge: Empathy is grounded in knowing the other person as they are, as far as possible, from their point of view. How does this person see themselves? How do they represent themselves to others? How do they see the world? What are their values and how do they express their perspectives? Do they walk their talk? What does their style say about them?

Background: Consider everything you know about the other person's history, culture, religious views and practices, attitudes, family of origin, possibly previous relationships; in short, everything that comprises where they've come from that influences their needs, values and perspectives.

Personality: What sort of person are they? Are they passive or pro-active? A leader or follower? Are they thick-skinned or sensitive, or sometimes one and sometimes the other? Are they outwardly emotional or reserved? Are they caring or not caring? Are they happy or sad or depressive? Are they generous or mean? Who is this person and how do they operate psychologically? Are they narcissistic or altruistic? Introverted or extraverted? Are they vengeful or forgiving? Are they emotionally balanced and rational or more impulsive and reactive? Are they angsty and anxious, edgy and tense, or calm? There is so much to personality and, of course, mood can make a huge difference as to which tendencies come into the foreground. Personalities may be more or less consistent; some people always seem the same while others are changeable, sometimes radically.

Mood: Try to work out what mood they are in, and what may be influencing them. Have recent events made them light-hearted or morose? Are they stressed or care-free? Are they casual and easy-going or serious and intense? Some people's moods vary more than others, and some people's moods are far easier to read than others. A mood can be momentary, short term or last a little while. Mood and present context can be closely entwined. Mood is internal while context is external.

Present context: What is affecting this person in the present moment? How does the immediate situation pertain? What are they dealing with? What's playing on their mind? Are you aware of how this person is affected by you at this moment? Present context can refer to work or family, financial or emotional, friends or colleagues, physical health or mental health, or any combination. Context can refer to a particular domain of experience.

What do you now understand about their point of view? What is affecting them most? How do they feel and what do they want? What does it mean to be this person right now?

Application: Having considered the above, can you imaginatively put yourself in their position? As far as possible, try to be in their shoes, in their world, as they are. This is *not* being who *you* are and then considering their position as you would feel in it. Rather, it is trying to 'be' who *they* are, in *their* way of experiencing the world – as far as you can reach to it.

Remember: you can never *be* anyone else. Any sense of the other person's experience will always be mediated through your own self, inevitably. You cannot get yourself out the way completely because your self is the screen upon which empathy lights up your perceptions and apperceptions, your intuitions, your way of understanding and interpreting. It is only through knowing yourself that you can begin to get yourself out of the way, even if you can never be out of the way completely.[19]

Empathy is an imprecise 'science'.[20] If you put yourself aside and attempt to occupy the other's world, as they do, from their point of view, it is a rich mine of information. The gold in this venture is a deep understanding of how the other person experiences their world, and that includes you as a part of it. You can gain crucial insights into how others are affected by you through the practice of empathy.

The goal of empathy is to know, as far as possible, how the other person feels and why. If you are attuned you resonate with the feelings of the other person, as they take shape, form and meaning.

---

19. This is one reason why therapists and some other mental health professionals have their own personal therapy, and often quite a lot of it. Some psychotherapy trainings require this.

20. I am using 'science' here in its original sense derived from the Latin *scire*, meaning 'to know'.

My meditation upon empathy leads me to consider The Golden Rule: *do unto others as you would have them do unto you*. When I think about it in the context of understanding the principle of empathy as outlined above, I realize that The Golden Rule is wrong. Why?

The Golden Rule is narcissistic. First, we are directed to think about how we would like to be treated. Then we are meant to treat others as we would like to be treated. What if the way others would like to be treated differs from the way we would like to be treated?

> *Don't do unto others as you would have them do unto you.*
>
> *Do unto others as they would have you do unto them.*

True empathy is counter-narcissistic. The gold in The Golden Rule needs to be empathic. The Golden Rule needs to be modified accordingly. Let's understand how others would like to be treated and consider how that may differ from how we would like to be treated.

Do unto others as they would have you do unto them.

Nowhere is empathic negotiation needed more than in the domains of sex, money, child care and domestic duties, all primary elements of the ecology of love relationships.

a) Sex

Co-sexuality works better when it is informed and shaped by empathic negotiation. Most commonly, negotiation around sex is about when, how and how often.

- She wants to come first, but he can't help it and comes in a few minutes.
- He wants her to go down on him before having intercourse, but she refuses because he hasn't had a shower and smells.

- He likes to use a vibrator on her and watch her orgasm, but she feels self-conscious about being watched. She would rather he had contact with her whole body, but he is into sex toys and doing things to her.
- She has her period and doesn't want to have sex, but he isn't bothered and wants to anyway.
- He's been working in the mines for 10 days straight and needs to rest and recover before having a romp with his wife but she is horny, having been on her own for all that time.
- She loves for him to go down on her but it can take her over half an hour to orgasm and he gets worn out giving her oral sex for that long.
- He likes her to dress up in lingerie and high heels, but she feels like a hooker and feels annoyed that he needs her to perform to become aroused.
- He wants an exclusive and monogamous relationship, but his male partner wants to be exclusive emotionally but not sexually.
- He likes pornographic videos playing while they make love because it turns him on, but she feels he becomes distracted. She also finds them degrading to women and is turned-off by them.
- She isn't sexually attracted to him since he put on weight around the middle. He says if she *really* loved him, it wouldn't matter.
- She needs to be warmed up to get in the mood. She needs to be seduced slowly, gently and gradually, or she just isn't into it. Her female partner can't wait to jump in; she is passionate and sexual and feels impatient with gently stroking her lover's hair.
- He wants her to tie him up and tease him, dominate him and maybe even cause him a little pain, but she finds this weird and uncomfortable.
- She would like to make love with two men at once, but he finds this threatening.

These are all examples from my therapy practice. How will these couples negotiate their differences? It can be difficult, or impossible. Relationships that last find ways to negotiate differences in sexuality.

The best forms of negotiation involve a willingness on each side to give something up, and there has to be a corresponding relinquishing of demand. When everything *has* to be *exactly* as you require – when it has to follow a set of specifications providing little room to yield – negotiation becomes harder.

A loving empathy mediates your attitude toward negotiation, encouraging you to consider how your partner feels and to accommodate them, thereby reaching toward a fair resolution of your different positions. Resolution becomes more important than holding out for what you want, for squeezing the last drop of your partner's willingness to give. Empathic negotiation contributes to the making of love whereas power-driven negotiation makes for a dynamic of domination and submission.

Being prepared to negotiate brings to sexual differences the possibility of evolving your co-sexuality within the environment of relational ecology. It is a move away from being driven purely by individual need or the ego-driven striving for your own satisfaction, to the inter-erotic gratification of mutual pleasure as a part of your ecosystem's dynamic functioning.

Successful couples tend to discover different ways of being sexual with each other that satisfy both individual and relational needs. Here are just a few examples:

- 'Quickie' sex – grabbing an opportunity when both parties feel the urge. The sex can still be loving.
- Intimate sex – may take longer and usually benefits from privacy and time for physical and emotional contact, sensuality and a high level of involvement in each other's body, mind and soul.
- Relief sex – one gives relief to the other, or both to each other, such as from sexual frustration, physical tension or anxiety.

b) Money

Money is a difficult subject for many couples. There is a tendency for the one who earns the money to feel they should be able to control how the money is spent, invested and distributed. Some 'breadwinners' love to give, and some do not. I have known people who give their partner nothing or practically nothing. Where is the love in that? Some do the opposite and give everything. Sometimes too much is given, which is not in the best interests of a family's future or their love.

Some breadwinners earn the money and the partner controls it – does the bookkeeping, pays the domestic bills, saves for holidays, buys food and clothing, looks after the kids' needs. Some couples keep their money completely separate. Many couples have a balance between joint expenses and separate accounts. There is no right or wrong way. It is a personal choice, but one worth negotiating so you both feel the arrangement is fair and balanced. Imbalances of financial control are a common source of disempowerment and subordination.

> Daniel, a mining engineer, was referred because he was unable to control his anger. When we investigated, the reasons for his anger were always the same.
>
> His girlfriend increasingly expected him to support her two children and herself. She didn't receive much from the kids' father. She worked but didn't earn much. Her family believed that it was the man's responsibility to support his loved ones and so assumed Daniel would support them all without question.
>
> Daniel loved them but didn't see why it fell to him to pick up 90 per cent of the expenses for all of them. I said that he didn't so much have an anger problem as a failure to negotiate the financial terms of engagement in his relationship.

This problem is not gender specific. There are many variations, of course. Sometimes one earns a lot more than the other.

Do they share equally or do they operate entirely based on their individual resources?

If he earns $100 a day and she earns $200 per day, should she pay twice as much of the electric bill? If he earns $1,000 per day and she earns nothing, who should allocate how the money is spent? If she wants to buy an expensive sports car for herself and he doesn't care what he drives and has an old run-around vehicle, is that unfair? Or is it okay?

> One family was in serious debt, not an uncommon situation. The husband felt that it was his problem because he had lost money through a poorly judged investment. He had exposed them to risk (though it all sounded sweet and certain when it was presented to him).
>
> He took it all on himself; he didn't discuss it with his wife or family as he didn't want to stress them. He didn't even tell them to be careful about their spending because he felt guilty about the debt. He just worked longer and longer hours to cover the interest payments. He carried the anxiety entirely on his own.
>
> In time, the house had to be sold to resolve the debt but they were able to rent a home and live as well as before while they re-built their fortunes. Five years later he was diagnosed with cancer. It was a very slow growing tumor and probably began shortly after the time the debt originated.

Too much debt can be toxic both for individual health and for the emotional health of the relationship. In the above example, I wonder if they could have negotiated so that the psychical burden of carrying debt was more equally shared within their partnership. It might not have made a difference financially, but it might have lightened his mental burden in carrying the anxiety, guilt and responsibility. He wore this heavily, it weighed on him inside. What if he could have avoided cancer through a more shared and negotiated approach?

Could the ecology of our primary relationship be reflected in the personal ecology of our physical health?

The combination of empathy with negotiation in managing money means you are mindful of your partner's emotional disposition as you navigate the tension between love and self-interest.

c) Child care and domestic duties

Many couples both work, and divide child care and domestic duties more or less equally. The classic conflict over child care occurs where one is working significantly more than the other, or when preconceived or stereotypical gender roles are assumed.

> If Jamie works full-time and Lisa works part-time or not at all, Lisa will pick up the greater responsibility for looking after their children. What should Jamie's responsibility be?

My experience of parenting has shown me that raising one child is at least a three-person job. Raising two children is at least a four or five-person job and raising three children is a much bigger job, exponentially greater than one or two children, perhaps a seven or eight-person job. That is a long way from raising children as a couple and an even greater distance from being a single parent!

> Jamie works hard and sometimes long hours. When he comes home he needs to switch off, relax and have dinner. Lisa has been looking after young children all day and is also sleep deprived, having been woken up three times the night before.

> Lisa is exhausted but pleased to see Jamie home from work, even though he was supposed to be home at 5.30pm and hasn't appeared until 7pm. There is perhaps a little disappointment and resentment but on balance, Lisa is still happy to see him. However, Jamie pours himself a drink, sits down and switches on the TV news before dinner.

> It's like a match to a fuse. Why didn't Jamie think Lisa might like a drink, too?

> Why should Jamie get to sit down when Lisa has been at it not just all day but much of the night?
>
> Jamie feels justified because work was so demanding – he just wants to think of himself for a moment and besides, home should be a respite, a space to relax and unwind. He just wants half an hour and then plans to help with the kids and whatever needs doing. He feels entitled to that.
>
> Lisa feels this attitude is unjustified because it is based upon Jamie's needs at the expense of hers. Early evening is one of the most demanding times, with the kids tired, cranky, hungry, and often needing more attention than usual. They are excited to see Jamie after spending all day with Lisa. Meanwhile, Lisa is preparing dinner and that makes it difficult to attend to the kids as well.
>
> Why doesn't Jamie understand this without Lisa having to spell it out?
>
> And if Jamie is entitled to a half-hour break, isn't Lisa just as entitled? (Try telling the kids that, she thinks.)

There are many variations on this classic example. One couple found the morning routine was worse.

> Marie owned and ran her own business – a small boutique employing a few staff. Nick was a stockbroker and fund manager. He was responsible for significant assets and ran discretionary trading accounts for a number of high net worth investors.
>
> Nick agreed to help with preparing the kids' breakfasts and school lunches, but he found it hard to get up in the morning. He was just not a morning person. He also needed some time to read the paper and check what had happened on international markets overnight. He watched the TV business news while getting dressed.

They had three young kids, two in primary school – who Nick took to school before going to work – and one who Marie took to the child care center.

Nick didn't get up early enough to do his share, and that meant that Marie had to do more than she had time for.

Nick resented the time Marie spent *beautifying* herself in the mornings when he was under pressure. His work is important.

But Marie ran a boutique; it was part of her job to look the part, it goes with the territory.

Marie resented Nick for not being on top of things; he could have achieved everything if he had got up early enough and organized himself. Her work is important.

The phone invariably rang when the market had some event overnight. That took Nick's attention; part of his job was to take these urgent calls, it goes with the territory.

At these times, shouting broke out, frustrations became arguments, everything was expressed aggressively, and this became the usual morning currency of transaction between them. The kids, of course, reacted to the hostilities and became more difficult – often fighting broke out between them, mimicking their parents.

Marie and Nick felt terrible about how they reflected to their kids an example of inharmonious family living. They knew they weren't modelling a loving relationship.

Shouting tends to occur when we become distant from each other. We have to increase the volume of our voices to get through, to reach across the abyss. It is intensely frustrating to be physically close but mentally and emotionally remote. Increased shouting can be a sign of a deteriorating relational ecosystem.

> *Though we stand face to face, shouting aims to span the distance.*

Most of us do not have eight people to look after three children. The scenarios described above, and similar examples from other parenting partnerships, are complex to resolve. Raising kids is possibly both the hardest and most important job there is. And these days, it is rarely the only job we have.

Empathic negotiation is crucial. Otherwise, the unavoidable task of domestic duties becomes an issue between you and family living becomes a nightmare, the mornings become hellish and the evenings become something you would rather avoid. Quite a few people confess their guilt at feeling at the end of the workday that they would rather not go home.

> One chap played games on his phone for half an hour or so before leaving work. He made the executive decision that he would take a half-hour break for himself, and keep that to himself.
>
> He knew it wasn't negotiable.

Here self-love competes with both partner-love and children-love. The relational ecosystem is a delicate balance, just like the environmental ecosystem. If we tip the balance too far in one direction, that of self-interest, the ensuing imbalance can have global consequences.

Affective compromise

In affective compromise, you make the compromise not only willingly but also with heart and good grace. You understand that affective compromise enables the compromise to be put into place without resentment, guilt or indebtedness. The prefix 'affective' in this context means with feeling. As such, affective compromise becomes effective compromise.

> *The first step toward compromise is* wanting to.
>
> *Compromise is easy if you want to, impossible if you don't.*

Perhaps we begin to compromise begrudgingly. However, if we can increase our willingness to compromise as a part of how two love as a couple it begins to come more naturally.

In some situations, compromise appears impossible, though if you dig a little deeper, you can find ways to make it possible. Mundane examples occur regularly in everyday living. So, we decide to go out for dinner. You are craving Chinese, but I want Italian. We can't go for Chinese for half the meal and Italian for the other half. It's one or the other. But is there a third possibility? Could we both be happy with Indian food or Thai? Maybe, but maybe not, maybe there is no third possibility. Maybe you *really really really* want Chinese. *Oh, all right, let's have Chinese, it doesn't matter that much to me.*

But what if our desire for our respective choices is exactly equal. We could argue about it. *We always have Chinese. I'm sick of Chinese. I'm not going for Chinese again. I'd rather not go out then.* What does this attitude do for your relationship?

Even when no other choice will suit us both there is still a possible compromise, if we are willing. With a bit of lateral thinking: *what if we go out for Chinese tonight but the next time we decide to go out for dinner – it's my choice!*

- She wants to paint the bedroom purple, but he wants white.
- He wants to save up for a large, ultra-high-definition television but she wants to save up for a new cooktop and oven.
- She wants old colonial furniture in the sitting room, but her partner likes contemporary furniture.

- He likes vegetarian food, but his partner is a body builder and needs heaps of protein, ideally from meat.
- He wants to go to sleep early, but she isn't sleepy by then and wants to stay up.
- She wants to make love twice a day, he wants twice a week.
- He wants to live in New York, she wants to live in Berlin, and their teenager wants to live in Sydney.

How will they sort out these differences? It depends entirely on their willingness and ability to compromise. With affective compromise, across a range of issues and time, each partner yields, and therefore sacrifices, in equal measure. Decisions operate according to a principle of fairness.

If we move to Berlin as you would like, then what are you prepared to do for me? This is a whole-of-life change. How can compromise be affected? How can my life in Berlin be compensated in ways that make giving up my life where we live now worth it? There may be sacrifices that make this decision viable and more agreeable.

Most of us would understand what it feels like to have a craving for some food or other but what is your craving worth? Are you willing to give anything up? Are you willing to make sacrifices in the service of love? If you answer yes to these questions, you are the beneficiary.

That is one of the key paradoxes of love.

> *Letting go of what you want can bring you more of what you want.*

There is empowerment in letting go of control. There is satisfaction in letting go of egocentric desire. And there is fulfillment in letting go of an obsession with perfection. Holding out for perfection prevents you from feeling satisfied with what is possible.

Interesting that the word *promise* is part of the word *compromise*. 'Com' means together. Compromise involves making a pledge to each other to privilege the 'between'. The between is the middle ground, where we arrive through arbitration. The between is where we dwell as a couple; it is the place reached by compromising. We could say the between is compromise's destination. And this is an example of how the environment of relational ecology is co-created.

A promise is an example of what is called a speech act[21] This is because we do what we say in the act of saying it. A compromise needs to be a speech act too. It needs to be lived as it is said. So, compromise not only brings us to a particular *place* but creates a sense of occasion. It is an event that occurs in a particular *time* as well. It is through the actioning of compromise that the 'between' is formed and given meaning, as a loving environment. It is the tie that connects you.

Consider *I love you*. Are you loving your partner when saying this or are you just saying it?

Love requires a compromising attitude and disposition. Even if I *need* a half-hour break after work, it is more loving if I give this up than stay back and play solitaire in my office. What if we took turns having a half-hour break? Each of us might feel better about going without, knowing we each get a turn next time and we are giving something to our beloved through what is given up.

Affective compromise happens by meeting in the middle. When there is no middle, another approach is needed and often possible.

- You choose the restaurant, and I choose the film.
- You relieve me of having to clear up after dinner and you can choose the entertainment after the meal.
- I hate clutter on the kitchen counter. Maybe I have to become more pro-active about clearing it up even if I didn't create it.
- Maybe you will make more of an effort to prevent clutter there if I clean the bathroom sink after I use it instead of leaving hair trimmings and toothpaste, which I know you dislike.

---
21. In Wittgenstein

Can you compromise affectively such that you are both happy about the outcome? Can you be attuned to each other and when you reach the limit of your attunement, communicate with emotional honesty and negotiate empathically? If so, you truly have the making of a viable, functioning ecosystem.

The relational ecology of successful relationships requires ongoing assessment and practice. Be mindful of the four elements that contribute to a well-functioning ecosystem, and be alert for signs of weakness, deficiency, deterioration or, worse, breakdown. Most of us get tired or worn down over time from work, from looking after children or our other responsibilities, from not having enough money (aka life). Nevertheless, relationships require relating to each other with emotional engagement. This is what keeps you connected and co-creates the environment of your relational ecology. Putting your relationship first makes success possible and gives it personal meaning.

CHAPTER 10
The Best Relationship You Can Have

"When the power of love overcomes the love of power, then there will be true peace."
— **Sri Chinmoy**

You fall in love. All goes well, you feel you have made it. You are in the best relationship you can have. And then it changes.

The in-love feeling wanes. While you are not so high on the relationship, you are still happy to be in it. Maybe the feeling wanes a little too much, and you wonder: *What happened? Where did it go? Can I get it back to where it was?* But there is no going back, only forward.

Rewarding relationships do not rely on the in-love feeling lasting forever but rather upon the establishment of an equilibrium of harmonious balance between the feeling of love and the sense that the relationship works operationally. The in-love feeling may need to be renewed though it may feel somewhat different from the initial in-love feeling. Often, relationships oscillate on the the highs and lows of love's emotional rollercoaster. Ideally, the relationship should be satisfying and feel fulfilling with the passage of time albeit with some variations.

For better, for worse

Successful relationships don't have to involve marriage or making an explicit vow. Some people just get on with it. Some never seem to have discussions about being together, about what this relationship is all about or what frames their unity. There is nothing that says you must.

However, many couples find it necessary, helpful and positively clarifying to define what they are in with each other. As we discussed in Chapter 8 'Partnership Unity', through the concepts of 'rules of engagement' and 'the contract', a couple's status can range from *we'll see what happens* to a formal binding agreement. People in de facto relationships often find, after a time, that they want to take it to another level and marry, if that option is available to them.

> *Two of my friends were together for about 38 years before they married, in their seventies, prompted by the wedding of their oldest daughter.*

You may wish to sanctify the bond of loving unity through a formal ritual or ceremony, such as marriage. Sanctification means to make sacred or holy. Sanctification gives spiritual reverence which means that you enter into something bigger than yourselves.

Sacred (and also consecrate) come from the Middle English *sacren*, which refers to devotion. While the word carries a religious connotation, this doesn't have to be adopted personally. To function well as a couple you are called upon to transcend 'self', as an individual being. Devotion is to each other and the relationship.

> *Devotion is the underlying meaning and operating principle of weddedness.*

To evolve into 'weddedness' – to enter a sacred vessel that contains and joins the two of you – is a radically different way of being from being a couple in a more casual sense. 'I' becomes 'we'. Being becomes being-with. This doesn't mean that you cease to be an individual, or that you are joined at the hip, or 'in each other's pockets'. A measure of psychological separateness often makes for a healthier connection and relationship, as we said earlier. Weddedness means fealty – a commitment not to a Lord in the medieval sense, but to a binding union between two people. (Here 'Lord' can be understood metaphorically as something higher than 'self'.) This is why we make a vow in the wedding or marital ritual. During this ceremony, we agree to enter 'holy matrimony'. Holy means whole; two becomes one.

Many people write their own vows these days, but the standard traditional wedding vow still expresses a principle that is worth considering:

> *I, (Name), take thee, (Name), to be my lawfully wedded wife/ husband, to have and to hold from this day forward, for better for worse, for richer for poorer, in sickness and in health, to love, honour, and cherish, 'til death do us part, and thereto I plight thee my troth.*

"I plight thee my troth" is an unusual phrase and not one I have ever heard in any setting other than a wedding ceremony. 'Plight' means pledge in this context and 'troth' is a Middle and Old English word for truth. So, this phrase means:

> *I pledge my truth to you.*

This is an extraordinary principle in a modern social context. How many of us live this with our partners? Not Craig! (Chapter 9). How many amongst us can stand up and say: *I have been thoroughly honest and true to my partner in every way, and always?* Yet we marry, we pledge our truth to each other, then what?

How many married couples walk their talk and live their vow to each other? How many of us think about what we say when we marry, and mean it? How many have considered this undertaking, their vow, before finding themselves at the altar, saying it? "Repeat after me ..."

I need to be careful not to sound too sanctimonious. While we are not Hindu, Cath and I married in a beautiful Hindu ceremony in Mumbai during which we danced around a fire seven times. While I espouse the importance of knowing fully the commitment you avow, perhaps I hadn't studied well enough the symbolic meaning of my own wedding ceremony. Afterward, someone asked me if I knew exactly what I had just agreed to (in a foreign language), and I shrugged my shoulders. They informed me: *You just married her for seven lifetimes.*

Unreal! I cried out:
From commit-o-phobic to married for seven lifetimes!

You may find yourself standing before the community of your family and friends, saying your vows, publicly. The celebrant reminds you of the solemn and permanent nature of the commitment you are making. You place a ring on your partner's finger as a symbol of union and seal your promise with a kiss.

You enter into this ritual sanctification of your relationship with reverence. You consecrate your relationship by making your commitment to your partner sacred before the community of those who matter to you. Again, these terms are not confined to religion despite their religious origins and overtones. You can take a sacred vow to each other equally in a church, synagogue, temple, registry office, garden or standing in the Indian Ocean (as we later did). All are sacred.

Why place a symbolic ring on the fourth finger of the left hand? How many of us know what our symbols mean as we enact them?

This tradition originated with the ancient Greeks. Some centuries before the Common Era, physicians mistakenly believed that there was a vein that ran from the fourth finger of the left hand directly to the heart; it was called the *vena amoris* – the vein of love. The ring symbolizes the other with whom you join your heart.

When the Romans adopted this practice they gave it a religious significance. It became a symbol that reflected our pledge to the broader community – those who can see the ring as you wear it – to honor your vows and marital contract. By the 16th century, the English designated the fourth finger of the left hand as the ring finger.

In many languages and traditions, the fourth finger was believed to be magical and was called 'nameless'. This suggests a vow that cannot be spoken; it transcends the earthly, material realm. It is a spiritual union that cannot be conceptualized.

Here, my discourse on love arrives at its natural limit. There are no words. At a certain point, we must not quench the fire of love with words.[22] Yet, though words tell only part of the story, we should still consider the words we say.

We promise to love, honor, comfort and cherish but what happens when these noble qualities turn out to be a one-way street? Remember Gabby (Chapter 3) who discovered that almost every representation Dean had made to her was a lie? He wanted to impress her, he said. They had planned to marry. She might have found it harder to bail if they had. Or there is Harriet, who had always trusted her husband.

> Harriet discovered her husband had been visiting brothels regularly throughout their relationship including the period of their wedding, her pregnancy and birth of their child and spent in excess of $20,000 on his 'sex-capades'.

Should Gabby and Harriet be expected to stay with their partners in the spirit of a sacred commitment, for better and for worse? Some would argue they should. Both left.

Despite emphasizing the sanctity of making such an undertaking, I have compassion for anyone who has to repudiate their marital partnership and exit. This especially applies when they entered the marriage in good faith when their partner did not, or when their partner did not live up to their promise.

---

22. '... as soon go kindle fire with snow.' (Shakespeare)

> *The spiritual significance of marriage does not outweigh the conditional nature of a relationship.*

The wedding vows call upon family and friends to offer ongoing support to the couple. Should we continue to support couples if one member has been unfaithful, or mistreated the other, or if the mutual feelings of love and respect have died?

As a therapist, I have seen massive damage caused by rigidity in a couple's family and community. Some people hold a dogmatic adherence to a principle of staying together at all costs, which does not help the couple. It would be more valuable to hold a flexible attitude that supports their emotional needs, as the wedding ritual prescribes.

In an ideal world, the best relationship you can have happens once and lasts a lifetime. Maybe those people never come to therapy, and I never get to meet them, but ideal relationships that begin during youth and last until 'death do us part' are incredibly rare. Divorce statistics suggest that the longevity of marriage is not assured, no matter how committed the couple feels on their wedding day, or how many lifetimes they promise to stay together.

While it may appear that this discussion has moved a long way – from sanctification to divorce – couples often need help in a whole range of situations. Just as they need help to work things out and stay together, they need help to separate when their relationship's 'best-before' date has passed. So, let's be real about it. Let's support couples in doing their best to stay together. Let's support them when it gets tough and issues need to be addressed. Let's support them if they cannot go any further and have to go through the painful ordeal of separating. And let's support them more when they enter the next relationship so they can make that the best it can be. What would you want?

The implication of the traditional wedding vow is for the couple to be honest, to pledge their truth, to love each other through adversity, and persevere to work things out and stay together, within reason. What 'reason' means is personal and must be left to the individuals to determine. At that point, when reason means they are no longer willing to keep going, then couples need the support of their family and community even more.

The discussion above idealizes the sanctification of a relationship and the making of a sacred vow of devotion; it should be understood as an ideal to aspire to rather than a reason to beat yourself up, if you don't live up to it perfectly. Part of love's beauty and depth lies in the lessons we learn during our stumbles, and the wisdom gained when we pick ourselves up from a fall.

> *Loving is a human art form that inevitably includes our failings as well as our successes.*

Each other's best interest

It is easier to find reasons to stay in a relationship when you privilege each other's best interests.

> Todd realized one day that he had been almost completely self-focused and rarely, if ever, thought about his partner, Tina. He decided he would try to be a better partner – that he would make a point of thinking about her and acting on what he came up with, and see what happened.
>
> Tina was flabbergasted. Because she wasn't used to Todd's new attitude, she didn't know what was happening. She asked Todd: *Are you feeling all right? Is there something you're wanting from me?*
>
> He laughed and confessed that he had been selfish and wanted to rectify it. He explained that he wasn't trying to

get anything from her, he just wanted to show her he loved her, and wanted to be a better partner.

Tina had always been giving to Todd and thought about him a great deal. It was just her nature. She hadn't complained but was aware that Todd had always been in the business of serving Todd. This change in Todd transformed the feeling of closeness between them. It also stimulated her sexual desire for him even though he hadn't set out to arouse her sexually. Not only was she desiring him in a new way, the sexual intensity between them became charged and deepened, making the sex more powerful and fulfilling, and also more frequent.

Todd discovered how beneficial it could be for him to be more focused on her best interests. She said: *I don't recognize you!* referring to his change of behavior.

He said: *I don't recognize you!* referring to her newfound sexual interest in him.

Functioning less as individuals and more as a couple with a focus on each other's best interest changed the way they 'looked' to each other.

The power of love and the love of power – Part 1

You want what you want, and that may be fair enough. However, when you are so driven by what you want that it becomes more important than how your partner feels, you are purchasing individual satisfaction at the expense of love. This places you as an individual in opposition to the best relationship you can have as a couple. In other words, you are working against the relationship in the service of yourself, as Todd (above) realized in good time.

You may succeed in getting what you want for yourself by compromising your partner and, so, by compromising the relationship. This is a precarious trade-off and one which, ironically, can become a self-defeating one.

> *When power walks in the door, love flies out the window.*

Maybe you get caught in a narrative that goes something like this: *I do a lot. I give a lot. I am always at it.* This could refer to the home, kids, or maybe to earning an income that supports the two of you, or simply what you give to your partner. Perhaps you find yourself thinking: *I take you out for dinner. I take you on trips to exotic places. I buy you flowers. I give you beautiful orgasms.* Or: *I work crazy hours to provide the lifestyle we enjoy.* Or: *I look after your children, your pets, your house, and garden. And most of all, I look after YOU!*

This can lead to self-justified requests or demands that your partner does something for you. *I want you to cook dinner while I put my feet up. I want you to look after the children all weekend. I want you to surprise me with something romantic (and not just red roses because you did that last week). I want you to clean the house and keep things far neater. I want you to lose weight and start some physical exercise (like you used to do). You look miserable, where is your happy face? I don't want a depressed partner; I want someone to have fun with.* There are so many possibilities.

The bind is this: *If I don't put pressure on my partner to meet my requirements then nothing will happen. I'm sure I won't get what I want.* This is where power often comes in the door.

You might express what you want, but that hasn't worked. Maybe you think that is because you haven't stated it strongly enough, and so desires become demands. Demands become requirements, and requirements ultimatums. The more you up the ante, the more oppressive the dynamic of power becomes, and the more damaging. Then the imbalance between you grows greater.

Sometimes the dynamics of power are expressed in the form of a competition. Remember the previous discussion: on whose terms do things happen? Who is the boss? Who is in charge? Who calls the shots? When I asked this of one couple, each pointed to the other in children-fighting cartoon-style. Although amusing, it was also revealing that each perceived the other as the boss of the relationship.

- Are you a democracy or are you a dictatorship?
- Are you equals or is one subordinate?
- Is your love a form of tyranny and my submission a form of masochism?
- Do you take advantage of me out of power or do I surrender to you out of love?
- Perhaps I'm the boss because I'm a man, and that's how it's always been.
- Or perhaps I'm afraid to be the boss because men have dominated women for most of history and it's about time that changed.
- Maybe you wish I'd grow some balls, be decisive and put my foot down but I'm afraid to; I don't want them chopped off!

If a woman asserts herself is she a 'castrating bitch'? Or is it about time she stood up for herself and stopped him (or her?) from treating her like a doormat? Maybe it's time she grew a pair of balls and put her foot down. What if he cuts hers off? The usual stereotypes are up for grabs in the high stakes of sexual politics.

What it means to be a man and what it means to be a woman is increasingly challenged.

While each of us needs to work out what it means to be oneself, there is an important principle at play in love relationships that I call 'the power of love and the love of power'. Have you ever found yourself in a relationship with a partner who was critical and undermining?

> I had a relationship with a partner who was always right, and she became an authority on 'what is wrong with Jan Resnick'. Over time, it drained me of self-respect. I had to fight for credibility and to feel worthy. The harder I strived to be good enough, the further away the goalposts moved. Despite a sense of devotion, I didn't feel accepted as I was.

It was rare that I received acknowledgment or validation. Consequently, I became more drawn to grab little bits of gratification for myself. I might spend too much money on myself. I might flirt a little when the opportunity arose. I cultivated some close friendships with other women where there was an ambiguity around what we could become to each other, though no overt infidelity occurred. I might also spend more time at the office because I was 'working' and this is a legitimate thing to do. But it also gave respite from the pressure and was a sign of discontent; it was also a strategy of avoidance.

The feeling of being under pressure grew over time to a feeling of being under siege. The more I 'looked after' myself, the more the discourse intensified of me not being right. I could see the truth in it and I grew to dislike myself in some ways, internalizing the negative view of myself. But then, the need to find things to make myself feel better grew. I felt a competition develop between serving my own interests and our interests as a couple and this resulted in developing doubts about my integrity. Often, I felt either selfish or deprived. Correspondingly, either feelings of guilt and shame made me feel like less of a person, or I felt like a greedy child.

With the benefit of hindsight, I grew to see there was an ideology that permeated our relationship under the banner of what was called 'feminism'. It became a reference point that came with a personal agenda. It was as if our relationship was a battlefield on which all of the historical and cultural imbalances between men and women had to be fought and corrected. I'm not against feminism, but rather the use of an ideology that became a form of tyranny. It felt to me that power had usurped love.

It wasn't that I thought I shouldn't have to do the clearing up after dinner or the laundry because I worked 60 or more hours during the week. Rather I had to do so many domestic things because we were 'equal' and so it wasn't negotiable. It felt like I was required to make up for something that had nothing to do with me. It politicized the relationship in ways that meant tasks like washing up were loaded with layers of meaning beyond what it was in itself.

Feminist ideology was used as an instrument of power, and because I agreed women have been treated unfairly, and still are, I succumbed to what felt like punishment. Bullying occurs in many varied subtle and unsubtle ways, by men to women and women to men and within same gender couples. This does not make for an equilibrium of harmonious balance between the feeling of love and the relationship working operationally, as referred to at the beginning of this chapter.

In contrast, my wife Cath has given me the opposite experience. She exemplifies what it feels like to have a partner who is 'on side' – she defends and supports me. Her usual disposition is one of sympathetic understanding.

She is not a 'yes lady' – she is not compliant or acquiescent – rather she is a strong woman with a mind of her own. She advocates for me and goes to considerable lengths to see things from my point of view. That does not mean that she always agrees with me and, indeed, she may well not agree. It might seem that her attitude could make it easy for me to get away with things *because she will be on my side and make allowances.*

In practice, what actually happens is I feel that I want to live up to her faith in me and not take advantage of her generous attitude. I aspire to be the best man I can be when I feel like my efforts are valued. I know I am a long way from being the perfect partner but I don't feel drawn to grab things for myself individually, as if I needed to seek compensation.

If I stay later at the office to work, it is because work needs to be done and not because I don't want to go home to avoid negativity. I limit closeness or even avoid involvement in friendships with other women because I don't need to seek the blurred boundaries. There is no place for ambiguity in my external relationships. We each wash pots and pans and it isn't an issue. No one is keeping score.

I am seen as a good person and because of this feel good and that makes me act in good ways for the good of the relationship; it's like living on a different planet.

This is the power of love, and when we are lucky enough to receive this gift, it is transformative. It brings out the best in us. It empowers the relationship instead of creating a relationship of power.

When a love relationship goes well, it affects every aspect of your life. While this doesn't mean everything is perfect, a powerful love partnership provides a foundation from which to move forward, in all activities; family, broader social connections, work, creativity and more. The benefits are pervasive.

When a love relationship goes badly, it affects every aspect of your life. While it doesn't mean you must fall apart or that it won't get better, it means there is a dark shadow hovering over you or the feeling of an anchor weighing you down, in whatever you are doing. It detracts, it distracts, and it diminishes. The consequences are pervasive.

To recap, some relationships have a power structure where one or both aim to call the shots. Some relationships seem to be negotiating issues of power all the time, while other relationships – where power is not an issue – are more informed by love. This creates a positive spiral where love breeds love.

I am against the domination and subordination of one party by the other especially where this results in suffering. In couples therapy, actively empowering the latent strength of the oppressed feels right even if that destabilizes the relationship further. At the same time, not every person in a couple partnership is necessarily equal to the other, nor should they be. Not every person wants to be equal to their partner or has to be, or even could be. While having equal rights is critical, that is not the same thing as equal qualities, abilities, resources or achievements. It is each couple's balance, and it is more important that it is a balance that works for them. Again, we can understand relationships that work and last through the analogy of a balanced ecosystem as explored in Chapter 9.

Relationships establish their own balance through complementary differences or through a symmetry where each is roughly the same as each other.

Complementary differences include the following examples. In relation to your partner, you may be:

- stronger
- smarter
- more beautiful
- richer
- older and more experienced, while they may be younger and more energetic
- better qualified
- more accomplished
- more of an emotional supporter
- more of a financial supporter
- more insightful or psychologically-minded
- more knowledgeable or have expertise in a given field
- more sociable, affable or popular
- more articulate or communicative, better with words and ideas
- more expressive of feelings
- more confident, self-assured and outgoing.

If you are equal to each other in any of the examples above, you have a symmetry.

> *Unequal qualities do not justify unfairness.*

The dynamics between unequal complementary positions inform the attachment between partners. Such dynamics change with time, and sometimes with personal growth. For example, you may have needed your partner to be:
- a parent
- a guide
- a mentor
- a teacher
- an instructor
- a healer
- a rescuer
- or a coach

but now you no longer do.

The complement would be if you needed your partner to be:
- a child
- a subject
- a student
- a patient
- a dependent
- an apprentice

but now you no longer do.

You may have tired of the former role or developed a newly evolved symmetry and now seek a more balanced reciprocity and fairness; perhaps you have grown to be more equal or at the same level. This can require an adjustment for the relationship when one person who occupied an 'inferior' position develops to occupy an equal or even 'superior' position. For example, one person takes a step back from their career to raise children and earns little or no money and is supported financially. Later, they resume a profession or embark on a new career or business and out-earn their partner. The change can create a different feeling and alter the balance between you; then the relationship needs to adjust accordingly.

The power of love and the love of power – Part 2

Relationships often begin lovingly, and then shift in the direction of power. For many of us, this may be parallel with our experience of childhood and growing up.

Maybe some of us start off in a loving bond with our mothers or primary carers, and then, as we get a little older, the parenting becomes more about control. Are you repeating a pattern of your childhood in and through your long-term relationships? What if being a couple turns you back into being a dependent child? Do you find yourself reaching toward autonomy, self-sufficiency and a feeling that you will have to leave home to establish your independence?

Can you stand the thought of the other person having something 'over' you? If your primary orientation is to accommodate your partner, will you lose yourself? Or your self-respect? Do any of the following thoughts worry you:

If you become stronger, then I am sunk.
This must not be allowed.

If you get your way too much, then I have lost myself,
then I have lost everything. No, I will never go there.

Of course, I love you but I am not going to be your
accessory or your slave. I do not want to revert to the dependent
child position where you assume parental control over me.

But if I don't give you what you want then
will you still want to be with me?

If being a couple means assuming a counter-developmental position or a position of servitude, what happens to love? This formulation can be demeaning or degrading. Where is the love in that? If I regress, then my love becomes reduced to that of a dependent child for a parent. That is not the same as adult inter-dependency.

How can I sustain my self-esteem if I have to conform to be what you want? To be 'good' is not the same as devotion. To be subordinated by coupledom is not healthy for us as individuals.

> *You only need power to do harm, otherwise love is enough to do what matters.*[23]

A power imbalance between two individuals creates a hierarchy. The 'inferior' one has to fight for self-determination or self-preservation and your love as a couple becomes a casualty.

> Bruce and Margaret had been together for 30 years and had three grown-up children. Things had become stale, and though they each shared a strong sense of being a family, the relationship was in question. Margaret found Bruce distant, not present emotionally, and frequently preoccupied with work. She started to demand that he do something romantic because she was dying of boredom.
>
> He didn't know what that meant. *What do I have to do? It's not like we've just met.*
>
> Bruce bought flowers, but Margaret hated formal flower arrangements. She liked one type of flower in a bunch, not a mixture. He should have known that. He failed there.
>
> He took her to an expensive restaurant but they didn't have much to say to each other and the evening was a little flat.
>
> He suggested they go away for a weekend, but she said she had more fun going away with her girlfriends.
>
> He bought her a ring. She liked that but it didn't really change anything.
>
> Margaret had a big social group and liked inviting people over for dinner. They had dinner parties where Margaret cooked fancy dishes and Bruce served his best wine.

---
23. I have paraphrased a quote attributed to Charlie Chaplin. It is naïve, but I like it anyway. I wish it was as simple as that.

The trouble was that every time Margaret invited people over, she became extremely stressed by the pressure of having to make everything just right and on time. Consequently, she would bark orders at Bruce. He would run around, following her directions, but invariably failed in some small way. Then Margaret would fly into a rage and become what Margaret herself called a 'crazy bitch'.

Once she wanted French butter, it had to be French, and there were only two shops open on a Sunday that sold it. She dispatched him with the words: *and whatever you do, don't be long.*

Bruce went to the closer shop, but they were out of French butter. The other shop was quite a distance and so Bruce decided to return home empty-handed because Margaret's words were ringing in his ears. He had been practicing listening to her to avoid getting it wrong. *Whatever you do, don't be long.* He understood that it was more important to get back than to get butter.

Once back home, Margaret exploded about the lack of French butter, and Bruce felt crushed.

He didn't want their marriage to break up, but this had become unbearable. The next day, they had quite a good talk about it and felt better. In the course of it, Margaret made a reference to Bruce needing to 'score points' for her to stay with him.

When we discussed this, it was clear the structure of their relationship had become one in which he was being scored as a partner – 'husband assessment'. Were his grades high enough? Or was he being marked down? The relationship had become a test that he was repeatedly failing.

I said that bullying was not love. Based on his account of how she treated him, I failed to see her love for him.

As a result of a few sessions, he managed to stand up for himself with Margaret. He stopped her from pushing him around and said that he was no longer open to striving to do better on her scorecard. He didn't want to be with a crazy bitch, and she would have to contain her aggression or he would go somewhere else, and she could have her dinner parties on her own. If she didn't want to be with him, maybe it would be better to put the house up for sale.

It was a shock to her that Bruce voiced the prospect of their marriage ending. The implication of putting the house up for sale was also shocking as they were just finishing with a two-year renovation project.

Bruce was willing to make efforts to improve things, but it was the message that he was not open to being treated like a gofer that made the most difference. Margaret wasn't happy, but she seemed to respect Bruce more and that opened a potential space for love.

Equalizing the balance of power enhanced the prospects for a better connection. And sometimes, you can win the battle but lose your home.

Consuela and Pete had both been married previously. Each had successful businesses and owned their own homes. They both had children, all of whom were grown-up and lived independently.

Increasingly, they enjoyed being together. They went out, socialized, made love and sailed around on his yacht on the weekends. It was a good life. Then they got married and moved in with each other.

While initially all was good, Pete then decided to sell his 40 per cent stake in his software business and retire. Consuela moved her office into their home. She felt she could continue working for some years and this suited Pete well.

However, something started to change after they lived together for some months.

Pete had always been a stickler for tidiness, but he had never been quite so insistent and cross about it as he then became. He could give Consuela a hard time just for leaving a jumper on the bed. Everything had to be in its place, and when it wasn't, it became a serious problem. Consuela found herself saying things like: *you've got too much time on your hands*.

Pete got angry when Consuela spoke her first language, Spanish. He disliked not being able to understand what she was saying even if she was on the phone to her mother in Spain. At a party where many of her relatives mainly spoke Spanish to each other, he became belligerent and obnoxious *to her* because she responded in Spanish. He became aggressively righteous, saying it was rude of her to exclude him.

Consuela's work involved consulting that required her to visit clients' businesses from time to time. This was never a problem in the past but now Pete would interrogate her about where she was going, who she was meeting and for how long. If she was longer than expected, Pete was unhappy with her and suspicious. It was as if he no longer trusted her or believed her accounts. There was no reason why this should be the case, nothing had changed for her. She was not doing anything wrong, nor did she want to. She couldn't understand why he had become so controlling and nasty.

Pete maintained his 'demands' were not unreasonable. It should present no hardship for her to put her clothes away and to respect him by not speaking Spanish. When I spoke with him about it, he seemed to understate the importance of the issue to him. When I spoke with her about it, she said it had become a very big deal and he could be extremely unpleasant, bordering on abusive.

We had just three sessions discussing these matters when Pete not only bailed on therapy but also bailed on his marriage. He said that things had irretrievably broken down, he was unhappy, she was uncompromising and that he'd had enough. (I thought he was uncompromising and she was highly willing to compromise.) He moved back to his own home and presented her with his draft settlement agreement. Their friends and family were stunned.

Consuela was surprised but not overly disturbed about Pete leaving. She had been fine on her own for 10 years before Pete, and she would be fine now. Interestingly, her lawyer said that Pete's financial calculations had failed to take into account about $150,000 that she had contributed to their joint home renovations when they moved in together. Pete then claimed he was being cheated and that she was after his money.

Pete couldn't be on the same level with Consuela. He required her to comply while he was not prepared to negotiate their differences as equals. The combination of her unwillingness to acquiesce and accommodate him and my unwillingness to back him was untenable for him. He bolted from their home, their relationship and the couples therapy process they had sought to improve their relationship.

The power of love and the love of power – Part 3

Another variation on the theme of power in love relationships occurs when one uses sexuality as a bargaining tool or even as a weapon. While I have seen this done more frequently by women, men sometimes behave in this way too. I've also seen women cornered by their partners, usually men, such that there is nowhere to go without resorting to the use of their sexuality in the service of their survival. And sometimes it happens just because it is a device that works.

Sandra found that her husband often said 'no' when she wanted to buy something for herself before he even considered it. She discovered that if she danced him over to the settee and gave him oral sex, in the way he loved, and then asked, he always said 'yes'!

Sandra sometimes found herself thinking what a pushover her husband had become. Formerly, she regarded him as mean. But, either way, she did not respect him.

Their co-sexuality has moved away from love and is now employed by Sandra as a technique to get what she wants. Their co-sexuality has become utilitarian for her, a device of power to achieve an end. She grew unhappy that her formerly loving relationship now required her to prostitute herself, as she saw it, to her husband. She felt alienated from the original romance they had enjoyed and alienated from her own sexuality that had once been a way of expressing love.

She countered his automatic 'no' – his device of power – with a device of power that turned it into a 'yes'. Emotionally honest communication, empathic negotiation, and affective compromise were nowhere in evidence here. The need for power had introduced a toxic element that was now contaminating their relational ecology.

> *In the dance of power, it takes two to tango but only one calls the tune.*

Irene worked out that if she withheld sex her partner Ben would not overly pressure her to be intimate. And the more she withheld sex, the more pliable he became when she wanted something. Irene would sometimes stop herself from being sexual with Ben *even if she felt sexual*. She could turn herself off for days and sometimes stretched it out to weeks.

When Ben was in a sufficiently heightened state of sexual frustration, she would time her proposals for a holiday together, an event she wanted to attend or even a new car.

She loved hopping on a plane with a friend and going designer-label shopping for a weekend in another city, and withholding sex could usually get this wish granted. She grew to be ever more calculating to the point that she could predict exactly how long it would take before Ben would go along with whatever she wanted.

She laughed coyly and said cheekily to me: *You must think I'm the most terrible bitch in the world* ... I responded: *Maybe there is a trace of your own conscience in that thought?*

Such manipulation reflects an imbalance in their co-sexual ecosystem. In a different sort of example:

Samantha and Jeff had a very loving and strongly sexual relationship. They both enjoyed sex, were ready for it most of the time, and it was usually a powerful shared experience. They looked after each other sexually, and both felt loved in and through their usual sexual repertory.

Every so often, Jeff would drink too much. He liked beer. He liked fine wine. He liked vodka, tequila and, in the right mood, a gin and tonic.

Samantha liked a drink too, but she didn't like the feeling of being drunk. She often stopped drinking before Jeff.

When Jeff was drunk, something about the sex was different. He seemed not to care about Samantha as much. He would manoeuvre her into positions she found uncomfortable. Sometimes he would go too hard or be rough with her. It was as if the part of him that monitored how she was had gone. It felt like Jeff was in it for himself.

Sometimes Samantha would not reach orgasm because Jeff had finished before her and passed out. Sometimes, even when she did get to finish and felt reasonably satisfied, she didn't feel as happy afterward; she felt a bit used.

She didn't like that feeling and wondered if it was just something she had to put up with or whether she should address it with Jeff. She hated to spoil his fun. She wanted him to have a good time and prided herself on how good their sexual relationship was, but this was different – it had a different quality. It lacked heart.

What's more important: fun, or the feelings of your partner? When you love each other, is it okay to be an object of use for your partner? Your answer to this makes a difference to the best relationship you can have. Put differently, can it be the best relationship if one feels it is, but the other doesn't? Or if sex sometimes lacks heart?

When care for each other dies, issues of power are born. We move from loving relationship to a tug-of-war between individuals.

> *An emotional deficit in the balance of give and take skews the relational environment, your moral compass loses true north and points to the greedy child.*

Darren would come in week after week complaining about his wife – how negative she was, and that he felt browbeaten and pushed around. They had four kids and Kaye had given up her emerging career in the biotechnology industry to raise the children. She always seemed to prefer attending to the children than paying attention to Darren. He felt that she didn't really desire him, rather her focus was upon the family and the way of life that he could provide. He was a director in a successful company and earned a substantial salary and held a sizable equity stake in the company that had grown hugely over the years.

After Kaye left the biotech company she had worked for, they made a significant discovery, developed a profitable drug, and were then taken over by a large pharmaceutical company. She felt she had missed out on her potential success and making her own money, while Darren constantly received recognition, both for his financial successes and for being a charming person.

She carried a good deal of resentment that was expressed frequently by pointing out his shortcomings and making demands on him. He had hoped that if he was more compliant and appeasing she would feel less resentful. But the more acquiescent he was, the more annoyed she seemed to become. She oscillated between being overtly and passively aggressive.

One day, Kaye saw a text message in Darren's phone from a person she didn't recognize. The message simply said: *Want some oil?* He said it was from someone he had met and didn't mean anything.

Kaye persisted: *Well, it has to mean something? Cherie doesn't sound like one of your industry mates. Are you visiting hookers?*

Eventually, Darren caved in and admitted that he had been for a massage. He didn't have sex, but she had given him relief in the end. Kaye flew into what Darren called 'incandescent rage' and said that she hadn't given up her life so that he could get relief from other women.

Now she had the moral high ground on top of an underlying reservoir of resentment. She punished Darren, either through verbal attacks, cold stonewalling or through a seemingly endless stream of demands that he felt obliged to fulfill. This went on for months and months.

Sometimes it seemed to settle down and they would be calmer and happier together, and then an event like a reference to a massage on TV would light her fuse. She would erupt in anger, recrimination and indignation.

Sex became more problematic and less frequent. He started to find it difficult to maintain his erection. Kaye's reaction to this was to be more hurt and more enraged. *I'm clearly not sexy enough for you, you aren't aroused by me any longer. Maybe you should go off and have one of your massages!*

If Darren said anything suggesting that her treatment of him might be affecting his behavior or the way his body was reacting, she became angrier. *Don't try to shift the blame on me when it lies entirely at your feet.*

Darren said: *it's not a question of blame but in a relationship two people share a responsibility for what happens.* Kaye wouldn't hear of it. The responsibility was his, not hers; she did nothing wrong.

He said that he felt there was nothing he could do to elicit her forgiveness and that he felt no love from her at all. Kaye reacted with disbelief: *you should have thought of that when you were having your dick oiled, shouldn't you?!*

Darren felt an obvious vacuum in his marriage because of Kaye's negativity and barely veiled hostility. He thought a massage was harmless and just gave him a bit of relief from an otherwise stressful grind where he believed he was doing all he could for his relationship and family. He claimed to love Kaye a great deal, was attracted to her and only wanted to have sex with her. But he felt so ground down by her attitude that he felt justified in seeking a 'little something extra' from outside the relationship.

I asked him why he had left a text message like that on his phone and suggested he might have wanted Kaye to discover it, perhaps unconsciously, but Darren didn't accept a concept of the unconscious. To me, that and scarcely concealing other tell-tale signs of indiscretions, reflected an intention. He needed to find ways of showing her or conveying to her that she had disconnected from him, pushed him away and that he felt marginalized. However, what he achieved was her feeling even more aggrieved with him and him feeling hopeless about the future of the relationship.

Notice the power play in this situation. Kaye feels compromised by the loss of her career, relegated to looking after children and outdone by Darren. She is envious of his success even though she is a beneficiary of it. She is resentful of his freedom, his frequent trips around the world, the recognition he receives and the gratification from his considerable financial rewards. She feels owed something.

Kaye's feelings of being owed something make him feel he must compensate her but he feels owed something too. In that context, he has a massage she regards as much insult as injury. Now she feels owed even more, the opposition between them is greater, and he has to try harder to make it up to her while feeling futile, defeated and depressed.

These two people loved each other a great deal in earlier, happier days. Now, there are four children and a substantial estate between them, and both are wretched most of the time.

Of course, regarding a sexual massage as 'harmless' is a long way from devotion and the sanctification of vows. Each has good reasons to feel cheated by the other. How are they ever going to improve the environment between them and reach to the best relationship they can have?

'Best relationships' involve giving up:
- willing to be powerful
- being right
- grabbing entitlements
- being owed
- occupying the moral high ground.

They also require you to let go of:
- holding something over your partner
- using sexuality as a lever or a weapon
- using guilt as a method of subordination
- using money as a device of manipulation and control.

And they also demand we relinquish the need to be or to appear:
- smarter
- stronger
- higher earning
- more accomplished
- more beautiful
- more talented
- more enlightened.

*Ultimately, you have to give up
competing and assuming a superior position.*

And most of all, you have to move on from:
- your feelings of hurt and woundedness
- anger and resentment
- deception, betrayal, disloyalty and abandonment
- being a victim.

It is up to you to take responsibility for your choices – the benefits and consequences – while operating in an equal and reciprocal partnership with your beloved. To be a victim or a martyr does not make for a better relationship. Self-pity also tarnishes the relational ecology.

In the example above, of course Darren is responsible for deciding to have a massage with a dash of illicit sexuality and therefore for the after-effects on his marriage. Kaye also has responsibility for the position she's assumed, her behavior toward Darren and her aggressive attitudes and negativity.

She wanted to have children. She chose to give up her career in biotech to be a stay-at-home mother. And she urged Darren to pursue his corporate career and encouraged and supported many of his business decisions. However, her frustrations mean she is unable to receive his gratitude and appreciation of her and conversely to feel gratitude and appreciation for what he contributes. For example, he thanked her publicly at his company's annual general meeting but she scarcely registered it because it was him who sat at the front of the room with the rest of the Board of Directors.

While her feelings of having missed out are understandable, and she was probably just as capable as him, punishing him for those feelings via a power struggle doesn't help their relationship or her individual happiness. And it certainly doesn't contribute to his.

The 'love' of power over your partner becomes the unmaking of love between you.

Realizing the dream

The dream of a happy, enduring, successful relationship needs to be circumscribed by what is possible. If the dream is so idealistic that it is unreachable, you are set up for disappointment. The dream can only be realized by keeping it real. The word realize means to make real.

We return to where we started. Keeping it real depends upon knowing your partner. What is possible is determined by who each of you are, and what you are capable of. We can all work at developing ourselves, to increase our capacities for loving, for giving and forgiving.

> *The less required to be satisfied, the more easily you arrive there.*

You develop your capacity for satisfaction inversely. In other words, the more you need to be satisfied, the harder it becomes to arrive there. The less you need, the more easily and the more frequently can you arrive at a fuller sense of satisfaction.

At the same time, the more you can be and do for your partner, the more likely they will want to be and do for you. The chance of this working and therefore of you realizing the dream is exponentially enhanced if both parties are devoted to serving the relationship at their fullest capacity. If you are not already doing this, an adjustment is required: what is in the way needs to be removed, what must be lived with needs to be accepted.

When you were in love, you didn't need to think too much about all this. The relationship was easy. No effort was required. It felt perfect all the time. Perhaps your dream is to feel like this always, but that is not usually how it goes.

A relationship of reciprocal devotion is the ideal – where the giving flows organically and the receiving reaches you in the depth of your soul, where you feel met and known, recognized and understood, valued and appreciated, respected, admired, and loved. The feeling of being desired as you desire the other is absolutely delicious. You can feel passionate toward each other, intensely sexual, irresistibly attracted. None of that requires you to be in love. If you are, that's even better.

If you can see your partner's defects and flaws and you can also see beyond them – into their core, to that inner quality that best defines them – then you really don't have to worry about the imperfections that come with the passing of time. Love and care see beyond the weight and wrinkles gained and the hair lost, they scarcely register. This is what Patty (Chapter 7) needed to understand to feel as free as she once did with her husband.

You can love how your partner looks but the true object of love is the person and not the package. When you love the whole substance of your partner, you love the package and its imperfections. Perhaps it is odd to speak of substance in the context of a dream but to realize the dream of the best relationship is to bond with the substance of the person of your partner. Bonding is a process that requires constant renewal and reinvigoration, which is itself the task of relating.

Relationships are always unfolding. Remember the image of dance. The movement involved is a choreography of form and meaning, as you dance your way with and around your partner. You have no artistic director to guide you; it is an improvisational art, impromptu and spontaneous, as you weave your very selves around and through each other. Who you each become depends on this movement.

There is an elegant beauty in a dance of love that generates satisfaction and fulfilment – two people transcend the limits of their individual selves and join to create and re-create a dynamic union of two souls. In that flow, we never want the music to stop and the question: *is this the best relationship I can have?* is answered.

CHAPTER 11
Couples Therapy

> *"Women might be able to fake orgasms.*
> *But men can fake whole relationships."*
> — **attributed to Sharon Stone**

Love needs to be made, and often re-made, but what can be done when love has been unmade? One option is couples therapy.
- What do you do when there is damage or emotional injury?
- What approach can you take when resentments and disappointments have built up over time?
- How do you cope with frustrations that grow to unmanageable proportions?
- How do you respond when doubts have crept in, and you are noticing other options and feeling tempted?
- Where do you search for a remedy to feeling deeply unhappy with your partner?
- How can you reverse acting-out when you notice that little misdemeanors risk becoming major relationship crimes?

Sure, you can leave the relationship, but many people want to feel that they have done all they can to try to restore a love relationship before giving up, especially where children are involved.

People come to couples therapy for a range of reasons. Often their relationship is at the point of breakdown, or there has been a crisis, a loss of trust or infidelity. Sometimes fighting has taken over and become the norm. Sexual contact may be infrequent or non-existent. Some couples have not had sex for years.

Sometimes, one wants to leave and the other doesn't or isn't sure. From a position of feeling that love has gone and *I've had enough* it is hard to imagine how the relationship can be redeemed.

A common scenario is when one person realizes that the other is near to leaving and wants to prevent this. They realize that to avoid a parting of ways they need to restore the relationship and become the kind of partner that would make the other want to stay. The undesirable prospect of being alone becomes motivating. Perhaps a realization dawns about what dividing a joint estate would mean or co-parenting without cohabiting. What would this mean for the children?

Sometimes there isn't a crisis but a sense of impasse. The couple is at the limit of what they can do about it, on their own. They are blocked, so a third party – a therapist – is enlisted to help and a process of regular sessions is launched. Bringing an independent perspective helps clients to negotiate the obstacles and improve all of the situations outlined above.

On occasion, couples present for therapy feeling relatively okay, and then as issues emerge and we begin to address them, 'bad' feelings intensify. It is as if the 'mud' has been churned up and rises to the surface. It can almost seem like conflict has been created in the session but we have only uncovered something already there. Sometimes, negative feelings emerge out of historical issues and clients wonder why they are doing this when they felt fine before the session. But what's muddy down below only gets cleaned up once it surfaces and becomes accessible to attention. Then we have to work to clear such negative feelings or they easily return to being submerged. Latent issues or conflicts can fester like untreated infections. It becomes a strategy of deferral, and putting it off can make it worse later.

These days many couples come for therapy before they are

due to marry with a view to anticipating what can go wrong. Often, those happy in love fear losing it or discover fantasies in themselves of what can happen to ruin it. Even though these couples are traveling well, this is a useful discussion and one worth having.

One person might have reservations prior to marriage or about a decision to live together or to have a child together. The process of addressing reservations often leaves us feeling better about them even when they are not fully removed.

Going to counselling in the spirit of anticipating problems and issues creates a legitimate situation in which to take the lid off the potential can of worms that might be hidden within your innermost thoughts or fears. You are invited to speak freely and can be surprised at what emerges.

- You can prevent an issue from developing.
- You might learn of a problem or issue that you weren't aware of and that your partner has kept to themselves.
- You may get to know your partner a little better such as by discovering something in your relationship that they are anticipating causing them anxiety.
- You partner may also reveal something they are seeking from you that you didn't know about.

A problem preempted is as good as a problem solved – no, better, because you haven't had the problem in the first place. If an issue is already there in one, the other needs to know about it. The process of couples therapy opens lines of communications not previously opened on your own. Once established, an improved facility for communication can be brought home.

An independent perspective

Every so often, it is worth reflecting together on how you are traveling and what needs attention. An independent perspective adds value. There are times when relationships *appear* to be fine but in reality one person is harboring private discontent. You can bury your unhappiness so deeply that you don't even know it is there (I've done this).

Consequences will unfold and acting-out becomes more likely. All that has been buried may erupt without warning; you may both be surprised by the destructive potential. The suppression of feelings takes energy and buried feelings create distance. They present obstacles to intimacy that appear mysteriously as if for no reason. They can affect our moods and even our physical health. You might wonder: *I am so tired all the time and can't see why because work has become easier.*

If resentment builds and hostility percolates under the surface of the relationship, couples therapy presents an opportunity to bring such thoughts and feelings out in the open. If problems are left unchecked, love can be eroded in myriad ways.

Making your views explicit with a third party makes them *feel more real*, and gives weight to a sense of mutual understanding because there is an independent witness.

> In one session, Sally said to her partner Jesse that she felt single because Jesse was so immersed in work. Jesse worked so late at home and also on weekends that Sally felt she hardly saw her partner. *You go to bed with your laptop!* Sally exclaimed.
>
> Though they had argued about this before and not found common ground, in the session Jesse replied: *I am at a point in my career where I am going to have to work extra hours in order to achieve the advancement I am aiming for and I want to be supported in that because success will, in turn, serve both of us in our joint goals.*

These differences are common for relationships, and couples therapy is often used to arrive at a fair and agreeable balance between two relatively reasonable positions.

I have been amazed at what comes out in such conversations. In the example below, the couple had been together for years and had come for counselling because Perette had become moody and bad-tempered. It was difficult to discover why things had changed.

I started with an extensive investigation into their way of living and their relationship together. Despite this, nothing emerged to account for Perette's irritability. I asked about their physical relationship, and both said it was fine. Harry, her husband, said that it was wonderful but could happen more often. She said she was happy.

Perette asked for an individual session with me and in that she confessed that she had never had an orgasm with her husband. He believed that she was anorgasmic, in other words, incapable of having one.

She didn't know how to tell him that she could orgasm without any difficulty with the right amount of pressure usually from a vibrator on exactly the right spot. He was confident sexually and believed that he did all the right things. She couldn't find a way of telling him because she was afraid it would be crushing for his male pride. But she was frustrated and fed up that their sexual activities always ended well for him but not her.

In the next couple session, I prompted her to raise the subject and reveal her true feelings about their sex life. He was quite shocked at what he heard, especially as he was a gynecologist. I suggested that she show him exactly what worked for her (at home!) and invite him to practice with her as part of their sexual interaction together.

With encouragement, and dressed up as therapeutic homework, she became less inhibited and was able to tell her husband specifically what to do and how and where. With a bit of practice, her moods changed, and she stopped feeling bad-tempered and moody.

> *When couples are bogged in the mud of unspeakable subjects, therapy is an opportunity to clear the water.*

Often a reason for moodiness can be uncovered by looking at the point in time that such moodiness commenced. The gynecologist was a little embarrassed that he needed another person to discover how his wife could orgasm, but he got over that quickly and thanked me for it. Happy wife, happy husband.

In this example, her moodiness and irritability reflected her internal timing. She got to a point where she was fed up and didn't want to accept things as they had been any longer. Her unexplainable unhappy mental (and physical) state was the catalyst to invite a therapist into their relationship as an agent for change.

Clear the air, clean the water, bring light to dark places – all express the function of couples therapy.

> Isaac was distressed that Martha wouldn't make love with him anymore. He couldn't get her to say why.
>
> When I asked her the same question in a couples therapy session, she had no difficulty in saying that his hair smelled because he didn't wash it often enough. The smell turned her off, in fact, she found it quite revolting.
>
> He responded directly saying that he would wash it twice a day if that made a difference.
>
> And he did.
>
> And it did.

Why couldn't she just tell him when she could tell me directly with him present? I don't really know how to answer this question. It can be easier to speak freely to a third party than to one's own partner. While it seems that a love partner should be the person with whom it is most easy to speak, sometimes this is not the case and it is impossible to say a simple truth like: *your hair smells, and you need to wash it if you want me to feel like being sexual with you.*

Perhaps there is a sense of blunting the pointy end of the knife when speaking to a third party about such matters? You are not just sticking it into your partner directly. That said, some people find it embarrassing for a third party to be a witness to such private revelations. In that event, the customary non-judgmental attitude of the therapist and a disposition that says *these sorts of things are quite normal in relationships* helps to reduce any discomfort. The sooner it comes out, the more directly things change for the better. Getting over any discomfort about such revelations also helps disclosures to surface more readily in the future.

The therapy process

Couples therapy is different from individual therapy. In individual therapy, we allow someone as much airtime as they require to voice their own personal narrative. This is not the case in couples therapy.

If one person needs to speak about themselves at length, they need to undertake individual work. There is a place for this in couples therapy but it is important that the needs of the relationship are privileged over the needs of the individuals.

Sometimes, I see each party of the couple individually as well as seeing them together. This can help each of them give their point of view without having to worry about dominating the space of a joint session. They can speak freely and without being overly concerned about their partner's feelings or reactions. Often, issues are raised in these sessions that I can bring into the joint sessions. This is done with sensitivity to the feelings of each party. Getting to know clients also enables me to support and facilitate them in coming to their own ways of expressing themselves to their partners.

There are both potential problems and benefits with this approach. Confidentiality has to be carefully managed as I can be told things that one doesn't want the other to know. This can place me in a compromising position of colluding to keep secrets at one party's expense – a position I was able to avoid in the Craig and Marjorie example from Chapter 9. While it's not hard to keep a private feeling on behalf of one party, major deception is different and I won't be drawn to collude with that. I use discretion in considering how best to serve the relationship and the interests of both parties separately.

There is also the potential problem of allegiances where one party feels I'm on the other's side. Sometimes, 'I' am used to support the position of one against the other. Remarks have been attributed to me that I haven't actually said.

> *Dr Resnick agrees with me that you are too flirtatious at parties.*

'I' have also been used in a teasing way.

> *I'm going to dob you in and tell Jan about this at our next session, and he'll sort you out!*

The most important point is that every couple could read this book and a hundred other books and it would not achieve the same result as entering a personal process where issues are worked on as a couple. To read about fitness does not achieve the same result as exercise.

I have written this book to be used for self-help but the therapy process helps in ways self-help cannot. The process works most of the time if people are committed to it and the therapist is up to the task. Commitment to therapy involves opening up, speaking your truth, revealing your experience and taking responsibility for your actions.

Frequently, I notice that couples that have been at war with each other can come for a single session and by the next time I see them, peace has 'broken out'. They are much nicer to each other, and are thinking about what they appreciate about one another. That is not to say all their problems are solved. The intention of reconciliation makes confronting issues a relief and not an ordeal to be dreaded. The couple re-position themselves in quadrant 2 of the Matrix of Desire – desire to desire – they want to improve the relationship and so feel better for undertaking the task.

I have seen couples who have said the feeling of love has died, and they cannot imagine feeling that way again, but they don't want to split. Sometimes they recover surprisingly well after the source of resentments has been removed, and feelings aired fully. Acknowledging responsibility for causing hurt, frustration, anger or disappointment goes a long way to reviving more positive feelings and re-connecting. Contrition is healing. And a shift in attitude toward repair enables repair to begin.

Relationships suffer depression much as individuals do, and it often lifts when the future outlook improves. Sometimes grieving the loss of what was is necessary to make space for what could be. It won't be the same but does it have to be? Few relationships escape the need for adjustments over the longer term; therapy sheds light, enhances understanding, promotes movement and initiates change.

Therapists love to tell their success stories. With time, we all have them but it usually takes longer and is much harder work than the case snippets in any book reveal. That said, occasionally there are beautiful and rewarding outcomes in couples' work that happen quickly and easily. Remember Gail and Carl (Chapter 8), who said that their relationship had grown to a place that was better than it had ever been since they met? They were both adamant that where they had arrived was a product of our work together, and said that it couldn't have happened otherwise. They sent me an email saying: *you have made an indelible impression on our lives, and we will be forever grateful.* This is sheer magic for me; something you can't buy or find in most other types of work.

There is also the opposite scenario. Sometimes the work is harrowing for the therapist and sometimes outcomes are not what we would like. We can see that the whole future of a person's life is going to change, and that of their children, if this relationship breaks down and this couple breaks up. We know that generations that follow will have been affected by the outcome of what happens in this process.

I have felt like tackling one person to the ground out of desperation to get through to them: *if you can just get this one point, if you can just do one thing differently, then everything changes for the better!* Most of the time, it doesn't just depend on me. I do what I can to get through (tackling them metaphorically rather than literally). When clients reflect fully and bring a willingness to make changes in themselves to the therapeutic process, it can make all the difference.

> *Therapy depends on your readiness to take responsibility for your affect upon your partner. If you are not there, we work toward readiness.*

Many couples come wanting to blame each other and enlisting support from me for their perspectives. This is a dead-end track. No amount of pounding home a particular point is going to get through and change the dynamic unless each individual is prepared to look at themselves.

> *No one can get through if the phone is 'off the hook'.*

Many people find it hard to see themselves clearly in their role in the relationship – their part in what happens – until they reach their forties, fifties, sixties or even older. Some of us never see ourselves at all, though we get into intense relationships, or marriages, in our teens or twenties or thirties. It can take a long time for some of us to mature, develop emotionally and grow up. A deeper and fuller sense of what responsibility means is a hallmark of maturity. However, it is not only about age or experience, as some people are incredibly mature, responsible and insightful at a young age. Some precocious young people see themselves more clearly than their parents see them, or more clearly than their parents see themselves.

Some sessions seem to position me as judge. Each party presents their case, and I am to decide which case is stronger or more correct. That is not my role nor is it an approach likely to bring joy to either. Even if I could judge – and one party felt gratified through being deemed right – this is not nearly as good as both parties feeling closer with each other.

> *Letting go of being right, and needing to be acknowledged as right, serves closeness more than winning on the imaginary scoreboard of an argument.*

You are given a gift: the ability to see yourself as others see you. Caring about the consequences of your way of being upon others, and realizing your responsibility for what happens, are essential parts of how two love. They light the path of conciliation.

My approach

There are many different approaches to couples therapy. There is no best approach though there are certainly some ineffective ones. Many of the models are theory based and therapy then follows a set model based on the current theory. Theories abound as to how and why couples get into strife with each other and then what they need from therapy to make their relationship work better. Sometimes theories are backed up by what is called 'evidence', the outcomes of studies or research. This psychological methodology produces general conclusions whereas competent therapists recognize that clients are always different from each other and different at different times. No amount of research can succeed in reducing the personal to a generality that applies to everyone and still be therapeutically useful. And what is universal is usually already obvious.

> *In effective therapy, one size does not fit all.*

I am not attracted to any of the theory-based models because I dispute that anyone knows exactly why couples have problems in advance of them walking through the door. I have tried to elaborate what happens in love relationships, but that does not mean that I know in advance exactly what to do before a couple has arrived. I have to hear from them. Though there are themes and patterns, it is better to suspend 'knowing' and learn from each couple what these themes and patterns mean for them. Better to regard their issues as unique even if I've heard about similar issues many times before from others.

As with individual psychotherapy, the one-size-fits-all approach is going to miss what is important for each person or each couple and the immediacy of their experience. No amount of theory or knowledge can fully capture that in advance even if clinical experience helps to be prepared.

> *Relationship is an improvisational art and so therapy must be as well.*

Knowledge and experience are indispensable resources on which therapists draw but these do not take the place of the therapy process; sitting down together, focusing on your issues, reflecting and discussing possible ways of improving things.

The best approach is a fresh perspective brought to every session; this is called a 'phenomenological' approach. This philosophical term refers to focusing on the experience of the people who consult me at the time that they come. Phenomenology is more concerned with descriptions of experience than with explanations, psychological theories or fixed methods to change things.

Both individuals and couples appreciate an open attitude of interest in what is going on with them at the time, what they are feeling, what they understand about their situation and what needs attention from their point of view. Usually, they don't expect me to know how to fix it before hearing from them. My view is based on their account of things and that gives it directness, relevance and immediacy; a pertinence that is personal and timely.

These are some of the important points I want to understand:
- What is the source of suffering or dissatisfaction?
- What does each want from the other?
- What would each need to be happy in the relationship?
- What causes resentment, hostility or disaffection?
- What is it that diminishes libido towards each other or the eros of the relationship in general?
- Are physical conditions or medications an issue?
- What works in the relationship? What can be acknowledged or appreciated about each by the other?
- How long is it since it was 'good' and what made it so?
- When did it change? And why?
- What are the relationship strengths?
- What are the challenges?
- What do you love and hate about each other? Or, if that is too strong, like and dislike?

A number of principles are important to me in couples therapy. I try to connect, establish a rapport, and form a working relationship with each party as equally as possible. During sessions, I give each person roughly equal airtime to talk.

Sessions are based on what comes up at the time – much easier for the experienced therapist to improvise than the novice.

In day-to-day living, underlying feelings often precipitate behaviors characterized by argumentativeness, nastiness, contempt, aggression, acting-out or shutting down, sulking or stonewalling. There is a kind of discovery process in therapy that uncovers the driver or source of the challenging behaviors that couples fall into.

Often we hear one saying:
- *I don't want to be a nag.*
- *I sound like my mother (or father).*
- *I don't like it when I become aggressive; it's not me.*
- *I don't recognize myself when I regress to childish behaviors such as name-calling, sarcasm, or sulky withdrawal.*
- *I cringe and recoil when my partner touches me.*
- *It's not like me to be so dependent.*
- *I can't stop myself from nit-picking; every little thing irritates me.*
- *I feel numb, or indifferent. I have gone cold when I used to feel the opposite.*

We work to identify underlying feelings and develop capacities to express them in ways that bring the two together rather than continue to create divisiveness and hurt.

Many times, I have heard one call the other a 'slut' even though they have been loyal and faithful. Where is such a nasty attribution coming from? The underlying feeling might be expressed as: *When you dress up and go out with your friends I feel threatened that someone else will be as attracted to you as I am, and that I could lose you.*

Another example: one is happy that the other is home early from a party but despite that, appears cold and withdrawn. What they struggle to say is: *I feel abandoned when you go out to a party without me even though I don't want to come. I don't like parties; and I recognize that you can't just stay in and have quiet nights at home with me all the time. But then I fantasize about you making a connection with someone else or having fun, dancing in a sexy way and then I feel threatened. I drive myself crazy by making up unbearable scenarios in my mind. Then when I see you, you look pleased to come home to me but I'm already feeling so hurt by all the possibilities I've imagined. I'm not pleased to see you because I'm terrified by what news you might bring from the party.*

A central theme in couples therapy is how people communicate when feelings have turned negative. If communication has become a weapon to cause pain, a means of retaliation, or a device to overpower their partner, the therapy process focuses on the underlying reasons, how to approach each other differently and how communication can become a medium for resolution rather than war.

> *If you attack your partner, you may succeed in injuring your partner.*

Over time, enough injuries will amount to irreparable damage.

You may feel entitled to hold hostility toward your partner for whatever reason. You may feel your partner deserves to be attacked. Vengefulness might even make you feel better. But your partner is more likely to understand how you feel if you express your feelings with a soft voice rather than an attacking one. Retaliation breeds retaliations. Aggressive communications spark friction that can easily degenerate into fighting or bickering and all the diverse ways you can be offside with each other. Even if your feelings are extreme – murderous – if you stretch to exhibit empathy for your partner then the possibility of empathy grows in your partner for you. That creates an opportunity for reconciliation and opens the prospect to be closer rather than descending into hot conflict (again).

I work in one of three modes depending upon what couples are seeking from therapy.
1) To improve the relationship.
2) To disentangle the attachment and separate.
3) If clients don't know at the outset,
    we work to determine if they want to work to
    improve the relationship (1) or separate (2).

Sometimes they don't agree, or one wants number 1 and the other wants number 2. Then number 3 means we try to work out which way to go.

The first mode accounts for the great majority of couples, while the third mode accounts for more than the second. Sometimes couples arrive at the second mode via the third and then don't want to continue with therapy. Game over. This could be a mistake because there is much involved in separating and so much to go through emotionally where a therapeutic process could be valuable.

Normally, I am in charge of the session, of its structure and flow, though there may be exceptions to this, for example when something is 'breaking-through'. Breakthroughs happen as insight, as emotion, as an epiphany, or any combination of these. Often a breakthrough occurs when one person sees themselves and sees their part in the relationship dynamic clearly, and often sees the consequences for their partner. Breakthroughs also happen when someone sees how they are creating conditions in the present for past experiences or traumas to recur. In these cases, it is better to allow it to emerge organically and without interruption. Such light-bulb moments can be life-changing, dramatically altering the course of a relationship for the better.

In sessions, I stop each person from interrupting, from indulging in blame, from pathologizing their partner and from descending into hostile aggression. I try to cool the temperature of conflict before it heats up to a full-blown row.

The golden rule for both individual therapy and couples therapy is that the space needs to be safe for everyone, including the therapist. Protecting the space is the therapist's job. Each person needs to be protected, and therapists have to look out for themselves. This is easy to say but not always easy in practice.

> Once I had a very unusual couple in which I realized that the man was both psychopathic and also quite regressed and broken down. The psychopathic personality organization is

so focused on being on top that it is rare to meet someone who is also regressed and prone to floods of tears. It became apparent that his emotion was enlisted in the service of trying to position me to manipulate his girlfriend, according to his design.

He kept on protesting his innocence over allegations from his partner. In one session, she brought in a mountain of documented evidence that showed that he was guilty of all that he was being accused of. Despite his multiple infidelities and deceptions, he still wanted me to convince her that he was a good guy and deserved another chance.

Shortly after, I had a dream of him bursting into my consulting room, spraying the room with an automatic weapon and killing me. I felt terrified when I realized that his next session was on a Saturday when the whole medical center in which I work was unoccupied. I was going to be alone in the building. When he came in, I scanned his clothes; he was wearing the local uniform of shorts, T-shirt and thongs with no weapons that I could detect. A momentary paranoia perhaps, but I believe the dream was telling me something that I needed to know. It was hard to feel safe in this session and keep my mind in focus with such fears activated.

Part of a therapist's job is to manage their own thoughts and feelings while sessions unfold. I tried to hold the responsibility for the work, despite feeling anxious. Soon after, his partner ended their relationship in no uncertain terms and made it clear that the therapy process was finished. He wanted to continue but I didn't think I could work effectively with him individually and referred him to another therapist with whom he could make a fresh start.

While safety is paramount, I don't *always* stop a fight between warring couples. Sometimes, people need to fight. It can be a demonstration of what happens between them that is being enacted as a communication to me. Perhaps they need to get it out of their systems and will feel better for it. I stop fights when I feel that one is unsafe, can't handle it or that it is becoming harmful. I also stop fights when I can't stand it any longer.

It can be incredibly difficult to stop a fight. I have felt like a referee in a boxing match. On one occasion, I yelled STOP! On another occasion, employing humor to lighten the intensity, I said: *If you don't stop attacking each other I'm going to attack both of you myself!* I have also insisted on a minute's silence to let some steam out of the pressure cooker atmosphere.

Some clients need to vent their feelings and frustrations when on their own with me. It can help for the therapist to be the one who receives the negative sentiments about the relationship. Some clients feel better for getting it off their chest and can then address their partner more positively.

I will endeavor to show a sense of hope even if I feel doubtful about a couple's prospects for the future, but I won't pretend if I don't feel any hope at all. In that event, a lack of hope can be used to communicate a rather grave message: *if you both want to redeem this relationship and avoid a painful and costly separation then you are really going to have to change your attitude.*

As I said to Craig (Chapter 9) I work in the truth business. If I cannot be emotionally honest and authentic in this situation, I'd rather not do it at all.

Communications about the challenges couples face need to be balanced with communications about what couples have going for them, their positive attributes, courage to confront problems and strengths to endure hardship. This might be hard to see when couples present the worst of their relationship in the consulting situation. That is, after all, what they want help with and what they come for. But it is incredibly important to balance the negatives with the positives, even if we have to dig a little to find them. Remember: it is the positives that brought a couple together and is keeping them together, even if mostly based on a memory of the past.

It is desirable to remain neutral where that is possible but sometimes I agree with one and disagree with the other, and I may say so. I don't have a rigid rule about neutrality like many therapists. If I take a position and demonstrate why, the party that disagrees can consider my point of view and remains free to accept or reject it. These days, I find many clients want to know what I think and are tired of the cliché therapy approach that puts it back on them: *and what do you think?* Many clients already know what they think and want an independent opinion from me, an opinion that may well be different from that of their friends and family.

I am usually drawn to help couples work things out, and families stay together, where they want to – even if I think the relationship is problematic or even dysfunctional (whatever that means). Like most therapists, I strongly believe that emotional engagement and intimacy is better than isolation, distance, estrangement or alienation.

> *Emotional engagement is a fundamental value of therapy and intimacy is its reward.*

At the same time, therapists must be cautious about not imposing their personal values and agendas upon clients. While the primary agenda of therapy is the client's best interest, with couples I also advocate for the best interest of their children (who I may never meet).

Many couples manifest patterns that are found to be transgenerational, discovered by investigating in depth and detail the genealogy of each party. Such patterns can be handed down from parents (or primary carers) who learned them from their parents who learned them from theirs, and so on, like links in a chain that stretch over time.

Family-of-origin dynamics and patterns influence our adult relationships in ways that are determining and self-perpetuating.

These are worth working through, whether in individual or couples therapy.

> *One aim of therapy is to break a link in the chain of negative patterns that recurs through the generations.*
>
> *That may be the best gift you could ever give your children, and their children.*

The work of therapy functions like a stone thrown in a pond. From the epicenter where the stone lands the water ripples outwards, and so the benefits to one person ripple out through them to their significant others and, in turn, to others still. A lasting benefit, even in the detail of one person's life or self, reverberates over time as an ongoing legacy of positive influence. We may never know how much benefit has been paid forward or what disasters may have been avoided as a product of the therapy process.

Healing and repair

Effecting healing and repair are amongst the most important functions of couples therapy. Healing refers to the recovery from injury and repair refers to the mending of damage, and these functions have considerable overlap. Emotional injuries and damage can occur within the relationship or come with you from way back in your personal history. Damage can be minor, as when one party offends their partner, or it can be major, such as the traumatic damage caused by an affair, a deception or another breach of trust, abandonment or perhaps a physical altercation.

Healing from injury or repairing damage in therapy ranges from straightforward and relatively easy, to complicated or even impossible. Hurt is experienced differently by different people, and the 'same' hurt can be felt as massive by one and inconsequential by another. For example, Xavier had lunch with his ex and never mentioned it to his wife Lisa. When she asked him about the charge on their credit card statement, he told her that he had taken his ex out to lunch. Lisa asked why he hadn't mentioned it but that was the end of it. However, in the identical situation, when Bill's wife Sandra asked him about a credit card charge and he said he'd taken his ex out to lunch, Sandra exploded with anger and outrage. To her, his omission was evidence that he 'was up to something' that he had attempted to conceal from her. She was already suspicious of Bill's ex and regarded any contact they had as a betrayal and a threat. Bill's action caused Sandra an emotional injury and risked damaging their relationship whereas Xavier's action barely ruffled Lisa's mood.

An injury can cause damage but doesn't have to. Damage suggests a hurt that is lasting. Hurts can be repaired or be irreparable, cured or incurable. This is the case emotionally just as it is physically.

While injuries can scar, it may be possible to go on in a relationship despite extensive scarring. Just as the body can feel like a battlefield of aging, with time many relationships become similarly scarred. For those of us lucky enough to reach the twilight years, few arrive unscathed emotionally or physically. What can therapy do about it?

Therapy is an opportunity to go right into it. Air the feelings surrounding the injury. Explore the reasons for it and examine the context and extenuating circumstances. Seek an understanding of how the injury happened and of how you have been affected. Deep pain and hurt need expression. By giving them space to breathe, to be suffered and acknowledged, the pain of emotional injury is made meaningful. Full expression and mutual understanding bring relief to emotional hurt. And going through a therapeutic process with a partner helps the relationship to move on.

There is no agenda to wallow in misery or suffering. Quite the opposite; the point of going into it is to go through the healing process so you can come out the other side. When you emerge, you grow to be more fully implanted in the present, and then more rewarding possibilities open up. Pain demands attention and consumes energy. Once pain is not so dominating, it is not in the way and we feel freer.

It is said that time heals all wounds but sometimes time is not enough on its own. Many wounds of an emotional nature heal more quickly and comprehensively with the assistance of a sensitive and compassionate therapeutic process. However, certain types of trauma (and specifically complex trauma) have been found to not benefit from the process of airing and going into it advocated here. Sometimes too much talking about injuries can re-activate traumatic memories, trigger a re-experiencing of traumatic experience, and so re-traumatize. At these times, a trauma-informed, body-orientated and mindfulness-based practice to help us stay in the present may work better, even if not normally a part of couples therapy.

Repair has a different quality. Repair is often called for in response to the damage caused by a transgression by one party against the other, or against the love relationship itself.

> They had been together for 11 years. They argued, they bickered, they quarreled and they squabbled, but they never fought physically. While they usually recovered from their verbal shots at each other, one day she said that he was becoming more like his brother (who had recurring psychotic episodes). At that moment, she found his most sensitive trigger.
>
> He lost control; he had never hit her before, but this time he did. He punched her across the chin. He hit her so hard her jaw dislocated. It needed to be wired back into place and took a long time to heal. However, the emotional damage caused by this blow was far greater.
>
> Her whole orientation to the relationship changed. She had always said that if he ever struck her, she would be out

> of there in the blink of an eye. She had told him: *Hit me and I'm gone. You will never see me again. There will be no discussion, no room for apologies, and no forgiveness. I will just leave, and that will be the end of it.*

In one way of looking at it, maybe that is what he wanted. A psychoanalytical perspective would suggest that unconsciously, without any forethought or premeditation, he wanted to end the relationship. He'd had enough. He was fed-up but too attached to leave. He needed to break the bond and cut through the attachment. But that is not what he said.

> He was adamant that it was an aberration – he didn't want to end the relationship, he loved her dearly and he didn't want her to leave. He acknowledged that his behavior suggested the opposite. He was deeply remorseful. He begged her to forgive him and swore nothing like this would ever happen again.

> She was in a crisis of faith. She didn't know whether to believe his words or his actions. He had always said in the past that he would never hit her, and now he was saying it again. But he had. How should she regard this?

> She was in conflict with herself. How could she stay when she had always maintained she would be gone in a flash? Now that it came to it, she didn't want to leave. She was afraid, however, that she would lose credibility if she didn't follow through. Would she set a dangerous precedent?

> She wondered if she might have 'deserved it', much as she knew this was never the case. She had provoked him and provoked him until finally he snapped. Maybe she wanted to discover the limit of his self-control? She had certainly found it. She wished he hadn't hit her quite that hard. Did he have to dislocate her jaw?

Once, privately, in a confessional moment, she told me that some part of her liked it and felt relieved when he whacked her. She was confused by this. It was opposite to all that she believed. She couldn't understand how this could be. The last thing she wanted was to give him the message that hitting her was okay, or that it might be okay for it to happen again. That's how some domestic violence cases get started; she knew this. She was in a quandary.

I suggested that perhaps some part of herself was acting like a provocative child who then felt guilty for finding his Achilles' heel, while also feeling angry for being punished. She said that she could see that she had 'hit him below the belt', where it hurt most. She knew he was anxious about the mental illness that stretched back through his family history. At the same time, it wasn't okay for him to hit her and dislocate her jaw even if it did relieve guilt and confronted a childlike tendency. She said that even though she didn't like the idea, it made sense that some part of her was acting like a provocative child who needed to be punished. This was too reminiscent of actual childhood experiences with her father, and that connection made her feel uncomfortable.

With the help of therapy, this couple took the event of physical violence as a wake-up call and started to be more loving and caring to each other. Both realized that the worst thing each could think of was to lose the other. But there had been damage that needed repair, both physically and emotionally. Neither could live with the idea that it is okay for a man to strike a woman, let alone to cause her a physical injury and put her in hospital.

I, too, faced a difficult quandary. I had to censure him and say: *this behavior is unacceptable* whilst not wanting to foreclose possibilities for understanding, insight and personal growth.

If I only assume the role of stern father and morality police, that is unlikely to make a meaningful or lasting difference to either partner in the future. At the same time, behaviors that cross a line cannot be allowed to pass without an authoritative NO!

> This is what I said to him: *Being a man means we have to control ourselves. There are some things that are non-negotiable and striking a woman is one of them. There are no extenuating circumstances that excuse this. Your authority as a man resides in your ability to stop her from provoking you, through effective verbal communication. If that doesn't work, you have to walk away. I don't know if you realize it, but you could be charged and go to jail. What you did is not only against the law, it is also against the law of love.*

We went on to examine the frustrations and disappointments that had built up in each toward the other. Through a detailed investigation of how they had got to the point where violence erupted between them a sense of repair was effected. Each was able to take responsibility for their part in the build-up of tensions, of ways they had hurt each other, and ways they had been obstructive and demanding.

They had both been 'violent' to each other in many non-physical ways. We recognized that each party was primarily orientated around getting something out of the other rather than giving to each other. They had fallen into a joint power struggle; each trying to get their needs met by the other yet each finding the demands of the other impossible to satisfy and an ongoing source of pressure and aggravation.

We were able to trace back some of these dynamics to childhood patterns – to dynamics between him and his mother, and between her and her father. They had fallen into a negative complementarity whereby each had become like the frustrating and punishing parent of the other. This was a formula for an explosion of violent feelings.

Repair was affected as they worked through how to accommodate what had happened between them. Neither of them knew that he was capable of whacking her like that. She thought better of provoking him, and he realized that he had to control himself no matter how provoked he might feel. He understood that he had to rise above the petty squabbles and resist the temptation to fall into their former pattern of hurtful comments, heated arguments and retaliation. As his capacity for emotional self-regulation grew, he learned to manage his frustration. Accordingly, he could mitigate tensions between them and be more conciliatory and, in this way, made convincing efforts to recover his credibility.

He also needed to undertake therapeutic work on his fears about mental illness in his family and his sensitivity to being associated with his sometimes-psychotic brother. Her body was repaired and, thankfully, the relationship was able to be repaired too. If anything, their mutual commitment strengthened, and their closeness was renewed and reaffirmed. A crisis was turned into an opportunity.

This is not typical of physical domestic violence situations where women are brutalized by men. This example is not an excuse for anyone to think they can get away with striking someone else. Exploring the meaning of experience and behavior should not be mistaken for condoning it.

Another less salubrious outcome is the example of Roz and Ross.

> These two had been together for nine years. They had one rule. They could do whatever they liked as long as they did not have sexual contact outside the relationship.

> At a New Year's Eve party, after quite a lot of alcohol, Ross fell asleep in a chair upstairs. He woke with a start for no reason and walked over to the internal balcony on the first floor that overlooked the sitting room. When he peered over, he saw Roz kissing his best friend. It was not an innocent peck; they were full-on 'snogging', their tongues in each other's mouths.

> Ross nearly fell off the balcony, and swore loudly at them. They were shocked and realized he had witnessed their momentary passion. Each was overwhelmingly guilty, which was further proof to Ross that this intimate kiss was sexual and a gross violation of their one agreed rule.

> *What's the difference between his tongue in your mouth and his penis in your vagina?* Ross bleated with all the pathos and gravitas of a Shakespearian actor.

Quite a good question, I thought.

> To Ross, his trust in Roz was shattered, and his trust in his best friend was destroyed. The damage was cataclysmic; he thought he would never recover.

My assessment, following our best therapeutic efforts, was that the recovery was partial.

> Roz expressed regret and acknowledged that it was a traumatic beginning to a new year for Ross. She knew what it meant to him, but that just made it worse. She didn't know what else to say or do to make amends.

It was also hard for me to know what I could say that would help repair the damage. Their relationship needed to accommodate the damage and somehow go forward, but Ross seemed to nurture his wound. It was almost as if he didn't want to get over it. He seemed to prosper by having a moral advantage over Roz, and this kept him quite attached to his hurt. I said to him that it *almost* appeared that he didn't want it repaired.

Remember: we have to let go of being a victim or a martyr. Repair is much more likely to be effected through a genuine willingness to make amends, to forgive even if forgetting is not possible, and to make convincing efforts to make it up to the injured party. On the other hand, maybe Roz's infidelity was too much for Ross to forgive, much less forget. He felt that something had broken for him. He wondered openly whether he needed to find the strength to end it with Roz. For him, a non-negotiable condition had been breached.

What would it take to enable repair? I asked another patient, and he replied: *Compensation.* It was a wry joke, but it did reveal a truth in his attitude. Like Ross, he also seemed to profit from the damage. This slows or impedes repair, but sometimes there can be more damage than anything can repair.

> *Healing happens when you let go of being the innocent victim and release your partner's guilt from an infinite debt that can never be absolved.*

Holding the pressure of a guilty debt over your partner polarizes the power dynamic and sustains an ongoing imbalance between you. And as we said before, when power comes through the door, love flies out the window. Relationships are conditional, as we also said before, and sometimes those conditions are broken. Does that signify the end of the relationship or are healing and repair possible? That is an essential question that couples therapy aims to answer.

> *Some transgressions are simply unforgivable. When healing and repair are not possible, the courage of your convictions is required to de-couple.*

Therapy aims to discover and remove the obstacles to healing and repair, where possible. The pre-condition for healing and repair is to want to feel better together more than your attachment to the gratification you feel from having been wronged.

The previous example of Ross and Roz may be one where the essential condition of their 'contract' had been breached. Therapy can help to face up to the unhappy realization that some damage is too great to be mended. If trust has been comprehensively destroyed, it can be too big a job to re-build it.

From the position of having let it go, injury healed and damage repaired and, correspondingly, the relationship revitalized, you wonder why it took so long. Why didn't you let it go sooner?

And equally, from the position of having left when injury could not be healed or damage repaired and, correspondingly, the relationship has been terminated, you also wonder why it took so long. Why didn't you leave sooner?

The answer to each of these questions is the same. A state of affairs has arisen that brings you to a crossroads. The path you choose to follow will alter the rest of your life; it is that dramatic. Of course, we want to choose the right path, and to feel as sure about that choice as possible. That takes time. A therapeutic process facilitates this movement – the weighing up, the thinking through, the feeling your way – until the right path comes into view. It is better to get it right than to decide too quickly. I have often counselled clients *not to decide,* at least not yet, when they are pulled in opposing directions, and the right choice has not yet crystallized. Then, once you know, no further time is required, only action.

Just as *How Two Love* is a call to action, for getting it right, so too is couples therapy. At the end of the Introduction we said: it takes two. In couples therapy: it takes three.

CHAPTER 12

Ever After

"True love stories never have endings."
— **Richard Bach**

All of us would like to look to the future as a happy place, as the expression 'ever after' implies. With no insurance policies to guarantee future happiness, learning from the past improves our chances. Your own experience and that of others provides ample lessons.

This book is an accumulation of such lessons, and the lessons that love teaches present higher and higher peaks of aspirations to climb. No one ever gets to the top of this mountain. Being human means that we don't ever love perfectly or completely. The lessons of love show us what we need to work on, for we are all a work in progress, and so is our capacity to love.

The lessons of love

What can love teach you? The most important lessons you ever learn about yourself are learned through the experience of love relationships – through the tension of courting, passion, sexual ecstacy and intimacy, romance, fun, the challenges of maintaining long-term partnerships, and then through love's demise and pain of loss to the next relationship if there is one. Love is an opportunity to be the best of yourself or the worst. Love holds possibilities of feeling your most intense feelings. If you are open to learning what it has to teach you, love is an education. There are no Bachelors, Masters or Doctorate degrees to be gained, just the higher degrees in your capacity to give and receive love.

> *Who is the greatest teacher of all?*
> *Love, if we are willing students.*

If you have arrived at this final chapter, you are likely to have felt confronted by deficiencies in your and your partner's behaviors and that of past relationships. You may have adventured through your own personal lovescape including disappointments, emotional injuries and traumas, even failures and the exhilaration of the best love has to offer – compelling closeness with another person with the corresponding hopes and dreams for the future. Few people have experienced love without getting hurt. I certainly don't know any. Getting hurt tends to go with the territory. The preceding chapters aimed to minimize the conditions that produce hurt and maximize the conditions that produce rewards. If hurt is the unavoidable cost, the profits of love must be worth it.

In summary, *How Two Love* has endeavored to identify some crucial themes, provide a thoughtful perspective upon them, and offer some useful recommendations. These themes are outlined below:

Balance functioning as an individual with functioning as a couple

The overarching theme throughout has been to show how functioning as a couple differs from functioning as an individual. Coupling is a partnership of individuals in a love relationship. We are always individuals but can and must choose to prioritize the relationship as a third entity if the relationship is to prosper and avoid the issues I commonly see in the therapy situation.

The essential message is that a transition is required to function well as a love partner – we must transcend the natural tendency toward self-interest as an individual. Making this transition is a form of personal development that embraces the very meaning of love and the experience of giving and receiving it.

Grow your self-awareness and your partner-awareness

Consider how you affect your partner. It is natural for our initial focus to be upon ourselves – *how do you affect me?* Alongside this, cultivate awareness of the converse – *how do I affect you?* This will benefit your relationship immeasurably.

Break the circularity of negative relational dynamics

For example, he criticizes her, she shuts down, withdraws her sexuality and goes cold. He feels rejected and so criticizes her more, and so on. There are many variations of destructive circularity. Blame does not reside solely in one; each position is the cause and effect of the other.

Communication is often the central issue

Communication is often the facility with which couples have most difficulty. Communication is benefited greatly by cultivating a space for private reflection. Getting in touch with feelings and then connecting your emotional experience to events or situations promotes clarity and an understanding of what needs to be communicated. From there, how you communicate becomes the guiding question. It helps to take ownership of your feelings while identifying how you are being affected by your partner. Then, listening becomes an essential adjunct. Honesty, empathy and respect are enablers of communication.

Respect and trust are paramount

Being trustworthy, crucial as it is, may not be enough to ensure your partner feels safe. Being seen and felt to be trustworthy takes this to the next level. Transparency and accountability make trustworthiness visible. Respect needs to be 24/7, without exceptions or excuses. Loss of trust and respect is one of the worst, most damaging pitfalls in relationships.

Vulnerability is essential

We are forever vulnerable in love because we have everything at stake and everything to lose. Vulnerability is the ground of love. It refers to our emotional investment and so involves risk; as such, it gives love meaning.

> *Paradoxically, vulnerability gives love the possibility of strength.*
>
> *There is no strength if you are invincible and so could never be hurt.*

Know thy partner

Knowing each other is enhanced by keeping your perceptions fresh and refusing to rest in the knowing of the past or the 'knowing' that is based on your constructions or conceptions. Mindful knowing is a refreshing of your sense of each other as you go based upon perception; it involves honest and straightforward representations of self to your significant other.

Love should not be confined by definitions or foreclosed by theory

We have considered love as esteem, as fantasy, as madness, and also as romance. Love's relation to sexuality and desire is inextricably intertwined with the meaning and experience of intimacy. Ultimately, love belongs to you two to make of it what you can and give meaning to how it feels.

Desire is infinitely complex

This has been explored as a matrix and a dialectical dance.

The matrix describes our positive or negative relation to desire while dialectics consider desire as a lack. There is a waxing and waning of desire as we move toward and away from the feeling of having that which we want. When diminished, desire needs to be renewed – sometimes by leaving space – in order to keep sexuality alive and promote the longevity of intimacy.

Co-sexuality is the unique sexual dynamic created by each couple

The term 'co-sexuality' focuses on the particular quality of eros that belongs to each couple's sexuality, and is uniquely co-created by them. Co-sexuality refers to the way we make love, how we create eros between us and how love informs eros and eros fuels love.

Contracts give shape to relationships

Whether the formal vows of marriage or a less formal agreement, contracts and rules of engagement frame relationships. Within that frame, freedom is enhanced by virtue of an understanding of what is permissible and what is not. The boundaries are clear when limits are undertaken voluntarily.

Acceptance is a vital attitude and has a limit

The expression 'for better for worse' reflects acceptance as a central feature at the heart of love. But this does not mean that anything can and should be accepted without question. The limits of acceptance are as important, and something that each person must work out and express as part of their ongoing negotiation with their partner.

Fidelity promotes a feeling of safety for relationships

It is difficult to love with an open heart and be vulnerable without a corresponding feeling of safety. Feeling unsafe by risk of infidelity generates suspicion, mistrust and paranoia. These all compromise love. Many have attempted open relationships and few have succeeded. Polyamory may seem easy, natural and desirable, but isn't usually compatible with feeling comfortable in a stable couple relationship.

Successful relationships involve a balanced system of essential and integrated elements within a 'relational ecology'

The four key elements within the relationship ecosystem are emotionally honest communication, reciprocal attunement, empathic negotiation and affective compromise. These four elements are a dynamic practice that require both parties to assess the health of their relationship and participate actively in supporting it.

A love relationship is a sacred commitment of mutual devotion

A spiritual practice that transcends individual egoic desires informs the meaning and practice of devotion. This involves taking responsibility for the affects of your actions upon your partner. Your partner becomes your primary reference point in all that you do. This is not the same as slavish devotion by one to the other but a reciprocal privileging of each other's best interests.

Love and power operate in an inverse relation for couples

The more power is exercised, the more love is compromised. You can be powerful to each other without subordinating each other. When subordination rules, love contracts in its wake. Surrendering to loving and being loved is a more powerful experience than the experience of power over each other.

Undertake couples therapy when help is needed

The great benefit of entering into a therapy process with your partner is individualized attention for you as a couple. Couples therapy is often shorter term than individual therapy and often employed when relationships need special attention, such as at times of emotional injury, ill feelings, distance or when sex is absent or diminished. Relationships also benefit from maintenance. Couples therapy can be challenging and can make a pivotal difference if both parties are willing to work at it.

Love is not unconditional, nor should it be

The feeling of love may well be unconditional but there is a crucial distinction between love and relationship. Much of this book consists of an elaboration of the conditions which enable relationships to work and last and those that cause erosion or deterioration. Ideally, the feeling of love and the conditions for a good relationship align so they can both be sustained.

Living lovingly

When I look out at the landscape of love relationships from the perspective of my personal and professional experience, this is what I see.

Many of us live our waking lives in a dream. The dream is of finding a partner. For some, that includes having a family – for others, not. Either way, the dream is of sharing our lives, being emotionally and sexually intimate, having our needs met and our interests supported, enjoying material benefits, having fun and feeling happy together. Part of this involves being recognized, accepted and understood for who we are, receiving care when needed and sharing our suffering and successes. Most of us want a fellow traveler, a good friend and soul mate, someone we can talk to, who will listen and really be there for us. Most people want to love and be loved.

The dream is a love story, the narrative of which we tell ourselves in our minds while we live our individual lives, sometimes in a relationship, sometimes not. We are the writers of our love story dream; we are author and audience, and, at the same time, the hero or heroine. We are the players who romance each other in all the glorious ways that love can unfold on the movie of thought. What actually happens may or may not coalesce with that story of love.

> *In practice, love unfolds on the stage of experience, based on how we interact.*

You might be lucky, win the love lottery and score your ideal partner. But you still have to make your own luck in love by how you love who you love. We have discussed what can happen, what to look out for, and how to protect love from the myriad dangers and mistakes to avoid the premature end of your dream of love. It's much better to prevent a nightmare than to wake up and realize you are living one.

Love is an ineffable subject; I've tried to say what can be said without destroying the magic in the process. Love, after all, is the most powerful catalyst that precipitates an almost mystical state between you. Those feelings lead some people to desire and chase after an imagined end goal but the real climax in love is feeling fully satisfied with your partner and your life together as it is. Dreaming of the 'happily ever after' is not the same as living lovingly throughout the waking day.

If the end of the chapter turns out to be the end of the book – the end of your love story – you have to go through what you must. Love's demise brings the wrenching emotions of separating or bereavement, getting over someone, moving on, and returning to yourself as a single person. Like an individual life, every relationship comes to an end, whether by choice or not. It is a matter of time.

Though loss can harden you, in due course you may find your attitude softens. You are drawn to someone, more open perhaps. There is an attraction. A sparkle in the eye of an admirer ignites your interest. You may not have had the chance to make a decision about it when you find yourself 'in' it. You are not back at square one, you are embarking on the next adventure in love.

The end goal of *How Two Love* is making the life of your relationship fulfilling and rewarding. There is no substitute for the feeling of closeness, companionship, connection and love that evolves over time. To love and desire each other as life partners co-creates meaning and direction for both of you. Through all that unfolds, as years become decades, relationships that work make the journey one of living lovingly, and I can think of no better way to live.

End Note

On the off chance that you have jumped to the end of the book and read the summary, you might be thinking you have found a shortcut to grasp what is essential; if so, this a mistake. What is most important in love is what you bring to it, and this applies equally to reading a book on love. The aim of this book is to stimulate your own reflections upon your experience, your desires, expectations, assumptions and perspectives on love relationships. I have said something about how I see love and what love means to me. Reading the summary is not the same as going through your own inner process of finding and creating meaning, and then living it. In the Preface, referring to reading the book through, I wrote *give this time* and this end note echoes that sentiment. The point of making your relationship work and last is to give love time, as time is what gives love value.

"Love is the single most important factor in what makes life worth living."

Share the love

If you enjoyed reading *How Two Love* please do me the kind favor of writing a review. You can spread the word by going to the Review section of Amazon, Goodreads and Google. Share the love more and 'like' us on our Facebook page, 'retweet' us on Twitter and share the ways this book improved your relationship on our website: meaningful.life

And, if you:
- want help with relationship issues
- could benefit from further insights on co-sexuality, intimacy and how to stay connected
- would be stimulated by an on going conversation
- are interested in other publications by Jan Resnick and the *Meaningful Living Series* please join us at: meaningful.life

Cheers

JR

About the Author

Senior psychotherapist, supervisor, teacher and writer Jan Resnick grew up in New York, and undertook his professional training in London with RD Laing and The Philadelphia Association, before immigrating to Australia with his family.

His expertise on love and relationships comes from nearly four decades of working with individuals and couples to heal their relationships. Those people provide most of the stories in this book. Jan believes that *in love, every wound, every mistake, and every missed opportunity is an occasion to heal, to grow and to learn how two love.*

He has about 100 publishing credits, including journal articles, talks, papers and videos across a broad range of subjects. *How Two Love* is his first published book.

He lives with his wife and six children in Perth, Western Australia.

Author website: meaningful.life
Personal website: janresnick.com
Professional website: amygdala.com.au

Index

A

abuse 132
   anonymous story 258–262
acceptance 126, 151–152, 273
   Alexandra and Derek's story
   136–137
   Brad and Jane's story 145–146
   Cam and Patty's story
   .... 139–142, 234
   of flaws 144–146
   Jan and Cath's story 216–217
   limits to 131–143, 271, 273
   Mia and Jonny's story
   .... 138–139, 161
accountability 269–270
   as part of trust 25
addressing issues
   see problems, addressing
affective compromise
   see compromise
aging 146
   see also appearance
alcohol
   Alexandra and Derek's story
   136–137
   Roz and Ross' story 262–265
   Samantha and Jeff's story. 227–228

anger 251
   Bill and Sandra's story 257
   therapy avoiding 252
   Val and Wyatt's story 185–186
anxiety 22
   see also insecurity
appearance
   see also body consciousness
   Brad and Jane's story 145–146
   of sexual partners 116–117
apperception 19, 191
arguments 251
   action and reaction in 128–131
   allowing 253–254
   anonymous stories ... 129, 258–262
   due to blame 125
   due to lack of communication. 183
Ashramas 139–142
attraction 1–16
   after breakups or bereavement. 274
attunement 15
   see also connectedness
   reciprocal attunement 180–184

B

beauty
   see appearance

before-play 109–113
betrayal
   see also cheating
   Bill and Sandra's story 257
   Gabby and Dean's story 44–47
   Ian and Kevin's story 29
blame 180, 252, 269
   causing arguments.................... 125
   negative effects of..................... 130
body consciousness
   Cam and Patty's story
   .... 139–142, 234
   inhibiting sex 90–91, 116–117
boundaries...................................... 271
   regarding sex 104–106
breakups...................... 210–211, 274
   Consuela and Pete's story 223–225
   Gabby and Dean's story
   .... 44–47, 209
   Harriet's story............................ 209
   as a part of life.......................... 267
   settlements and 163–164
   therapy to avoid 238

C

captivation 74
cheating
   see also betrayal
   Andrew and Aleta's story 56–59
   anonymous story...................... 169
   communicating about 178–179
   Craig and Marjorie's story
   174–177
   Darren and Kaye's story .. 228–233
   due to lack of communication. 183
   Gail and Carl's story......... 155–157
   Harriet's story............................ 209
   Lachie's story............................... 25
   Lara and Gil's story 155

Lauren and Neil's story......... 67–73
Roz and Ross' story 262–265
child care
   anonymous story...................... 200
   conflict over 197–200
   Darren and Kaye's story .. 228–233
   Jamie and Lisa's story 197–198
   Marie and Nick's story 198–199
children
   see also child care
   Cam and Patty's story...... 139–142
   Dakota and Darcy's story 188
   Lauren and Neil's story......... 67–73
   Naomi's story 147–151
   reciprocity of mother and........ 180
   therapy and
   .... 237–238, 239, 255–256
   Tyrone and Taylor's story..... 93–96
chores
   conflict over 197–200
   Dakota and Darcy's story 188
   Jan and Cath's story.......... 216–217
   Jan's story.......................... 214–216
closeness
   see connectedness
co-sexuality 103–124, 271
   see also sexuality
   anonymous story...................... 108
   dance of love and 32
   emotional safety and trust in
   78–79
   empathic negotiation for. 192–194
   inter-eros.......... 107, 110–111, 113
   Irene and Ben's story 226–227
   Jacinta's story.................... 114–115
   Leroy and Nancy's story 7–9
   Mary and Denise's story 34–36
   Michael and Wendy's story
   181–183

Samantha and Jeff's story. 227–228
Sandra's story 225–226
timing of sex 88

comfort zone 4–6
Joan's story 5

communication
  see also negotiation; therapy
  about problems 126–128
  about sex
    .... 81–88, 108–109, 113–119
  Craig and Marjorie's story
    174–177
  emotionally honest 168–180
  as a foundation of relationships
    269
  hostile 187
  Isaac and Martha's story .. 242–243
  Jacinta's story 114–115
  Perette and Harry's story . 240–242
  in relational ecology 168–180, 272
  Sandra's story 225–226
  Vince and Victoria's story
    .... 120–124, 183

communion 6

competition 213–214
  avoiding 184
  Jan's story 214–216

complementariness 218–219

compromise
  see also negotiation
  affective 200–204
  in relational ecology 168, 272
  Sandra's story 225–226

conception 17–22, 270

connectedness 245, 272
  see also relational ecology
  basics of 11–16
  closeness and intimacy 110–113

Darren and Kaye's story .. 228–233
George's story 13–14
Katy's story 11–12
Mal's story 12–13
Mary and Denise's story 34–36
Michael and Wendy's story
  181–183
reciprocal attunement 180–184
Sarah and Sam's story 14
trust and 154

conquest 30

contracts 162–166, 265, 271

cooperation 70

cosexuality
  see co-sexuality

couples therapy 237–265
  see also therapy
  addressing problems in 272–273
  healing and repair 246–265
  independent perspective .. 239–243
  Jan's approach 247–256
  therapy process 243–247

crazy love 55–60
  Andrew and Aleta's story 56–59

criticism, reducing 135–136

D

dance of love 30–36, 235
  see also space, giving as the
  dialectic of desire 70–72
  Karen and Kojo's story 33–34
  Mary and Denise's story 34–36

'date nights' 38

de facto relationships
  see marriage

de-idealization 53
  see also fantasy

decisions 41–47
dependence
    see self-sufficiency, emotional
desires 61–76, 270
    balancing.................................. 21
    becoming demands 213
    dialectic of ... 66–74, 113, 270–271
    Lauren and Neil's story 67–73
    matrix of desire ....
    .... 74–76, 245, 270–271
    negotiability of 133–134
    reciprocity of 234
differences
    leading to love 20, 22
discomfort zone 4–6
    Joan's story 5
divorce
    see breakups
domestic violence
    anonymous story 258–262
domination
    see power

E
emotional availability
    see connectedness
emotional need
    see neediness
emotional safety
    anonymous story 88–89
    fidelity allowing 271–272
    sexual 88–91, 104–106
emotional self-sufficiency
    see self-sufficiency, emotional
emotions and thought 55
    analysing relationships using 41–47
    balancing 49

    Gabby and Dean's story 44–47
    rationality as a balance of 92
    Sarah and Christopher's story
    47–49
    subjectivity and objectivity .. 47–51
empathy 269
    Dakota and Darcy's story 188
    empathic negotiation 184–200
    Jan and Cath's story 216–217
    in relational ecology 182, 272
    Sandra's story 225–226
    Val and Wyatt's story 185–186
equality
    see power
eros 106–107, 110–111, 249, 271
    see also sexuality
    Belinda and Tony's story
    .... 112–113, 160–161
esteem 61–63
    see also respect; self-esteem

F
fairness 217–218
    Declan and Carrie's story 28–29
    forbearance and 143–144
    leading to unity 184
faith
    see trust
family
    see children; couples therapy
fantasy 51–60, 270
    Andrew and Aleta's story 56–59
    desire and 65
    hypnoid state 51, 58–59
    risks of 18–22
    as the start of love 63
fear
    see anxiety

feelings
    see emotions and thought
'felt-knowing' 64
feminism
    Jan's story 214–216
fetishes 97–101
fidelity 26–29, 271–272
    see also betrayal; cheating
    anonymous story 129, 160
    Bill and Sandra's story 257
    Ian and Kevin's story 29
    Jan and Cath's story 216–217
    as part of trust 27
    therapy for 250–251
    unasked 135
    Xavier and Lisa's story 257
finances
    anonymous stories 143, 196
    Beverley and Blair's story . 186–187
    Chance and Courtney's story ... 187
    conflict over 195–197
    Daniel's story 195
    Harriet's story 209
food
    see hunger
forbearance 142–144, 151–152
foreplay 109–113
    Donna and Ronald's story 109–110
forgiveness 126, 146–152
    see also acceptance
    anonymous story 258–262
    Naomi's story 147–151
four dimensional communication
    169–170

G
gender roles 214

Jan's story 214–216
gestures, romantic
    see romance
getting to know someone 233–235
    continually 270
    types of 63–65
giving space
    see space, giving
guardedness
    Leroy's story 7–9
guilt
    anonymous stories ... 200, 258–262
    Jan's story 214–216

H
healing and repair 256–265
honesty 269, 270, 272
    see also trust
    Craig and Marjorie's story
    .... 174–177, 244
    emotionally honest
    communication 168–180
    in marriage 207–208
    as part of trust 25
hostility
    anonymous story 258–262
    therapy and 249, 251, 252, 256
hunger
    Joan's story 5
hurt, healing for 256–265
hygiene
    anonymous story 171–172
    complaints about 144–145
    Isaac and Martha's story .. 242–243
hypnoid state 51, 58–59
    see also fantasy
    Andrew and Aleta's story 56–59

I

idealisation
   see fantasy

immaculate attunement 15
   see also connectedness

independence 220
   see also self-sufficiency, emotional

infidelity
   see fidelity

insecurity
   see also self-esteem
   about the relationship 166
   Eleana and Jimmy's story 31
   reducing as trust grows 22

inter-eros 107, 110–111, 113
   see also co-sexuality

inter-psychic intimacy
   Michael and Wendy's story
   181–183

intimacy
   see connectedness; sexuality

intrusive thoughts 26–27

J

jealousy
   George's story 13–14
   Henry and Kathryn's story 23
   Mal's story 12–13

L

lies
   Gabby and Dean's story 44–47

life stages
   Cam and Patty's story 139–142

lifespan of love 125–152

loneliness 5–6

longevity of relationships 125–152

love .... v–xiii, 267–275
   due to differences 20, 22
   lessons of love 267–273
   lifespan of love 125–152
   living lovingly 273–275
   neediness and 6
   trust and 22

M

marriage 206–211
   see also relationships
   anonymous story 206
   Gabby and Dean's story 209
   Harriet's story 209
   history of 92
   Jan and Cath's story 208
   pressure to get married 50
   Sarah and Christopher's story
   47–49
   therapy before 238–239

metaphysical communication
.... 169–170

monogamy
   see marriage; open relationships

N

neediness 1–2
   see also self-sufficiency,
   emotional; vulnerability
   Josephine's story 2

neglect
   Henry and Kathryn's story 23
   Sally and Jesse's story 240

negotiation
   see also compromise
   Consuela and Pete's story 223–225
   Dakota and Darcy's story 188
   empathic 184–200

in relational ecology 168, 272
Sandra's story.................... 225–226
Val and Wyatt's story....... 185–186

O

objectivity
see emotions and thought 'the one'
see 'soulmates'/'the one'

open relationships 104
difficulties of 271–272
Ian and Kevin's story 29

P

paraphilias
see fetishes

parenthood
see children

partnerships
see couples therapy; marriage; relationships; unity

passion 91–97

pathologising................................ 252
anonymous story............. 171–172

perception 270
about sex.................................. 115
conception and 17–22

Plato.. 66

platonic love
vs sexual love........................ 65–66

polyamory
see open relationships

power 212–233, 272
anonymous stories
.... 252–253, 258–262
Bruce and Margaret's story
.... 221–223
Consuela and Pete's story 223–225

Darren and Kaye's story .. 228–233
imbalance causing conflict....... 184
Irene and Ben's story 226–227
Roz and Ross' story 262–265
Samantha and Jeff's story. 227–228
Sandra's story.................... 225–226

prejudice and pre-conceptions....... 20

problems, addressing 126–128
see also therapy

psychopathy, anonymous story
.... 252–253

R

reason
see emotions and thought

receptiveness............................. 30–31

reciprocity
forbearance and................ 143–144
Michael and Wendy's story
.... 181–183
in relational ecology
.... 168, 180–184, 234, 272

rejection
Nita and Ryan's story 83–84

relational ecology.................. 167–204
elements of.............................. 272

relationships ....v–xiii
breaking down negative circularity
.... 269
contracts in 162–166, 265, 271
maintenance.... 127–128, 205–235
mutual responsibility........ 128–131
realizing the dream 233–235
relating to each other .. 17–39, 234

religious concept of acceptance..... 132

repair and healing................ 256–265

resentment

avoiding 126, 200
  Darren and Kaye's story .. 228–233
  due to lack of communication
    .... 180, 187
  Gail and Carl's story 155–157
  Jamie and Lisa's story 197–198
  Vince and Victoria's story 120–124
respect 132, 135, 269–270
  Bruce and Margaret's story
    221–223
  building trust 30
  Jan's story 214–216
  Sarah and Sam's story 14
  Vince and Victoria's story 120–124
responsibility 245, 246
  mutual 128–131
  Naomi's story 147–151
'risk managing' your partner 135
  see also acceptance
romance 36–39, 270, 273
  Bruce and Margaret's story
    221–223
  within love 267
  through words and actions .. 61–63
  Vince and Victoria's story 120–124
rules of engagement 158–161
  anonymous story 160
  contracts 162–166
  Mia and Jonny's story
    .... 138–139, 161

S
sea lions, voyeuristic 86–87
seduction
  see sexuality
self-awareness 269
self-control
  anonymous story 258–262

self-esteem
  see also insecurity
  effect of power imbalance on
    220–221
  sexuality and 90–91
self-interest 272
  anonymous story 200
  conflicting with love
    .... 23–24, 211–213
self-pity, diminishing forgiveness
  149–151
self-sufficiency, emotional 73
  avoiding pressure to marry with 50
  developing 3–6
  Eleana and Jimmy's story 31–32
  Lauren and Neil's story 67–73
  maintaining in separation 73
sexuality 273
  see also cheating; co-sexuality; eros
  Ainsley and Aubrey's story 186
  Alex and Annabelle's story ... 80–81
  anonymous stories
    .... 82, 88–89, 116, 143
  as a barometer for the relationship
    119–124
  being a good lover 113–117
  Belinda and Tony's story
    .... 112–113, 160–161
  Craig and Marjorie's story
    174–177
  as currency 225–233
  Darren and Kaye's story .. 228–233
  function of sexual activity ... 79–80
  Isaac and Martha's story .. 242–243
  Jacinta's story 114–115
  Jan and Cath's story 86–87
  Mortimer's story 100–101
  Nita and Ryan's story 82–83
  Perette and Harry's story . 240–242
  vs platonic love 65–66

in relation to love
.... 77–101, 267, 270
romance increasing..................... 39
therapy regarding
.... 238, 249–251, 272–273
Todd and Tina's story...... 211–212
Tyrone and Taylor's story..... 93–96
unconventional sexual practices
.... 97–101
Vince and Victoria's story 120–124

shouting
Marie and Nick's story 198–199

snoring
communicating about 179
Paul and Rene's story....... 144–145

'soulmates'/'the one' 41–60
Andrew and Aleta's story 56–59
Gabby and Dean's story........ 44–47
Sarah and Christopher's story
.... 47–49

space, giving
see also dance of love
in balance with unity
.... 54–55, 268–269
in the dance of love 30–32
John and Anthony's story.... 15–16
Lauren and Neil's story........ 67–73

spiritual concept of acceptance.... 132

stagnation................................ 37–39

subjectivity
see emotions and thought

subordination
see power

T

'the one'
see 'soulmates'/'the one'

therapy................................ 237–265

addressing problems in
.... 126–128, 272–273
couples therapy 237–265
regarding sexuality........... 108–109

thought and emotions
see emotions and thought

thoughtfulness............................ 273
see also empathy
over self-interest 211–212
Todd and Tina's story...... 211–212

tolerance
see acceptance

transparency........................ 269–270
see also trust
Manfred and Maggie's story 26–27
as part of trust..................... 25–26
regarding expectations..... 158–160

trauma
influencing sexuality.................. 91
therapy revisiting..................... 258

Tristan and Isolde..................... 36–37

trust 22–30, 153, 269–270
see also betrayal; fidelity;
honesty; transparency
Cath's thoughts on 30
Consuela and Pete's story 223–225
Darla and Ben's story........... 27–28
Declan and Carrie's story 28–29
forming unity.......... 153–158, 166
Gail and Carl's story........ 155–157
Henry and Kathryn's story 23
Lachie's story............................. 25
Manfred and Maggie's story 26–27

U

uncertainty of emotions........... 41–47

unconditional love
see acceptance; love

unconscious, the............................ 4

une folie a deux............................ 21

unity 153–166, 235
   balancing giving space
   with 268–269
   due to equality and fairness 184

V

vanilla sex 97–101

violence, domestic
   see domestic violence

vulnerability 270
   connectedness and 181–182
   fidelity allowing 271–272
   as a foundation of
   relationships 6–11
   Manfred and Maggie's story 26–27
   sexual 106

W

wants
   see desires

'weddedness'
   see marriage

work
   Sally and Jesse's story 240